A DENTED BADGE

THOMAS BLANDFORD

ISBN-13: 978-1500457549
ISBN-10: 150045754X

This book is dedicated to my children and grandchildren:

Lauren Blandford
Andrea Maleki
Ron Blandford
Cheyenne Blandford
Katherine Maleki
Benjamin (Max) Maleki
Julianna Maleki

ACKNOWLEDGMENTS

I am indebted to my wife, Judy, for her patience and her expertise with computers—they are such miserable machines—and her invaluable understanding of the written word. *Mucho* thanks to Michaela Cameron for spending countless hours correcting my work, and it needed correcting. In addition to her grammatical skills, her insightful observations and suggestions were absolutely indispensable. I am especially grateful to Jinx Schwartz, a successful writer, for smoothing out the road that led to this finished product.

Two partners, Bill Dunn and Dave Reynolds, contributed to and corrected many of the stories found in these pages. A big thank you to Jerry Glade, an academy classmate, who helped me finish many of the rigorous runs and workouts on the PT field and provided the details of the Bolton-Brown shooting.

I sincerely believe that the Los Angeles Police Department is the finest group of men and women who have ever worn a badge. I wish I could shake the hand of each officer who has ever polished that badge and proudly pinned it to his or her blue-suit.

TABLE OF CONTENTS

INTRODUCTION

A Dented Badge is a collection of cop stories—vignettes—that I believe are true. I was directly involved in many of the incidents described in the book but not all of them. If there was some doubt about the truthfulness of a story, or if I was not directly involved, I'll let you know.

The book is an easy, quick read, which I hope is interesting to the reader. This is the real, unvarnished LAPD of the 1970s and 1980s: raw, exciting and rewarding for the officers. This is exactly what cop work was like in the city of Los Angeles forty years ago.

The book begins with LAPD's Training Division, quickly moves to Newton Division, then on to Communications, Harbor Division, 77th Division (my favorite collection of stories), Metropolitan Division and finally a very short section on the Underwater Dive Unit including an incident involving the Alaskan State Troopers. These were all divisions or units to which I had been assigned.

In 1966, long before I had ever thought about becoming an LA cop, I was fascinated by the publicity of a tragic accidental shooting that occurred in Los Angeles. It was known as the Bova-Deadwyler shooting. Bova, a young policeman assigned to South-Central Los Angeles, accidentally shot Deadwyler during a traffic stop. Deadwyler was driving his pregnant wife, who had gone into labor, to the hospital. Bova testified at a coroner's inquest, and a young lawyer named Johnnie Cockran represented the Deadwyler family.

Sensational snippets of Bova's testimony were televised; he answered difficult questions presented by an unrelenting and aggressive Cockran. Bova, however, held his own against Cockran and did an amazing job on the stand. He was articulate, polite, honest and incredibly professional. The coroner's inquest cleared Bova of any wrongdoing in this tragic shooting.

Watching Bova testify on television planted the seed about becoming a Los Angeles policeman. At the time it wasn't high on my list of careers, but his demeanor on the stand was incredibly impressive. Did I have the mettle, determination and "cashews" to become an LA cop? I had some misgivings, but the seed started to germinate.

I joined the department in 1972. It was a great job and a fine police department. I had outstanding partners and I was always proud to be an LA copper.

I sincerely hope you enjoy reading the book as much as I enjoyed reliving the incidents and writing about them.

CHAPTER ONE: TRAINING DIVISION

LAPD recruits spent six grueling months of formal training at the academy. During the first four months recruits learned how to write an arrest report, studied search and seizure laws, qualified with handguns and shotguns, practically memorized the department's shooting policy, learned patrol procedures and endured a robust physical training program.

Physical training (PT) focused on conditioning: long runs in the hills near Dodger Stadium and countless sit-ups and push-ups. (It's unusual, even today, to see a uniformed LA cop who is grossly overweight.) While on the PT field, recruits also learned how to use a baton, how to physically control a combative suspect and mastered the application of two choke holds: the bar-arm control hold and the locked-carotid. Both choke holds were effective at subduing aggressive suspects but were potentially fatal and eventually outlawed.

The fifth month found the recruit working as an observer in patrol, detectives, and traffic enforcement, usually as a third person on a two-person team. The fourth and final week was spent with the Driver Training Unit learning high-speed, code-3 pursuit driving. Finally, the last month at the academy focused on recent changes in criminal law and fine-tuning the skills that were learned during the first five months.

As in most high-stress occupations, the initial training was focused on weeding-out recruits that were not suited to be an LA cop. The department's philosophy was simple: The more you sweat on the PT field the less you bled on the street. If a recruit gave up during PT, especially combat wrestling, it's likely he (there were no female line officers on the department in the mid-seventies) would give up in a street fight. And giving up in a fight was never an option.

"GET YOUR HAT AND BOOKS!"

The physical activity began during the first week of academy classes. One of my classmates (we'll call him Smith) was an overweight but well educated African-American. He was the first recruit in our class to be told to get his *hat and books*—a phrase no one wanted to hear.

When a recruit was told to get his hat and books, it meant he had been fired. I don't know who made that decision but there was no appeal process. If you were told to get your hat and books—and this was not a phrase whispered quietly in your ear, it was a booming announcement made in front of the entire class—you magically disappeared, never to be seen or heard again at the academy.

Our overweight recruit simply could not cut it on the PT field. He gave up on the runs, and was unable to keep up with the class during calisthenics. He was a bright guy, articulate and well-liked by fellow recruits, but he did not perform.

About the end of the first week, the entire class was on the PT field doing push-ups, sit-ups, jumping jacks and just about any form of exercise that caused discomfort and pain. Our soon-to-be fired recruit managed to complete about five sit-ups and then stopped completely. Our primary PT instructor literally ran to the exhausted recruit and yelled, "Smith, get your hat and books!" It was no surprise to the class, but Smith appeared to be shocked. His response was, "But I have a degree in sociology!" It didn't matter; Smith was on his way home.

It was a painful process for everyone involved (including, I imagine, the instructors), but eliminating recruits who lacked stamina, desire, and determination produced reliable officers who could be counted on to save your ass when you needed help. Over the years I've seen a number of cops who risked their life and sometimes their career to help a fellow officer without giving much thought to their own personal safety. And these weren't rare events, they occurred nightly in many of the South-Central divisions.

"WHAT KIND OF PLANE IS THAT?"

Our PT instructor was a weightlifter with a nasty disposition and absolutely no sense of humor. He was also a private pilot and clearly had an interest in military airplanes. One of my classmates, Dave, had been a Marine Corp fighter pilot who flew an A-4 in Vietnam. On a hot July afternoon during physical training, an unidentified military jet flew over the PT field at a fairly low altitude. Our instructor, in his deep commanding voice, yelled, "Marine, what type of plane is that?" Dave jumped to attention and said, "Sir… It's an *airplane*, sir." The assembled class thought this instant comeback was outrageous, probably insubordinate and funny as hell. Bear in mind, PT instructors were nearly God-like—it seemed as if they could fire you on a whim—and mocking a PT instructor in front of the class seemed to guarantee a "Get your hat and books!" What was Dave thinking?

Years later I learned that our instructor was really a good guy and thought Dave's response was pretty funny.

"Hit the hill!" was an ugly, loathsome command, and our instructor didn't waste any time when he bellowed that order to the entire class for Dave's comment. *Hit the hill* meant the entire class had to sprint about one hundred and fifty yards to the base of a cliff that was approximately fifty feet high, scramble our way up the top of the cliff, return to the bottom—slipping, sliding and falling—and then race back to the starting point. One circuit was exhausting; because of Dave's comment, we *hit the hill* three times in a row that afternoon. However, the entire class thought the comment was worth the effort, and no one was critical of Dave for causing us so much grief.

PASSED OUT ON THE PT FIELD

The instructors at the academy were generally pretty bright guys. They were a dedicated group who took pride in producing outstanding, professional cops. However, they weren't about to hold your hand or coddle you if you were faltering.

I almost always carried a little extra weight, even when I was in good physical shape. I was always the Clydesdale never the quick-footed thoroughbred. Typically I was usually one of the last in class to finish a long, uphill run. To improve my running skills, I decided to lose a few pounds. I stopped eating breakfast and lunch, even though we were exercising vigorously every day.

While on the PT field and because of a lack of food, I got sick, and passed out. One of our PT instructors, ordered me to lie in my own vomit until I was able to resume exercising. I knew the department wanted tough cops, not someone who couldn't handle the rigors of academy life, so I continued working out as hard as I could once I regained my strength.

After PT, the instructor pulled me aside and asked if I had stopped eating; he had recognized the symptoms of hypoglycemia. I told him my plan to lose weight and why I thought it was necessary. He acknowledged my Clydesdale qualities and told me not to worry about coming in near the end of the class on runs. He said a few of the instructors noticed that I was a slow runner, but that I had finished every run, never walked, and worked hard on the PT field. I resumed eating normally, but decided to cut out junk food. I lost some weight, improved my running skill, and began finishing the runs in my assigned position.

FIRST HOMICIDE

During the fifth month of training, while assigned to 77th Patrol Division day watch, I saw my first homicide victim. It was a typical August afternoon in Los Angeles: hot, smoggy, and difficult to breathe. Tempers were short and the citizens were in no mood for arguments.

A *hotshot* radio call (a priority call, frequently designated as code-3) was assigned to my unit. I didn't understand the details of the call—recruits hadn't yet learned to listen to the radio—but I did hear the words "shooting in progress." Hotshots were broadcast citywide by a sworn, male dispatcher; routine radio calls were generally broadcast by a civilian, female dispatcher dedicated to your division. A hotshot radio call was preceded by three short beeps, and delivered by a deep, male voice—hotshots always stood out as serious, priority calls.

My unit was not the first unit to appear on the scene even though we were assigned the call code-3. When we arrived we observed two black-and-whites that had arrived before us and a rescue ambulance unit (RA unit). As is typical of most shooting calls, the shooting location was a little confusing, especially to me. The streets and sidewalks quickly fill up with black-and-whites, an ambulance, maybe a fire truck, possibly a fire captain, a police supervisor, and all the testy neighbors.

As we exited our car we were met by an officer who was escorting a handcuffed suspect, a very thin African-American male, back to his black-and-white. When he saw us he quickly flashed a code-4 signal (usually a display of four fingers) indicating no further assistance was needed. The code-4 is then relayed to the dispatcher who re-broadcasts it to all the units within the division so that unneeded responding units can resume patrol.

The arresting officer advised us the call was a family dispute that had escalated into a serious shooting; the husband had shot his wife. We entered the house and then the bedroom where the shooting occurred and found the victim lying in a narrow space between the bed and the wall. The victim was a female African-American who probably weighed more than three hundred pounds. She appeared to be conscious but had devastating injuries as she had been shot in the upper torso several times. The paramedics were unable to examine her as there was no room for them to gain access to her body. Both paramedics were fairly small men and had a difficult time dragging the victim out of the area between the wall and the bed. The big Clydesdale was quickly put to work; the paramedics asked me to grab one leg and they would grab the other leg and all three of us would pull her into an open spot. My first estimate of three hundred pounds was probably a little light.

Observing my first shooting victim was shocking. I had never seen so much blood loss nor had I observed anyone who was trying desperately to breathe (her mouth and chin were covered in pink, frothy blood). In addition to the serious physical problems this woman was enduring, I was equally shocked by the indignity of the entire incident. The poor woman had been shot—multiple times—in the chest with a .380 semiautomatic handgun. She was slowly bleeding to death, struggling for each breath and was clearly in a great deal of discomfort and pain. She had to know she was about to die. And during this time of fear and panic, three unknown white men were pulling, tugging, and trying to maneuver her on her back, through a maze of bedroom furniture, into an open spot. Her entire naked, lower body was exposed to these unknown men as her clothing had migrated toward her waist when we dragged her on the floor by her legs.

Once she was in the open, the paramedics attempted to stop the bleeding and restore her ability to breathe. They were quick, professional, and worked tirelessly for several minutes but their efforts failed. About twenty minutes after our arrival, the woman was pronounced dead. Her last conscious moment on this earth had to be terrifying. She had been fatally assaulted by someone she presumably loved; she couldn't breathe, was bleeding profusely, and suffered the humiliation of being dragged on the floor of her bedroom, half naked, by two paramedics and a cop. I'm not sure if there is ever a good way to die, but this poor woman died under horrible circumstances.

Her husband was booked for section 187 of the Penal Code, homicide. He was probably in shock, but did not appear to be upset by the death of his wife. I appeared

19

in court on this case for the next three years, it was eventually resolved with a plea bargain. I don't recall the details of his conviction, but it was essentially a slap on the wrist.

INDECENT EXPOSURE

After our fifth month, the entire class returned to the academy and assembled in a classroom to discuss our month of real cop work. Every recruit, almost without exception, had an interesting story to tell. My favorite concerned a man who was arrested for indecent exposure at some distant location in the Valley. There are actually two LAPDs; one is located in central Los Angeles, but includes the harbor and the airport, an exclusively urban area. And the other is located in the Valley, northwest of downtown. The Valley is essentially urban, but there are a few pockets of rural sections scattered throughout that part of the city.

While assigned to one of the outlying Valley patrol divisions, my classmate's unit received a radio call to see the woman about a 415 suspect. Four-fifteen refers to section 415 of the California Penal Code. It's a broadly defined, catchall section, which can be applied to anyone who is disturbing the peace. And it's used frequently as a description for a loud party, an assemblage of protesters, or a family dispute that has turned violent. The nighttime call was in one of the rural areas of the Valley where the goats probably outnumbered the humans. My classmate and his two partners were met by a PR (the "person reporting" the incident) who told the officers that she thought someone was under her outhouse—in the cesspool—below the toilet seat. The two patrol officers and even the recruit were skeptical of the PR. However, she didn't appear to be under the influence of alcohol or drugs; she was fairly articulate and clearly frightened.

She told the officers she lived alone in a small house with no indoor toilet. That evening, while sitting on the bench that forms the toilet seat, she thought she saw a light in the pit under the floor of the outhouse. After using the toilet, she stood up and illuminated the pit with her own flashlight. She caught a glimpse of a naked man hunched over, under her outhouse, looking up and holding his own light. She told the officers that she bolted from the outhouse, slammed and locked the door from the outside and called the police.

Still skeptical, the officers approached the outside toilet and—naturally—ordered the lowly recruit to open the door and see if anyone was really under the outhouse. My classmate cautiously opened the door and peered into the hole leading to the cesspool. Sure enough, he was looking directly into the eyes of a naked man standing up to his knees in effluent, wearing a shower cap and holding a flashlight. When the laughter died down, the suspect was advised that he was under arrest. The two seasoned officers had no idea what the charge would be, but they would figure that out later.

Veteran patrol officers rarely enjoy having a recruit, still in the academy, accompanying them on their watch. However, this night was an exception; my classmate was assigned the unpleasant duty of assisting the suspect out of the cesspool, washing him off with a garden hose, cuffing him and riding with him in the back seat of the patrol car to the station. What a way to break-in a brand-new uniform.

Lots of stories were told that day in the classroom, but none of them compared to the guy standing in the cesspool under the outhouse.

A FRIENDLY GAME OF BASKETBALL

The last week of formal classes at the academy was fairly relaxed. If you made it that far, it's likely that you were going to graduate. The recruits and the staff were preparing for the graduation ceremony, patrol divisions were being assigned to recruits, dress uniforms were being fitted and pressed, and the PT requirements had been lessened. In fact, one of the highlights of the last week was a basketball game between the academy staff and the recruits.

I was asked if I wanted to play in the game as I was fairly tall and everyone assumed I could play, at least a little. I actually detested the game, but I wasn't going to miss an opportunity to bang heads with the academy staff. My plan from the very beginning was to play as aggressively as I could and to make as much contact as possible until I was thrown out or fouled out of the game.

This was the first time in my life that I actually enjoyed playing basketball. I knocked down several staff members, applied a couple of very good elbow shots to one of our PT instructors, smashed into at least two classroom instructors, and nearly flattened our class advisor (who was really a pretty good guy). I was clearly the bull in the china closet. What a blast! They could dish it out on the PT field but pissed and moaned when they were on the receiving end of some aggressive play by a recruit. It didn't take the staff very long to figure out what I was up to. I, of course, claimed I was just a Clydesdale not Magic Johnson, and was never very good at basketball, which was the truth. My career as a basketball player didn't last long as I was quickly ejected from the game.

THE PERSONAL SAFETY OF OFFICERS

On a more serious note, there is one underlying theme that is stressed throughout your entire six months at the academy: *officer safety.* It's a subject that is hammered into the sole of each recruit. The hackneyed term *officer safety* is heard daily, sometimes hourly. The idea is for *every* officer to return home at the end of each watch. No cuts, no bruises, no torn uniforms, no emergency room visits and no bullet holes. A big part of the training is spent learning how to control a combative suspect with a minimum of physical force. Knock-down, drag-out fights are rare—and no fun. They usually result in a trip to the hospital, a detailed arrest report that must justify your actions, a torn uniform, interviews with Internal Affairs, and a possible civil lawsuit. In a nutshell, an officer is taught to be safe and do as little damage as possible.

Officer involved shootings are more rare than bar-room brawls, but they do occur. There is a memorial for slain officers that stood in front of the old Parker Center. The memorial names the officers who have been killed while on duty. One or two names, sometimes more, are added each year to that long list. A majority of those officers died from gunshot wounds, and many of them made mistakes; some as minor as a detective wearing two belts, one to hold up his pants and one to secure his revolver. Because he was wearing two belts, a savvy suspect—in the middle of an armed liquor-store robbery—immediately recognized the plain-clothes detective as an officer and shot him. The detective was entering the store to purchase cigarettes and had no idea that he was walking into an armed robbery.

Some of the mistakes were egregious. For example, a California Highway Patrol officer failed to remove a shotgun from its rack in the patrol car— knowing that he was about to face an armed and extremely dangerous suspect. The CHP required its men to write a report every time they removed the shotgun from its rack (a seal was placed on the rack to determine if the weapon had been removed). Because of that policy, CHP shotguns were almost never removed from patrol cars. Four officers died in a shootout with one suspect because of that mistake. This absurd policy was eventually changed.

The on-duty death of a police officer was always critically analyzed by the department, taken apart step by step. Precisely what action or inaction caused his death? Did he park his vehicle in the wrong location, was he too aggressive during a foot pursuit, or was he too casual in confronting potentially dangerous suspects? Every aspect of each death was carefully examined, and the officer was openly criticized for the mistake that took his life.

The detailed review and critique of each death included the display of photos of the dead officer lying naked on a gurney in the morgue, usually with one or more long, stainless steel rods passing through his body. The rods were used to follow the trajectory of the round and allowed the investigators to determine the relative position of officers and suspects. There is *nothing* more sobering than viewing photos of a slain officer with several of these rods entering and sometimes passing completely through his body. These were shockingly stark photos, vivid evidence of a costly mistake.

The critical analysis of the shooting, along with the photos, was an effective learning process for recruits. The entire review was brutally honest, clearly insensitive, and never forgotten. Young officers were sent into the field with these images imprinted in their memories.

We live in a violent world and officers are frequently criticized for actions that may be perceived as being excessive. One view of an officer lying on a stainless-steel table with a metal rod passing through his body clearly illustrates how deadly one simple mistake can be. Good, aggressive training—and that's exactly how the academy performed—helped eliminate mistakes.

CHAPTER TWO: SHOOTIN' NEWTON

After graduating from the academy, I was assigned to Newton Division as a probationary officer (formal probation lasted one year from date of hire). Initially I was disappointed in my first assignment; I wanted to work Harbor Division. Harbor was close to home and close to the ocean. However, as I happily discovered, there was no better place to learn about cop work than Newton.

FIRST NIGHT ON THE JOB

I was assigned to morning watch; this is the watch that generally runs from midnight to eight in the morning. My first experience in the locker room was sobering. I was getting dressed in my new uniform when I heard a veteran officer next to me whisper under his breath "son of a bitch!" while examining his badge. I looked at the badge and saw a fairly deep dent in city hall (there is a replica of city hall on every LAPD badge). I was a little unsure of why he appeared to be surprised, so I timidly asked him about the dent (new probationers generally don't strike up conversations with veteran officers).

He said he had just returned to work after being IOD (injured on duty) for several months and didn't know his badge had been dented. My curiosity prevailed and I asked him what happened. He casually told me he had been shot in the arm by an old gentleman while answering a radio call.

Surprised at what I had just heard, I blurted out, "How did that happen?" Stoically and unemotionally, he related the following story: The officer had been assigned a radio call to investigate the status of an old man who had not been seen by his neighbors for several days and was in poor health. He and his partner arrived at the scene, obtained the story from the PR and attempted to contact the old gentleman. The officer knocked on the door and identified himself as a police officer, but no one inside responded. He did this several times but still no response. He eventually knocked on the door with his aluminum flashlight, hard enough to leave dents in the wood and make the entire house shake.

Again, no one answered. He checked with the PR one more time to make sure that the old man was not away from his residence. He was assured the man almost never left his house, and if he did leave it was only for a short time.

The officer felt the old man was either dead or very sick and was unable to come to the door. He made the decision to force entry—kick in the door—to determine if the man was dead or needed help. Officers generally do not stand in front of a door when they knock; they usually stand to either side of the door where sturdy wall framing studs offer some protection. Most doors will not stop a bullet. However, when a door is being kicked-in the officer has no choice but to stand in front of the door and kick at the area adjacent to the door knob. Contrary to Hollywood's perception of forced entry, doors are almost never rammed open with one's upper body. It's a good way to damage a shoulder, and it's likely the door won't budge.

The officer, who was probably at least 225 pounds, stood before the door and shouted one more time, "Police, open the door!" When he received no response, he leaned back slightly and smashed his foot into the door as close to the knob as possible. Front doors rarely give way on the first kick, and this door was no exception. After the third or fourth kick, he heard a round go off inside the house and felt a sharp pain in his left arm. It seemed like he had been shot but he had a difficult time accepting that thought. *This wasn't happening to me* was all he could think of. The force of the bullet spun him around and he fell or was knocked to the ground. He realized that he was bleeding, but not severely, and his arm was beginning to throb with flashes of pain.

The old man finally opened the door. He appeared to be fine, although he was holding a handgun. The officer remembers looking up from the ground and seeing smoke slowly swirling from the end of the barrel and smelling gunpowder. It was at that moment that he finally understood he had been shot.

The officer's partner—amazingly—did not return fire. He quickly realized the man was confused and probably didn't intend to shoot a police officer. The old guy was taken into custody and an ambulance was summoned for the wounded policeman.

It was later determined that the shooter was almost totally deaf and had assumed that some bad guy—not the police—was trying to force his way into his house. None of his neighbors bothered to tell the officer that the man was as deaf as a door. He lived in an area of Newton prone to burglaries and robberies and maintained a gun for self-protection. He was actually a pretty good guy and felt terrible that he had just shot a policeman.

The injured policeman was off work for several months but eventually made a full recovery. When I met him, my first night on patrol and his first day back to work, he had not seen his badge nor had he been told about the dent. He had been shot with a .22 caliber hand gun from inside the residence. The round went through the door and struck him right over his heart where his badge had been pinned to his shirt (these were the days before body armor was commonly worn by patrol officers). The bullet hit the center of the badge, about the middle of city hall, and was deflected into the bicep of his left arm; it damaged some flesh and muscle but did not break any bones or do any serious tissue damage.

After our conversation, I thought to myself: *Holy shit, the first officer I meet in Newton has been essentially shot in the **heart** and is now back to work— Newton had to be a bad-ass place full of tough cops.* I also had a few lingering questions: Will I measure up to these guys? Do I have what it takes to be a good LA cop? Can I do this job?

MY FIRST TRAINING OFFICER

Training officers, like PT instructors, were feared, respected and usually admired by most probationers. These were officers you *had* to please. Your ability to remain employed was in their hands for the next six months. If you "screwed the pooch," you had to answer to him; he was the guy who was going to get you fired. Probationers worked with a number of different training officers during their probation. This insured that each probationer would be fairly evaluated and exposed to a variety of techniques and tactics. It was a good system that combined formal academy training with the practical application of real police work.

My first training officer, Larry Nichols, was a true warrior who had spent three combat tours in Vietnam. (Please indulge me in a short digression, but I've heard too many professional athletes refer to themselves as warriors and it generally turns my stomach. I only know of one pro athlete who qualifies as a warrior, Pat Tillman, who played for the Arizona Cardinals and was killed in Afghanistan.) Larry was a veteran officer who worked Newton for several years. His uniform was neatly pressed, his badge had been polished so many times that the thinly-etched windows in city hall had worn off, his shoes were spit-shined, his hair was cut short and his mustache was neatly trimmed. His actions, his looks and his attitude were impressive. He was a deadly serious officer who did not tolerate foolishness, bravado or incompetence. I liked him immediately and felt comfortable—as comfortable as a probationer could be—having him as one of my training officers.

During roll call we had been assigned to 13 A 47. The number "13" designated Newton Division, "A" meant that we were the primary car responsible for RD (Reporting District) 1347, a small geographic area within the division. After roll call we checked out the shotgun, shotgun shells, and two sets of car keys for the cruiser that had been assigned to us. Larry loaded the shotgun, placed it in the rack that sits on the floor of the car parallel to the front seat, and asked me if I was ready to go. We left the station and drove for a few minutes to a secluded location. Larry parked the car so that no one could approach on foot from the rear or the sides without our being aware of it. Clearly, he was concerned about safety. (The Black Panther Party had a strong presence in Newton Division and it was common knowledge they wanted to assassinate an LA copper.)

Larry told me it was time for a talk. He said he wanted to emphasize two points: I was to do everything he told me to do. He made it clear that if he told me to do something and my actions resulted in a problem, it's likely he could justify my behavior, but if not, he would take complete responsibility. He also advised me that if I failed to follow his direction, or if I did something really outrageous or stupid, I would suffer the consequences.

His second point concerned geography: I had to know my exact location—at *all* times—while patrolling in a black-and-white or on foot. For example, if we were about to make a traffic stop, I had to know that we were driving southbound on Broadway between 50th and 51st Street. The reason is obvious, if Larry had been unable to use the radio and we needed help or assistance, I had to know where we were—and know it instantly, almost intuitively—so I could direct incoming officers to our location. That sounds fairly simple, but it's not. Here's the problem: there could be a 38th Street, followed by a 38th Place, maybe even a 38th Court. No big deal, just remember to look at every street sign. But as Larry happily pointed out, there are no street signs in the back alleys of Los Angeles, and almost every residential street in Newton had a back alley, and Larry loved to cruise the alleys. I had to memorize all the streets within the division, and I had to do it within a short period of time.

Larry told me that at some point, very soon, he would drive down an alley for five or ten blocks in a residential area, stop the car and inform me that he had been shot. I had to know I was southbound in the alley west of Olive between 108th and 109th Street. Without the benefit of street signs, I had to know if I was on 108th Street or 108th Place. I probably spent far more time studying the map of Newton Division than I did for any law exam at the academy. And my class standing reflected that fact, but I had no intention of failing my final exam in LA geography.

After the lecture, Larry drove directly to one of the more active bars within the division and stopped the car in front of the location. He said, "O.K., where are we?" I told him we were in front of the Chihuahua Club at 51st and Central Avenue, across the street from the No-Tell Motel. He told me to advise communications that we were code-6 at that location. Code-6 meant that we were out of service, away from the radio, conducting some type of investigation. I picked up the mike, pushed the talk button but nothing came out of my mouth. I froze! I was terrified at the thought of talking into the radio. Larry patiently repeated what I was supposed to say into the mike, and somehow I managed to convey our code-6 location to the RTO (Radio-Telephone Operator, our dispatcher). The RTO then rebroadcast our code-6 to all Newton units. This alerted everyone that we were making a bar check at a location that could be problematic. Generally, nearby units would automatically head in the direction of the bar in case their assistance was needed.

Before getting out of the car, Larry said, "I want you to go into the bar, by yourself, pick out the biggest, loudest drunk, choke him out, cuff him and bring him back to the car." I thought back on our recent conversation and said to myself, *OK, I'm being given an order that I don't quite understand, but Larry seems to know what he's doing and he is my training officer.* I got out of the car and walked into the bar by myself. I began surveying the patrons to determine who was going to jail that night for being drunk in a public place. I approached the biggest guy in the bar, who was sitting on a stool, and placed my arm around his neck. Suddenly, I felt someone grab my arm. It was Larry. He led me out of the bar and said we had two things to discuss. First, he wanted to see if I would follow his directions, so I passed that part of the test. His second point was that I allowed someone to approach me from behind, in a dangerous environment, and wasn't aware of it. That someone, of course, was Larry.

I knew I was in a little bit of trouble, my situational awareness needed lots of work, but I had a feeling Larry was reasonably comfortable working with me as a probationer. Was I overly optimistic? Probably so.

MY FIRST "HYPE" ARREST

I did not actually make the arrest. A new probationer wouldn't know the difference between a "hype" and the chief of police. A hype was a person who injected heroin directly into a vein. In the seventies and eighties heroin was almost always injected. Today, heroin is so pure it can be smoked, snorted, inserted and, of course, injected into the body.

I was working with an outstanding training officer who would later become a prominent LA attorney. His name was Barry Levin. Barry was a Vietnam veteran, a court-qualified drug expert and, as a young man, had been a serious boxer. He had a quick mind and was whip smart. He was one of the most aggressive officers with which I had worked. He was constantly looking for Black Muslims who had made it known they wanted to kill an LA Cop. There was a Black

Muslim mosque in Newton, so there was no shortage of these anti-police extremists within the division. Nearly every contact between Barry and a Black Muslim resulted in a bloody fight, and Barry never lost a fight.

The hype arrest occurred on a warm day in Los Angeles. I observed two male blacks walking on the sidewalk in Newton Division and neither one of them appeared to be in a hurry. Barry, however, saw two men walking on a warm day wearing coats. He noticed they were not only walking slowly, but their gait was casual and flaccid. And they were in an area known to be full of hypes—which was almost the entire division. Barry looked at me and said that both men were "down" (under the influence of heroin). I saw two men walking on the sidewalk. How could he possibly know they were under the influence of a specific drug based on a casual observation and without examining them?

We stopped both men and Barry determined the following: They were walking with a loose, flaccid motion; they seemed to be unconcerned about being stopped by the police; their speech was low, slow and deliberate; their pupils were constricted below three millimeters (tighter than looking directly at the sun); and each suspect had a fresh puncture wound directly over a vein—they had been "geasing", shooting heroin within the last hour or so. Barry arrested both men for *possession* of heroin even though they did not physically have any heroin on their person. They were carrying heroin within their body. Barry was able to testify that both men were under the influence of heroin based on his observations and his expertise. While testifying in court a good hype expert—and Barry was one of the best—will prevail over the expertise of a medical doctor.

We transported both men to the station where Barry began the lengthy interview process. There is not much point in arresting someone for being under the influence of heroin unless you can obtain information that may lead to the arrest of a dealer or other valuable information. During the interview, I learned that one of the suspects was a sociology professor at California State University at Los Angeles—my college! I couldn't believe it. This was a smart, articulate guy, someone I might admire, who was using heroin. Working the street with Barry was a better education than my four-year degree. What a shock. This arrest stimulated me to learn more about illicit drug use.

In 2001 Barry was found dead at the Los Angeles National Cemetery—a cemetery that was the final resting place for many Vietnam veterans—from a self-inflicted gunshot wound. He had been battling a rare but fatal disease.

A NEW LANGUAGE

I was a white kid who had rarely been exposed to African-Americans during my formative years, and I had never spent any time in a low income, African-American community. I was working with Mike Reeve, my third training officer. Our first traffic stop was a car full of local gang members. After the suspects' vehicle stopped and without approaching the car, Mike ordered everyone out, directed them to a location on the sidewalk next to the car and told them to place their hands on top of their heads. Apparently they had been through this routine a number of times and complied without hesitation or comment. Mike directed me to search each gang member while he stood by as the guarding officer. After the searches, Mike singled out the driver of the car and completed an F.I. card (Field Interview card) on the guy. Mike asked him a number of questions called for on the card and engaged him in what appeared to be a casual conversation. He went through this routine with each gang member. After the interviews, Mike told me to stand by as guarding officer while he searched the interior of the car. We found no weapons and no dope, so everyone was kicked loose.

I carefully listened to each interview conducted by Mike. I understood about every third or fourth word that was spoken by each suspect. Mike, on the other hand, seemed to understand everything that was said. It was as if they were speaking and I could only understand a few of the words. I was completely confused. Mike was speaking English, but the suspects were using some foreign tongue that eluded me. Their language was a combination of unusual word selection and very poor word enunciation. After the traffic stop, I told Mike that I understood very little of what each suspect had said, and it sounded to me as if they were speaking in some foreign tongue. He told me not to worry about it, within a few months I'd be fluent in a combination of slang, slurred words, poor syntax and improper pronunciation. I was never a master of the English language, but now I was expected to learn an entirely new dialect. So far, cop work was not exactly what I had expected, but I was enjoying myself. My lingering self-doubts: can I really do this job, still persisted.

Three years later, when I was working as a training officer in 77th Division, I had this *exact* conversation with a brand-new recruit—fresh out of the academy—who had never been exposed to the ghetto. My advice to him was the same that Mike had given me: don't worry about it, you'll soon be fluent.

A "BURK" DEUCE-AND-A-QUARTER

During my first few weeks in Newton, Larry Nichols and I received a radio call that involved a serious crime and a getaway vehicle. Larry assigned me to interview one of the witnesses who had observed the suspect and the car that was used to speed from the scene.

During the interview I asked the witness to describe the vehicle. He told me that it was a "Burk" deuce-and-a-quarter. I had no idea what kind of vehicle he was describing. The only thing I could think of was a military truck that had the word *deuce* in it as part of an informal description. I asked him if the vehicle was a truck, and he said, "No, it's a *Burk*, a deuce-and-a-quarter." I could not have been more confused. I was certain the watch commander would not approve a crime report describing the involved vehicle as a Burk, deuce-and-a-quarter. I went to Larry and told him I needed an interpreter, and explained the problem. He told me that a Burk, deuce-and-a-quarter, was a Buick Electra 225. Well of course, why didn't I think of that?

A short time later I was interviewing another witness to a crime that involved a forced entry, robbery, and shots fired. When I asked him to describe what happened, he told me the suspect had kicked in his front door, forced his way into the premises, pushed everyone around, fired several rounds from a handgun and demanded everyone's money (a weekly poker game was in progress). Those, however, were not his exact words. He actually said something similar to this: *Man, the dude just "bogarded" his way into my crib, popped a few caps, and snatched the money.* I understood everything except bogarded. I had no idea what bogard meant. I thought about that phrase and felt that it might relate to Humphrey Bogart, the actor who frequently played a tough guy in the movies. No one really knows the origin of the word, but Larry was fairly certain that it related to the famous, tough-guy actor.

There were a lot more mispronounced words and unusual phrases that were commonly heard on the streets—and many were outrageously funny. I wish I had documented them, but a few do come to mind: *rat*-ta-shay case, *photogenic* memory, jury-box (jewelry box), jumped-on (an assault), bitches and hoes, "I loves that bitch," Whetto, Patti and Honkie to name a few. I always thought the origin of the word *Honkie* was interesting. It's believed that white men would drive into the ghetto to an area where prostitutes gathered and honk their car horns to attract the girls. So they became known as Honkies.

IN PURSUIT

I was involved in two vehicle pursuits during my first month on the street. During the first pursuit, Larry was driving and we were approaching a liquor store on one of the main streets of Newton. We observed a vehicle drive away from the store at high speed. The smoking rear tires lost traction, and the rear end of the car fishtailed away from the curb. Sensing a liquor store robbery had just occurred, Larry immediately fired up the red lights and hit the siren. When the red lights and siren are activated and the vehicle you intend to stop is obviously trying to escape, all of your senses are on high alert and your attention is focused solely on the escaping car.

Epinephrine, a powerful chemical that sharpens your senses and prepares your body and mind for a fight, is instantly blasted into your blood stream. If your emotions are not under control—and this is no easy task with all the adrenalin flowing—it's likely that your ability to think clearly will be impaired. And that is the main difference between a seasoned officer and a confused rookie.

After a few minutes of pursuing the escaping vehicle, Larry advised me to broadcast the pursuit. Officers were generally reluctant to immediately broadcast a pursuit, even if the pursued vehicle is clearly attempting to escape. No one wants to announce they are *in pursuit* followed shortly by a code-4 (short pursuits lasting thirty seconds or less probably should not have been broadcast). Whenever officers announce they are *in pursuit,* all divisional radio traffic is placed on hold until the pursuit ends. The announcement and broadcast goes something like this: *13 A 47, we are in pursuit; we are southbound on Broadway approaching 48th Street. The vehicle is a late model black Chevrolet, there are two African-American male suspects in the vehicle, and they are wanted for a possible 211* (the California Penal Code section for robbery and is usually pronounced two-eleven). The dispatcher then advises all units that 13 A 47 is in pursuit; she rebroadcasts the name of the street, the direction of travel, and the description of the vehicle, speed of the pursuit, the type of crime involved and a description of the suspects.

The pursuing officers periodically announce the current status of the pursuit: any changes in the direction of travel, the speed of the fleeing car, and any additional, pertinent information that should be known by the dispatcher and the other pursuing officers. The dispatcher relays all the information broadcast to her by the pursuing officers to the entire division. This rebroadcasting of information continues throughout the pursuit until a code-4 is finally broadcast.

After Larry told me to begin the broadcast, I grabbed the mike, crushed down on the key, but didn't say a word. Because of all the adrenalin flowing through my body, I was unable to think and talk at the same time. Larry had anticipated this and told me to settle down and start thinking about what I was doing. He told me what to say to the dispatcher and how to say it. His calming demeanor finally affected me and I was able to broadcast the pursuit; It was not, however, my finest moment on the radio.

About three minutes into the pursuit, an unmarked police car cut us off and forced us to pull to the curb. Larry recognized the officers as divisional vice coppers (I, of course, had no idea who they were). They told us the vehicle we were pursuing was another unmarked vice unit driven by two Administrative Vice officers that Larry didn't recognize. Unfortunately we had broadcast an accurate description of the car and direction of travel. And to exacerbate the situation, an air unit (helicopter) was now over our location and indicated they had the vehicle we described in view. Things were really getting complicated for Larry. He grabbed the mike and quickly changed the description of the suspect's vehicle and direction of travel. A moment later, he announced that we had lost the pursued vehicle.

Air unit pilots and observers are pretty sharp officers. It was clear to them we had accurately described the suspect's vehicle and we had not lost it until we were cut off by another car. They understood this was a pursuit that should not have been broadcast, although they didn't know why. Larry knew the two Administrative Vice officers could be in trouble if their supervisor learned they were responsible for a pursuit. Our watch supervisors and fellow officers assumed the confusion was caused by a rookie who didn't know where he was or what he was pursuing. We, of course, didn't tell our sergeant what had occurred, but Larry made sure the other officers on the watch knew the facts and that I wasn't a complete idiot.

I experienced my second pursuit a short time later. We were not the primary unit or even the secondary unit in this pursuit. We were one of many who joined in the excitement. Typically a pursuit involved the suspect's car, the primary unit (the unit that initiated the pursuit), a designated secondary unit, a sergeant, and about five or ten additional black-and-whites. According to policy, only the primary unit is allowed to drive code-3. All additional units usually follow closely behind—in a long string of police vehicles—with red lights flashing.

Typically, at the end of the pursuit, the suspect crashes his car and attempts to run from the pursuing officers. The suspect is followed closely by the officer who is in the best physical shape and an additional baton-wielding ten or fifteen "blue-suiters." Because of the adrenalin and nature of the chase, it was not uncommon for a suspect to take a few licks from a baton for his misdeeds.

In my second pursuit, after the crash, I was able to quickly bail out of the car and join the foot pursuit. This pursuit covered several blocks, but because of my Clydesdale-like speed I didn't arrive at the scene of the capture until just before the suspect was being cuffed. And like most vehicle pursuits that turn into a foot pursuit, this unlucky suspect decided to resist arrest—at least that's what I was later told. Apparently he resisted quite a bit as his white T-shirt was covered in blood.

One of the seasoned, veteran officers—the guy who had captured and bloodied the suspect—looked up and saw me approach the scene. He immediately recognized me as a rookie and, in a commanding voice, said, "Hey kid, I need a pair of cuffs." I happily obliged (it never occurred to me to ask about his own cuffs) and gave him mine, (individual sets of handcuffs are identified by a serial number and your inscribed name). The old-timer cuffed the suspect and said, "Thanks kid." He and his partner walked back to their black-and-white, got in and drove off. This mass departure was repeated by every officer at the site of the arrest, including the unit that initiated the pursuit. Everyone had split. When Larry finally arrived, I was standing next to a bloody suspect— by *myself*—with *my* handcuffs on his wrists. Seconds later we were joined by a sergeant who said to me, "What-da-ya got?" I, of course, had no idea. I had in my custody an injured, bloody suspect who could barely stand; he was under arrest, but I had no idea what the charge would be. How was I going to write an arrest report when I was completely ignorant of most of the facts? And how was I going to explain the injuries?

Larry quickly assessed the situation and announced with a chuckle, "You've been screwed." Because of his experience, we managed to complete the arrest report and get the suspect treated for his injuries. And somehow I managed to stay out of trouble, but I learned a good lesson.

A FATAL SHOOTING

Larry was an outstanding policeman. He applied for and was quickly accepted by LAPD's elite Metropolitan Division, commonly referred to as Metro. He had been assigned to the division for about a week when he was accepted as a SWAT (Special Weapons and Tactics) officer. It was a little unusual to be assigned to SWAT after spending so little time in the division, but Larry's combat experience was a valuable asset.

Many people, especially the news media, are grossly misinformed about the philosophy of the SWAT function. I've heard the phrase *SWAT mentality* used frequently as a pejorative by liberals, the media and defense attorneys. In fact, SWAT saves lives: the lives of officers, citizens and suspects. The use of tear gas, flash bangs, sophisticated tactics and special equipment results in fewer injuries and deaths. Long-range, sniper-type shootings are rare.

Larry worked Newton Division and SWAT for about six or seven combined years and was never involved in a shooting. And that's not atypical, that's the norm. He eventually left SWAT because of an outside business interest and was assigned to one of the slower patrol divisions. As much as he enjoyed working SWAT, the constant training and physical demands on his body consumed too much of his time and energy.

He was involved in his first shooting after working this relatively quiet division for only a month or two. He was paired with a recruit just out of the academy. They had arrested and were transporting a violent gang member to the station. Larry was driving and the recruit was riding in the back seat next to the handcuffed prisoner. While driving, he heard his recruit and the suspect struggling in the back seat. Before he could pull over, Larry heard the recruit yell, "He's got my gun!" (I've heard that chilling phrase before from my partner while involved in an altercation with a suspect, and it's scary as hell.) As the car stopped, Larry looked over his shoulder and saw his recruit's gun in the suspect's hands. The recruit had lost almost complete control of the weapon.

Larry quickly pulled his gun and shot the handcuffed suspect in the head, killing him instantly. Suspects under arrest are always handcuffed behind their back, never in front. Somehow this very flexible arrestee managed to work his arms under his ass and through his legs so that his cuffed hands were now in front. Although still handcuffed, he was able to grab the recruit's gun.

Ironically, Larry had spent a number of years working SWAT and Newton, where use of a firearm might be more likely, but he'd never fired a shot. He returned to a less violent division and was almost immediately involved in a fatal shooting.

THE MEDAL OF VALOR

Newton Division had a full complement of outstanding officers. One in particular was extraordinarily impressive. He was the recipient of the Medal of Valor, the highest award that can be given to an LA cop. He was impressive for a number of reasons: He was the sharpest looking veteran officer I had ever seen; every hair on his head was in place, his mustache was perfect, his uniform was always pressed, and he spit-shined his boots daily. He was a Latino officer who was in good physical shape; he was quiet, modest and shy. I believe he was a Vietnam veteran, but he never spoke of the war. And he always wore his hat whenever he left his cruiser (this was LAPD policy, but patrol officers generally disliked wearing a uniform hat and only put it on when a supervisor was present).

He won the Medal because he did *not* shoot a suspect who was firing at him with a handgun. What follows are the facts of the officer-involved non-shooting as they were related to me (I may not be entirely accurate or complete with the details, but the essence of the story is accurate).

The officer—I believe he was working by himself as a report writing unit (often referred to as a U-boat, don't ask me why)—responded to a radio call that required a written report, probably a stolen vehicle or burglary report. He parked the patrol car near the front of the house from which the call had originated. As he exited the police car and approached the front of the house, a woman burst from the front door with a revolver in hand and began firing the gun at the lone officer. He quickly returned to the black-and-white and momentarily used the car as a shield. The woman pursued him and continued firing her handgun. As she approached the front of the car, the officer positioned himself behind the trunk. He was attempting to keep the car between himself and the suspect. She continued firing the gun and eventually chased him around the car.

I'm not sure how many times the two of them circled the car, but for a few moments he was able to maintain some separation between himself and the woman. However, at one critical point he was unable to use the car as a shield and was completely exposed to her gunfire. Most officers would have shot the woman as soon as they observed her pointing the gun in their direction. But for some unknown reason he didn't, he must have felt that it was *not* necessary for him to use lethal force against this woman. No one really knows why he didn't immediately return fire. Did he sense the suspect was deranged, or under the influence? Could he tell she had a mental problem, was she wildly firing the weapon? No one knows, but as incredible as this appears to be, the officer did not feel he needed to use deadly force.

When he found himself fully exposed to the woman's gunfire—rather than shoot her, and most officers would have—he removed his hat (the hat most of us were unwilling to wear) and threw it at her. His aim was apparently very good as the hat struck her somewhere in the upper body and she was momentarily stunned. Taking advantage of the situation, he was able to charge her, knock her down and gain control of the gun. Incredible!

The officer could have easily and justifiably shot and killed the woman, but he didn't. All of our training emphasizes using lethal force to stop this type suspect. Training kicks-in and most officers would have returned fire. How he was able to overcome this ingrained—almost automatic—reaction and refrain from using his gun is a mystery. His action and reluctance to use lethal force obviously saved her life, and he received the Medal of Valor.

Ed Davis, who was Chief of Police at the time of this shooting, insisted every officer wear his uniform hat while in public. He believed the hat made the officer appear to be physically taller, stronger and more authoritative. Apparently he felt this intimidation factor would discourage altercations with his officers. He knew, however, most of the troops disliked putting on their hat every time they got out of the cruiser.

Most people didn't know the chief was also a college professor who taught a religion class at USC and police administration at Cal State LA; I was fortunate enough to be one of his students. As a student I had spent a fair amount of time in his presence, and I had a great deal of respect for his intellect and dedication. I can't say that I knew him well, but I'm sure he enjoyed gloating a little over his insistence that we wear our hats. The strict enforcement of his policy saved a woman's life;

however, he may have overlooked the fact that she clearly was *not* intimidated by our hat-wearing officer.

MY NEXT TRAINING OFFICER

After working with Larry for a month or two, I was reassigned to 13 A 51, with Dennis Walters, now deceased, as my training officer. Dennis was a great guy and a bit of a contrast to Larry. Dennis was truly an old-timer, and had at least fifteen years on the job. Physically he was not tall, burly or intimidating, but what he lacked in size and appearance was offset by experience. If I had to go to war, I'd want Larry Nichols, Barry Levine and Dennis Walters in my foxhole. Dennis and I hit it off right away, and I learned a great deal from his experience.

One night while patrolling in an area frequented by members of the Black Panther Party, Dennis recognized one of them walking on the sidewalk. He quickly told me what he knew about the guy: he had recently been released from prison, hated the police, was a weightlifter and had been known to carry a gun. Dennis felt it was likely this guy would be a problem.

Dennis stopped our car behind the suspect and we both quickly exited. In a loud, commanding voice Dennis said, "Hey man, I want to talk to you!" The Black Panther looked over his shoulder in our direction but did not stop walking. Dennis made one more request, but the suspect ignored us completely and continued on his way. We quickened our pace and soon caught up with the dude. I grabbed him by the arm and attempted to stop him from walking. He quickly spun around and pushed my hand off his arm.

We were taught at the academy to *ask* a suspect to comply with a command, and if that didn't work, we were instructed to *tell* the suspect to comply, and if that failed, we were taught to *make* the suspect comply. *Ask. Tell. Make.* In a nutshell, this was how the escalation of force was supposed to be applied. However, the moment the suspect pushed my hand off his arm, the third phase of this rule—*Make*—went into effect. I forcefully struck the suspect in the shoulder with the palm of my right hand to spin him around so I could use a bar-arm control hold and choke him out. He seemed to be prepared for that movement, and I was unable to turn him around. I had to get behind the suspect in order to choke him out. Failing to spin him, I attempted to step behind him to get into a position to apply the hold. No luck, he continued to face me as I moved. Clearly, I was not making any progress, so I placed one arm around his neck and my other arm around his shoulder. I attempted to bring him closer to me and spin him at the same time. Still no luck, this guy was much stronger than I was, and I clearly lost control of the situation.

Dennis, who was not very tall and weighed about forty pounds less than I did, moved me aside and regained control of the suspect. He quickly choked him out, cuffed him and had him in the back seat of the cruiser as I was still catching my breath from our earlier wrestling match. His experience clearly outweighed my advantage in size and weight.

At the end of the watch, which was about eight in the morning, Dennis asked me if I wanted to have a drink. A veteran officer, a guy who was respected by his peers, asked me—an inexperienced "boot" who couldn't control a suspect—to have a drink after work. I was a little surprised, but said sure I'd love to.

We changed out of our uniforms, jumped in Dennis' car and drove to the nearest liquor store. I assumed Dennis would grab a six-pack of beer, we'd consume one or two and I'd be on my way home.

After a liquor store stop, Dennis drove to a secluded industrial area within the division, parked his car and removed a bottle of Jack Daniels from a brown paper bag. He cracked open the top, gave me the bottle and said, "have a pull." I rarely drank hard liquor, never had it straight up and couldn't believe I was drinking right out of the bottle.

We discussed my tactics, and he explained why I couldn't choke out the suspect. (I was wearing a heavy leather jacket that made it practically impossible to effectively cut off his air supply with my forearm.) When the large bottle was about half empty, he said he had to meet his girlfriend, Lupe. At least I think that was what he said. He may have said I was loopy, I'm still not sure. He dropped me off in the parking lot of the station and somehow I managed to find my car and navigate all the way home. I made it into the driveway, but passed out on the steps leading into the house. I'm sure the neighbors were appalled.

I learned that Dennis was a quiet, unassuming, hard-drinking, experienced tough son-of-a-bitch; a man I respected a great deal.

When I first started working with Dennis, we booked a suspect at Central Jail. While there, I saw a family friend, an LA copper, who had been assigned to Jail Division as a supervisor. I approached him, said hi and had a conversation that lasted about five minutes. Dennis didn't join the conversation but he was watching us and seemed to be interested that we were talking.

When the booking process was done and we were back in the car, Dennis asked me if the sergeant was a friend. I explained he was and I had known him for several years before becoming a policeman. He asked me if I knew how long my friend had been assigned to Jail Division. I told him I wasn't sure but for at least several years. New sergeants, like probationers, were generally assigned to work the jail for six months and then rotated back to Patrol or some other function. Jail Division appeared to be a permanent, dead-end assignment for my friend.

Dennis told me that several years ago he had been assigned to Northeast Patrol Division and worked for that particular sergeant. During a busy night one of the patrol officers broadcast a help call. As Dennis was racing to the location, he observed the sergeant driving *away* from the call. At first Dennis thought a code-4 had been broadcast and he hadn't heard it. He continued to the scene and observed the officers still fully engaged in an altercation with several suspects. Dennis did not understand why the sergeant was driving away from an active help call.

Later during the shift, he asked the sergeant why he hadn't assisted the officers who were in need of help (it takes a big set of balls for a policeman to confront an LAPD sergeant—his supervisor—about inappropriate behavior). The sergeant told Dennis he didn't think the officers really needed any help. Dennis, of course, was furious with this guy. No cop can ignore a help call, especially when he is only seconds away from the location. Dennis went directly to the patrol captain and explained what happened. The sergeant found his name on the next transfer list for Central Jail, where he remained until he retired.

THE NEWTON B-WAGON

After I worked patrol for several months, I was assigned to work the divisional B-wagon. A B-wagon was nothing more than a bread truck that had been modified into a mobile holding facility. The arrestees in back are separated from the officers up front by a solid bulkhead. In Newton, it was used as a three-person patrol vehicle assigned specifically to investigate local bar activity and arrest drunks. The north end of Newton shares a border with Central Division. That border area was commonly referred to as Skid Row, and was chock-full of bars, liquor stores, and run-down motels and hotels. The original Hard Rock Café—not the same restaurant owned by a number of Hollywood stars—was located in the heart of Skid Row. Nearly everyone walking on the street in that area at night is homeless, drunk, or under the influence of some substance. And if they aren't in that condition, they soon will be.

The B-wagon, however, was primarily responsible for arresting 647 F suspects. Six-forty-seven F was the Penal Code section for being drunk in public. Being drunk in public is unlike being under the influence of alcohol. *Under the influence* suggests that one is impaired and shouldn't be driving a motor vehicle; being drunk means one is absolutely shit-faced, falling down, stumbling drunk, and shouldn't even be walking.

The B-wagon usually began its shift in the late afternoon. We'd hit all the bars until the truck was full of drunks, and then transport them to Central Jail where they would be booked and detained until they were sober. An assignment to the B-wagon usually meant you wore one of your old uniforms as it was likely you'd be exposed to urine, vomit, filth, wine, whisky, beer and the horrid, gagging smell of the homeless. It also meant you were probably going to fight with several drunks during the course of the evening. Fighting with a drunk, however, is usually not a big deal—unlike fighting with someone under the influence of PCP or some other stimulant. To minimize altercations, Clydesdales, like me, usually got the B-wagon assignment as drunks tend to be less aggressive with larger officers. A lot of officers didn't like doing bar checks in the B-wagon but I actually enjoyed it; I thought it was fun.

One evening, for some unknown reason, only two of us were assigned to the B-wagon. Generally, one officer would remain with the wagon while the remaining two officers would go inside the bar and look for drunks. It was unsafe for an officer to make a bar check alone, so we left the mobile jail unattended with the door latched—but not locked—from the outside. About half-way through the shift we had what we thought was a full load of drunks. However, we made one more stop and spent a little too much time inside the bar. When we returned to our little mobile jail, we observed about half of our complement of arrestees *sprinting* away from the B-wagon. Some kind soul had walked by, heard everyone inside complaining, and opened the back door allowing everyone to escape. At first we were really pissed. We had filled out all the necessary forms to book each suspect, and we had to account for each form with a body. We gave the situation some thought and decided that if a few of our drunks had the ability to run away, albeit without much grace or speed, they probably weren't really drunk. We laughed about that for a moment, but we still had the problem of too many forms and not enough bodies.

The obvious solution to our problem was to continue with our bar checks, collect enough drunks to match the number of forms that had already been completed (including the name of the arrestee), and deliver them to jail. That meant, of course, that each of our escapees, on paper, would still be officially booked for being drunk but was not physically arrested. Their replacements, however, were physically booked into the jail, but there was no record of the actual arrest. Skid Row drunks rarely have any I.D. and almost always give false names, so no real harm was done and we wouldn't be given any days off for allowing arrestees to escape. It was truly a win, win, win solution for everyone: my partner and I (we would not be disciplined), the drunks who were arrested but not booked and the drunks who were booked but no record of their arrest existed.

A NICE SET

We were conducting a bar check in one of the Hispanic bars located in the north end of Newton. The bar was absolutely packed and the music was loud, but the patrons, with one exception, seemed to be in a friendly mood. I was working with another fairly new officer who was smart, aggressive and a hard charger. And like most South-end coppers, he was alert and very conscious of his safety and the safety of his partner. I learned the hard way, however, that he was easily distracted by a low-cut dress and nice tits.

As we entered the cantina, we noticed that one of the bartenders was an attractive, young Hispanic woman. She had long, dark hair, was fairly tall for a Hispanic female and was wearing a peasant dress that displayed a foot of cleavage. My partner instantly stepped up to the bar for a closer look and some friendly conversation. And for some stupid reason, I made my way to the rear of the barroom looking for drunks.

Bar checks are generally somewhat casual. Officers tend to walk around slowly checking out each patron as they make their way through the bar. I rarely tried to put on an overly aggressive front. A smile and friendly nod to the customers usually made the intrusive presence of a uniformed officer a little easier to accept and it minimized the possibility of a physical confrontation. However, a few people are offended by the mere presence of a "blue-suiter" inside their bar. They just don't like cops. And if the person happens to be under the influence of alcohol and is aggressive by nature, the likelihood of bar fights goes up significantly.

I've been in hundreds of bars and observed and participated in scores of barroom altercations, and I've never seen a typical Hollywood bar fight where everyone is dukin'-it-out with another bar patron. Bar fights are usually isolated events involving two or three combatants. This night's main event, however, was fairly typical of most officer-involved altercations with one interesting twist. Well, maybe *two* interesting twists.

As I walked by a middle-aged, overweight Hispanic male, he said something to me in English. The music was so loud that I had no idea what had been said. I stopped walking, smiled at him, and started to ask him to repeat his question. I instantly realized, however, that this guy was not in a friendly mood. In fact he was downright hostile. My smile disappeared and with a strong voice I said, "What did you say?" The man, who really wasn't drunk, said, "Get the fuck out of here...asshole!" That comment, of course, was an invitation to remain and perhaps conduct a formal investigation regarding his sobriety. At least that's how it would read in the arrest report. In fact, it usually meant the fight is on or is about to begin. One simply did not tell an LA cop to, "*Get the fuck out of here... asshole!*" without some fallout.

I cautiously leaned closer to his ear and said, "Put your hands on top of your head and turn around—asshole!" He was apparently just as offended by the term *asshole* as I was. He responded with, "Fuck you!" and began to walk away. It was pretty clear, even to me, that he and I were not going to be bosom buddies. And now that we are on the subject of bosoms, I looked at the bar and observed my partner's back turned toward me. He was talking to the black-haired, brown-eyed beauty—with a substantial amount of cleavage on display—who was standing behind the bar. I could tell that his eyes were totally focused on one thing (actually two things). I don't think he even remembered that I was in the bar. Calling for help would have been a waste of time because the mariachi music was too loud, and my partner was clearly distracted.

The suspect, however, continued to walk away; he turned his back to me, but was not able to go very far as the back of the bar was packed with patrons. With his back facing me, it was the perfect time to go for a choke out. I'm not blessed with lightning speed, but I was able to quickly place my right forearm around his neck, grab my right wrist with my left hand, bury my head into the back of his neck and apply pressure to his throat. The effect was to slowly cut off the suspect's air supply and render him unconscious. It's a very effective control hold, and if applied correctly, the suspect is not seriously injured. A sore throat and a raspy voice are usually the extent of the damage.

Unfortunately, the once-friendly bar patrons did not hear my previous conversation with the suspect, and it probably wouldn't have mattered if they had. It must have appeared to them that I grabbed the suspect by the throat, from behind, and began choking him for no apparent reason. This clearly offended the sensibilities of his fellow Mexicans, and I found myself surrounded by a rather unfriendly group of would-be rescuers mumbling phrases in Spanish that I didn't understand but still had a clear meaning. These campers were no longer happy or friendly.

I didn't want to lose my grip on the suspect as his still conscious body was acting as a shield against the mob that had me cornered. My baton was in its ring and hanging from my Sam Browne, but to remove the baton meant I would have to release the suspect, and I wasn't sure a baton would have been effective against multiple suspects. (A Sam Browne is the heavy belt worn by officers containing handcuffs, gun, holster, extra rounds and the ring that holds the baton; it was named after its inventor, British general Samuel Browne.) I managed to drag myself and the still-struggling suspect into a dark corner of the bar hoping my partner would eventually come to my aid.

At this point everyone in the bar—except my partner—knew a fight with the police was imminent if not in-progress. Over thirty years after the incident, I still have a clear recollection of my partner leaning over the bar—focusing on a very nice set—as I'm being surrounded by a group of increasingly hostile drunk patrons. I can still clearly recall seeing the barmaid pointing to the rear of bar and saying something to my partner. That apparently got his attention. He was able to put out an *officer needs assistance* call and in a few moments we were joined by about half the officers in the division including the officer that had remained outside with the B-wagon. All ended well, and no one was seriously injured, but the asshole who caused this incident was booked for assault on a police officer (however, to be perfectly honest, I was the one doing the assaulting).

My partner realized that he had screwed-up and was apologetic. I agreed that he definitely had his head up his ass (he was not a training officer), but we were able to laugh about the incident over a beer at the end of watch.

DRAG QUEENS

The first drag queen I met as a young policeman was a complete surprise. My training officer stopped a vehicle for some infraction, and the driver was a fairly attractive female in her mid-twenties. He interviewed her for a few minutes, completed an FI card and sent her on her way.

When we got back in the car he said, "What'd you think of that guy?" And I said something brilliant like, "What guy?" He patiently explained to me that we had stopped a male dressed as a woman. No way! I couldn't believe it; we stopped an eight or a nine and *she* was a male. She had a very nice chest, a tight ass (I should have realized that it was just a little too compact), and a face that belonged in a glamour magazine. My partner asked me if I'd looked at her Adam's apple, and I admitted no, I was probably looking a little farther south. In addition to a large Adams's apple, he explained that her arms and biceps were well developed and nicely defined, and she had masculine hands and fingers. He then showed me the FI card he completed indicating the suspect's first name on *his* California driver's license was George.

No amount of money could have covered the cost of the education I was receiving at Newton. I was actually being paid to see and learn all these incredible things. If I didn't make it as a policeman, I was still getting one hell of an experience.

A PROSTITUTE, A PIMP, A COFFIN, AND FAMOUS HOLLYWOOD STARS

One night, while I was assigned to the front desk, an attractive woman walked into the station and said she wanted to report a crime. That's not unusual, but in this case she and her pimp were the *suspects* in the crime, not the victims.

She was African-American, fairly tall, thin, and had long, straight hair. She was dressed in tight pants and a loosely knitted top without a bra. She was articulate and somewhat regal in her demeanor, especially for a Newton prostitute. She displayed some skin, but not too much. She explained to me that she and her pimp were working the high rollers in Las Vegas. She hooked up with a wealthy Saudi Prince and was going to be well paid for her services (prostitutes generally won't tell coppers exactly how much they get paid). Her pimp, however, decided he wanted to rob the prince of all his cash, gold Rolex watch and jewelry. The plan was for her to collect the money for her services up-front, signal her pimp that she had the cash and he would force his way into the hotel room with his "hog leg" (a long-barreled, large caliber revolver) and rob the prince. Everything went as planned and the two of them made off with over $10,000 in cash and $30,000 or $40,000 in jewelry. After the robbery, they immediately left Vegas and drove to Los Angeles.

While in LA, her pimp dumped her and found another hooker. For reasons I will never understand, he left this unbelievably good looking woman for his new source of income. She, too, was surprised by her pimp; she was in love with the guy and couldn't believe she had been dumped. And now she was pissed!

I took her to the detective bureau and began making phone calls to the various law enforcement agencies in the Las Vegas area to determine if an armed robbery had been reported. I couldn't book her, or list her pimp as a suspect unless we had a reported crime. I made several phone calls and asked the local cops to check on any recent robberies where the suspects and MO of the crime matched my suspect and her pimp. Getting the results of the inquiry was going to take some time, so I poured her a cup of coffee and we began a long and interesting conversation. I was surprised by how transparent she was about her activities and her willingness to talk with me. Rarely do officers believe anything a prostitute tells them, and it's still difficult for me to explain exactly why she seemed credible, but she did. Most coppers have a pretty good idea when people are lying and when they are telling the truth. Even with my limited experience, however, I felt she was being truthful.

Our conversation was unremarkable in the beginning, but with a little prodding, she candidly told me a few stories about her customers.

One of her frequent clients was a big-name Hollywood director. He owned a huge house in the hills above Los Angeles, and he paid her big bucks for some very unusual services. I was somewhat surprised by his name as he had a decent reputation for someone who made a living in Hollywood, and he was married with a family.

When summoned, usually late at night, she would report to his home dressed in black, which was a requirement. He met her at the door and directed her to a room with a stunning view of Los Angeles and Hollywood. She remembers looking down on tall buildings and streams of cars traveling on freeways. Inside the darkened room was an open coffin, raised above the floor, and surrounded by votive candles. He directed her to slowly remove all of her clothing. When she was naked, he told her to lie down inside the coffin, close her eyes and remain motionless. After she had lain inside the coffin for several minutes, he sprinkled a fine white powder all over her body and slowly rubbed it over her dark skin. The process of covering and rubbing every inch of her body with powder took almost an hour.

On one occasion, while the powder was being applied, she opened her eyes and noticed that he too was completely naked; however, his penis was flaccid and he did not appear to be aroused. He rarely spoke and insisted she remain silent and motionless. When she was covered with powder, she was instructed to remain inside the coffin while he photographed her.

Other than applying the powder, he did not touch her, fondle her, or have sex with her. And as far as she could determine, he never once climaxed or engaged in any type of self-arousal. She told me that except for washing off the powder, it was the easiest $500 she ever made.

This director was clearly strange but he didn't hurt anyone. His wife may have known about his coffin and white-powder fetish but who really knows. I thought it was interesting that he covered a black woman with white powder. Was he simulating death or was the woman in the coffin supposed to be white? Could the woman in the coffin be his wife? Who knows what goes on inside the minds of some people, especially those who make a living in Hollywood.

This incredible looking prostitute spent about half of her time in Los Angeles, and the other half in Las Vegas. When in Vegas, one of her frequent customers was a famous Hollywood singer-actor. He was truly a superstar, a familiar name that everyone has seen on the big screen and TV. He was tall, handsome and funny. He liked to smoke and drink on camera, but there were no scandals in his background.

One summer evening our courtesan would be summoned to a residence—not palatial or ostentatious—on the outskirts of Vegas and met at the door by the superstar. Though married and usually surrounded by an entourage, he was always by himself while at this particular residence.

He led her through the house to the back yard where the pool was located. Typically, he removed all of his clothing and place a spiked, dog collar around his neck. He attached a leash to the collar and directed her to walk him around the back yard like a big dog. He got down on his hands and knees and she led him to a nearby tree. He remained on all fours and urinated on the trunk of the tree just like a big male dog. She scolded him for peeing on the tree, and called him a bad dog. After the scolding, she spanked him on the ass with a tree branch until his skin was red with welts.

She told me he had a number of different scenarios involving punishment and bad behavior, but peeing on the tree like a dog and getting spanked was his favorite.

She provided me with a lot of details from each encounter, much of which I do not recall. I felt her stories were believable as she related a great deal of minutiae with each individual incident. Could I have been fooled? Absolutely.

I don't believe it would serve any real purpose to identify these Hollywood superstars. I'm sure it would embarrass individuals and family members, and I do not know if, in fact, what she told me was the truth. However, whenever I see them in shows or hear their names in the media, an entirely different image of their persona flashes through my mind.

A BAND OF FIGHTING MEN

One night while on morning watch, my partner and I observed a group of about fifteen Hispanic men marching down the middle of the street armed with baseball bats, two-by-fours, and just about anything else that functioned as a handy weapon. I suspect there were also a few guns and knives present, but out of our view. They formed a group of men ready to do battle, but they were not in the least bit aggressive toward us. In fact, from a distance it seemed as if they were hailing us. As we cautiously approached this little band of friendly fighting men, a few of them actually laid down their weapons without being told to do so. Surprisingly, we didn't feel threatened by their presence.

The leader of the group approached our black-and-white and told us an interesting story. He said they were attacked by a group of young black men who didn't want Hispanics in *their* neighborhood. The resulting brawl involved hand-to-hand fighting; incredibly, no one used a gun or a knife. He told us they were outnumbered and eventually chased from the scene. They sustained a few injuries, but most of them were still ambulatory and they all wanted revenge. They did not appear to be gang members, just young men who lived in the community and resented being told to leave.

The leader, in halting English, politely asked us for permission to retaliate. They collected some additional reinforcements, bigger sticks and were ready to do battle. If we understood them correctly, however, they didn't want us to do anything. They simply wanted our approval to kick some ass. They seemed to be fairly reasonable and just wanted their own form of retribution. At the time my Spanish was practically nonexistent, but it sounded to me as if they hadn't planned on killing anyone. They just wanted to get even.

My partner contemplated their proposal very carefully and wanted them to assure us that no one had any guns or knives. They happily replied, *"No, no, solamente* bats." Once again, it seemed like they were only going to use baseball bats. Under the circumstances they sounded fairly reasonable. My partner finally said, "OK, I'll give you permission to find the group of men who fought you, and permission to kick their asses, but don't cut, stab, shoot or kill anyone!"

We could almost hear them cheering to themselves, smiles broke out on everyone's face and off they went. We had organized a small group of fighting men and sent them into the ghetto to battle, fight and seek justice. This is probably not what the chief had in mind when the "To Protect and Serve" ethos was painted on the doors of black-and-whites.

About thirty minutes later a hotshot radio call was broadcast to all patrol units in four divisions: Newton, Central, Southwest and 77th. The call went something like this, *All units and 13 A 41, respond to 51st and Central for a major 415 involving one hundred suspects.*

One hundred suspects involved in a major 415 at 51st and Central—what the hell had we done? And to make things worse, *we* were 13 A 41. There was no way we were going to show up at the call and take responsibility for a miniriot involving one hundred combatants and four patrol divisions. We quickly reported we were code-6 (out of service) at some distant location with suspects already in custody.

Unfortunately our little army of would-be Poncho Villas got their asses kicked, and about three ambulances were needed to transport many of them to the hospital. Fortunately, no one was killed or had life-threatening injuries, but the entire incident could have been a disaster.

The next day at roll call the watch commander, Lieutenant Bennett, told an interesting story. He said that he had personally interviewed the leader of this little band of fighting Mexicans, and the guy had made up some ridiculous story about the police giving them permission—and in fact encouraged them—to kick ass. The leader described the officers as two white guys with mustaches, which matched just about every officer on the watch. The boss said he was certain the story was made up; however, he was looking directly at my partner and me as he related this unbelievable story.

POLICEMAN FIRES SHOTGUN AT JUVENILES

There is at least one housing project in Newton Division, and like most projects, the crime rate in the area is high. Homicides, robberies, burglaries and illicit drug usage head the list of serious incidents. And the police are generally despised by the local residents—sometimes for no reason at all and sometimes for very good reasons. What follows is probably one good reason why the local gang bangers hated LA cops.

A group of the little cretins had gathered on a popular street corner not far from the projects. Many of them were drunk and disorderly and were causing problems. A few of them spilled onto the street and they began stopping cars and harassing the drivers. The police were eventually summoned and we were assigned the call. My partner was a Policeman-Two (P-2) not a training officer, but he had been on the job for over twenty years. No one knew the division better than he did, and no one, including supervisors, intimidated him.

The crowd was growing in numbers and was quickly getting way too rowdy. My partner parked about seventy-five yards from the main body of the rioters and positioned the cruiser so the crowd could only view the driver's side of the car. We remained inside the car but continued to monitor the activity of the crowd.

Someone from the middle of the group threw an empty beer bottle in our direction. The bottle landed harmlessly near the car, but it signaled the beginning of a constant barrage of rocks, bottles and anything that could cause damage or injury. I picked up the radio mike and started to call for additional units so we could disperse the crowd. However, my partner, whose name I do not recall, told me to hold off on the request. Instead, he went to the trunk of our car, removed his attaché case and returned to his position in the driver's seat. He removed two cherry bombs from the case and handed them to me and told me to fire up the car's cigarette lighter. Following that, he removed his baton from its holder in the car door and held it in his lap. He then told me to light one cherry bomb—on his command—and drop it out the window on my side of the car so no one in the crowd would be able to see it. He also told me to follow-up the first explosion quickly with the second lighted cherry bomb.

On his command, I lit the cherry bomb and dropped it out of my window. At the same time he extended his baton out the driver's side window as if he were holding a shotgun pointed at the crowd. When the cherry bomb detonated, he quickly raised his *shotgun barrel*—the baton—with his extended left hand as if it had recoiled after being fired. He did the same thing when the second bomb went off. To the crowd, of course, it appeared that a cop was firing directly into a large group of people. At that point all we saw were asses and elbows. I have never seen such a large crowd disperse so quickly. Poof, they were gone and all was quiet.

I thought the baton firing was a great ruse; the boss, however, had other ideas. About ten minutes after the incident we received a radio call to go to the station and see the watch commander. The watch commander that night was Sergeant Haig, an irascible but likeable supervisor who was infamous for picky corrections he made in written reports with his red pencil. He was not a happy man.

My unflappable partner, who was not awed by sergeants, lieutenants or captains, casually asked him if there was a problem. I, of course, was shaking in my boots. (We had already agreed, before going into the station, that the incident had never happened and the crowd was gone by the time we got to the scene.) The incredulous sergeant—who was nearly apoplectic—explained that he had a personnel complaint about officers firing a shotgun at a crowd of youths to disperse them. My partner explained that the crowd had already dispersed before our arrival. The watch commander gave us an unbelieving look and told me to get our shotgun.

It could have been my imagination, but I'm sure I saw the sergeant smile, just a bit, as he placed the end of the shotgun barrel under his nose and inhaled deeply. I saw the shock register on his face when he failed to smell the unmistakable odor of gunpowder. He looked inside the barrel and saw no indication it had been fired or recently cleaned; the firing mechanism did not smell like gunpowder, and the inside of the barrel was as clean as a whistle. The disappointment on the face of the sergeant was clear, and he really didn't want to waste a lot of time interviewing us if the real shooters were still on the street. We had a quick interview, denied everything and were allowed to return to patrol.

Every officer driving a black-and-white was called into the station that night and their shotgun was sniffed and scrutinized. No one knew anything, no one copped out and we had a great story.

THREE INNOCENT WHITE KIDS IN JAIL

Clang! There is simply no sound like a heavily-barred jail door being slammed shut. The loud metallic, piercing sound is truly unforgettable. I didn't realize how impressive the sound was until my three kids were locked inside a Newton holding cell. The cells in Newton were actually small jail cells. They were only about six feet by six feet, the front windows were made of thick glass impregnated with heavy wire, there was no place to sit and the bars on the door were thick and closely spaced. Spending time in any jail must be unpleasant, but a Newton holding cell with the pervasive, faint smell of vomit and urine was absolutely repugnant.

I had to go to the station to pick up my pay check on a day off. It was a Friday and I was caring for my three children: Lauren, Andrea and Ron. I thought the kids would enjoy seeing the station where dad worked and watching policemen in uniform writing reports and booking suspects. They seemed to be having a good time and were joking around with all the guys in uniform.

It's pretty common for coppers to ask a suspect, who may be under the influence of alcohol or drugs, if Mickey Mouse is a dog or a cat. The question is a combination of IQ and sobriety tests. Suspects rarely give the correct answer. As the four of us were walking down the hallway past one of the holding cells, one of the guys asked Andrea, who was about six- or seven-years old, that very question. She gave him a funny look and said, "He's a mouse!" She didn't say it, but I could tell she was thinking that this guy was not very bright.

As we passed the open holding cell door, I was struck by an idea. How would the kids react to being in jail? When I was about Andrea's age, I was shopping with my mother and decided to take home a small toy without paying for it. The new toy was discovered when we returned home, and I was forced to go back to the store and tell the owner that I had stolen the item. The incident had a lasting impression on me and it ended my short life of crime.

I suspected the kids would be extremely impressed when they heard the clanging sound of the jail door closing and they found themselves locked behind bars inside a real jail. I looked at the interior of the cell and it appeared to be relatively clean. I led them all inside, quickly walked out and slammed the door shut. Six little hands immediately grabbed the bars on the door and three sets of eyes grew to the size of small saucers as they watched their dad walk down the hallway without saying a word. However, every officer who walked past the cell made a comment, usually a pejorative, about the three incarcerated juveniles. Someone asked them if they had just robbed a bank. All three silently shook their heads back and forth as if to indicate they were innocent.

They remained inside the cell for about five minutes and never said a word. I returned to the cell, unlocked the door and watched all three of them sprint out of the holding cell.

Were they impressed? You bet. To this day, all three of them feel that I had left them behind bars for the better part of a day—at least eight hours. They are all now in their thirties and forties and as far as I know, not one of them has ever had a problem with law enforcement. My plan apparently worked.

MY FIRST BOSS

My first watch commander was Lieutenant George Bennett. He was almost an exact duplicate of Uncle Festus on the television program *The Adams Family.* He was totally bald, a little chubby, and had a fun-loving smile that was nearly always present. He was a great boss; his first priority was always his officers. His playful sense of humor was a rare commodity for a senior watch commander. He was a leader who was respected and admired by the officers who worked for him.

He hated being inside the station handcuffed to a desk. At every opportunity he was on the streets doing police work—usually by himself—and, not surprisingly, getting into trouble. I probably responded to at least two help calls broadcast by Lieutenant Bennett during my first month at Newton. Like many outstanding leaders, he was overly concerned about his troops, but seemed to be oblivious about his own personal safety. He was not a rear echelon commander; he led from the front.

THE ORDER OF THE GOLDEN BATON

One of those help calls found the Lieutenant—by himself—in the middle of a nasty family dispute involving a husband and wife and about half the neighbors. As is frequently the case, the folks who called the police and wanted their help turned against the cops, or in this instance the Lieutenant, and the fight began. George was surrounded by a hostile group but was able to fight, push and shove his way out of the house to reach his cruiser where the radio was located. The radio is probably the most important piece of equipment that's available to officers, almost as important as a hand gun. While holding one of the family members in a bar arm control hold as a shield, and with his back between the open door and the car body, he was able to reach the radio mike and broadcast a call for help.

A help call is a serious incident. The officer making the call needs *help*, and he needs it right now. The more help, in the form of officers, the better. Serious help calls are broadcast to nearby jurisdictions. For South-Central Los Angeles that would include the California Highway Patrol and the Los Angeles County Sheriff's Department.

Everyone who can respond to a help call usually will. One car within the division is assigned the call code-3, but everyone else responds as quickly as possible. Officers inside the station writing reports or eating will sprint out the back door, jump in their cars and drive as fast as they can to the scene of the call. Helicopter pilots and observers have been known to land their aircraft, sprint to the scene on foot, and do their best to help. Rumor has it that even Chief Gates, dressed in an expensive suit and tie, diverted to the scene of a violent help call while en route to an important city function. Everyone who was able and close enough responded to a help call.

When the first unit arrived at the scene, they observed Lieutenant Bennett wildly swinging his baton in an effort to keep this small crowd at bay. There is an unapproved use of the baton called *five-from-the-sky* that is definitely not taught at the academy. This forbidden maneuver involves the raised baton crashing down, vertically, on the suspect's head. Using *five-from-the-sky* can get an officer suspended; we were taught to hit the suspect anywhere on the body except the head. And batons crashing down from above don't look good on the nightly news, regardless of the circumstances.

After nearly every officer in the division had arrived at the scene, order was finally restored and a code-4 was broadcast. Lieutenant Bennett, always smiling, was cut and bruised and his uniform was torn, but he was clearly having a good time. However, he was missing his baton. Everyone assumed that he had dropped it and one of the bystanders (a large crowd almost always gathers at the scene of a help call) had picked it up as a souvenir. After a brief search the baton was located on the ground under his cruiser. It was, however, in two separate pieces. It is nearly impossible to break a baton if it is used in an approved manner (a horizontal swing at an arm or a leg, or a poking, thrusting move into the body). A broken baton is nearly always a sign that the forbidden *five-from-the-sky* had been used. When the good lieutenant was chided by a few of the troops about his use of the baton, he denied using the outlawed, vertical swing aimed at the head. Everyone, of course, knew he was lying—there's an old police adage: "Never cop out," so George wasn't about to admit to anything.

About a week after the broken baton incident and at the beginning of roll call, a presentation was announced by one of the old-timers. After getting everyone's attention—not an easy task with this group of rowdy, morning-watch officers—the old-timer proclaimed that Lieutenant Bennett was about to receive a highly coveted award. Knowing something unusual was about to happen, everyone in the room fell silent. The presenter displayed a gold-painted plaque that contained both halves of George's baton, also painted gold, and mounted in a crossed-swords pattern.

A polished brass plate was at the bottom of the plaque proclaiming that Lieutenant Bennett was now a member of *The Order of the Golden Baton.* Also inscribed in the brass plate was the following commendation which was read aloud by the presenter: "Lieutenant George Bennett is to be commended for the proper and effective application of *five-from-the-sky* while engaged in an altercation and being significantly outnumbered by a hostile crowd."

George quickly jumped to his feet—with a huge grin on his face—and vehemently denied that he used the outlawed technique. No one, of course, believed him.

A MONSTER SNAKE

George was also known for his practical jokes, some of which backfired.

One of George's sergeants was deathly afraid of snakes, and somehow, George managed to obtain a dead snake. The snake was non-venomous and fairly small, about four-feet long. While the sergeant was conducting roll call, George determined which car the sergeant was driving that night, and placed the dead snake on the floorboard directly under the brake pedal. I didn't see the actual placement of the snake, but I can picture George, with that huge smile plastered on his face, as he coiled the snake under the pedal.

George always wanted an audience for his practical jokes, so almost everyone on morning watch—the watch that was beginning—was aware of the dead snake. As a consequence, an unusual number of officers had gathered in the parking lot eagerly waiting for the sergeant to enter his patrol car. To add to the confusion, night-watch officers were entering the parking lot preparing to go off-duty.

Unfortunately, at this precise time, a night-watch patrol unit put out an *officer needs help* call. The parking lot, of course, was jammed with cars just getting off watch and cars that were preparing to begin their work day, all of which were now trying to speed out of the lot to aid a fellow officer. Officers, sergeants and lieutenants were flooding out of the station, jumping into anything painted black-and-white and racing to the help call. Our snake-fearing sergeant was just one of many responding to the call, but he, of course, had his own assigned car.

The sergeant ran from the station, located his car, threw open the door and jumped in. He was joined by two or three additional coppers who were without a ride. He fired up the engine, placed the gear shift in reverse and stomped on the throttle for a fast exit. At that moment, he felt something soft under his feet. A quick look revealed a massive, fifteen-foot rattle snake, coiled and ready to strike—that was his version of the story. As the sergeant's vehicle was accelerating in reverse, he flung open the door and dived out of the car. During the incident he tore his uniform, sustained minor bumps and bruises, and lacerated his arm badly enough to require stitches. The driverless car continued across the lot and collided with the side of an unmarked car assigned to the captain who ran the division. There is only one car that would have caused a bigger problem, and that would have been the chief's.

A TA (LAPD's abbreviation for a traffic accident) in a police vehicle was, at the time, a very serious incident. Regardless of who was at fault the involved officer was likely to relinquish four days off as punishment. An on-duty injury requiring stitches—though not as serious to police administrators as a dented police car—is significant and requires a few additional reports. Damage to the captain's car, however, is about as serious as a heart attack. Almost everyone knew the lieutenant was responsible for an injury, damage to a black-and-white, as well as the far more serious offense of denting the captain's car.

The lieutenant managed to cover his ass, get two police vehicles repaired *before* the sun came up, and stitch-up the injured sergeant—all without documentation. George had been assigned to Newton for a number of years and had many friends among the businessmen who worked in the division, including body and fender shops. I don't know this for a fact, but I suspect George rousted one of his buddies who owned or worked at one of the repair facilities and convinced him to work through the night to repair the cars. I have no idea how he managed to stitch up the sergeant's arm without generating any paperwork—but he did.

NEWTON STATION—UNDER ATTACK

Los Angeles police officers and firefighters tend to get along well. If firefighters or paramedics have a problem with their safety, they call for the police. If an officer is seriously injured, paramedics respond and transport the officer to the hospital. Not just the nearest hospital, but the best hospital available under the circumstances. There is rarely a serious conflict between the two agencies. In fact, most of the time there is a friendly atmosphere and a strong feeling of camaraderie between them. And, as in the following case, sometimes the joking and camaraderie gets a little out-of-hand.

One night during change-of-watch, water balloons began crashing down from the sky into the parking lot of the station. It was as if we were under a mortar attack with water balloons. The trajectory of the balloons strongly suggested that the attack was coming from the fire station located around the corner. It was, however, too far for the balloons to have been thrown by hand. Arriving night-watch units, driving past the firehouse, reported the firefighters were using a catapult to launch the balloons from the roof of the fire station. A few cars in the parking lot received direct hits, and a couple of officers were soaking wet from this sneak attack.

Lieutenant Bennett was not about to let the incident go unchallenged, and he immediately planned his revenge. He waited until the fire station received a call to respond to a structure fire. Except for paramedics, the station would be empty of firefighters. After the fire trucks left the station, he called for a paramedic to respond to Newton station to treat a minor injury. When the ambulance arrived they were met by several very large, very menacing looking officers. The coppers cuffed the paramedics and filled up the back of the ambulance with blue-suiters. The officers drove the ambulance to the fire station and used the automatic garage door opener to gain entry.

A fire station, of course, is about as clean as an operating room; almost everything is polished, scrubbed or waxed. The station kitchen is spotless unless the firefighters have been called away during a meal. It didn't take the guys in the back of the ambulance very long to turn this immaculate station into a pig sty. Trash cans were overturned on the floor, grape juice was poured all over the kitchen, and anything that had been neatly stowed was now adrift and on the floor. Pig sty, you bet. Lieutenant Bennett had his revenge.

I WANT TO GO TO THE HOSPITAL

Paramedics and firefighters frequently arrived at a dangerous crime scene before police officers. If both police and fire units were needed at a location, the fire department is usually notified ahead of the police department. The fire department can usually respond to a location much faster than a black-and-white as firefighters and paramedics are not as busy. A police unit in a busy division can clear from one radio call and immediately receive three new calls, and all of the new calls could be a priority. This delay in dispatching police units frequently placed firefighters and paramedics in a dangerous position. They were not allowed to carry firearms, batons or any other type of weapon. They were, however, authorized to carry a flashlight.

Most veteran paramedics working in high-crime neighborhoods didn't bother with small flashlights. The old-timers carried a heavy metal flashlight called a Kel-lite. Some of these Kel-lites contained as many as six D-cell batteries, and weighed about twice as much as a police baton. Clearly, they were an effective and formative self-defense weapon.

We received a radio call indicating paramedics needed assistance. When we arrived at the scene, we noticed a suspect lying on the ground with a nasty cut to his forehead. And the usually very attentive paramedics had not bothered to attend to this injured and nearly unconscious man. I also noticed the paramedic was holding a very long Kel-lite.

I asked the guy with the big Kel-lite what happened, and he related the following story: They had received a code-3 call to attend to an injured citizen. When they arrived at the scene, they determined the injured citizen was actually a drunk who had fallen down but was not seriously hurt. The drunk, however, demanded that they transport him to the nearest hospital.

The paramedics were almost always courteous, so I assume they politely told the drunk that this was not an emergency and that if he wanted to go to the hospital he would have to find a way to get there on his own. This information apparently outraged the man and he took a big, round-house swing at the paramedic, which of course was a mistake.

The man was standing next to a knee-high fence bordering a front yard. The paramedic was able to dodge the punch thrown by the drunk and quickly retaliated with his Kel-lite. A six-cell Kel-lite colliding with the head of the drunk contained enough kinetic energy to propel the guy over the fence and flat on his back. The drunk now had a nice cut to his forehead that would require several stitches at the local emergency room. The drunk got his wish; he was now injured seriously enough to be taken to the hospital by the paramedics. It was a pleasure to see a professional paramedic working diligently for the citizens of Los Angeles. We transported the suspect to the hospital, got his head stitched up and booked him for battery on a fireman.

WHERE'S THE HOT TUB?

Los Angeles County had a superior court judge who was another example of a reasonably bright jurist with extremely poor judgment and an inflated opinion of her worth. She was small, fiery and in general made life difficult for anyone professionally associated with her. She would publically reprimand officers and attorneys for the most insignificant reasons.

Like most judges she wore a long, black robe in the court room. But unlike her colleagues, she almost always had a small dog tucked away inside the robe. The dog would sit on her lap—invisible to the courtroom spectators—while she considered legal issues from the bench.

She was once stopped by an LA motor cop for a traffic violation. She displayed a handgun and advised the officer that if he wrote her a ticket she would shoot him in the balls. It was, of course, unlikely that she would have carried out that threat, but anyone who had appeared before her knew she was capable of this type of language.

A good looking, middle-aged sergeant assigned to Newton spent most of one day on the witness stand testifying in her courtroom. Everything that happened that day in court was fairly typical, but the sergeant apparently made a favorable impression on the aging magistrate.

While at home with his family that evening, he received a phone call from the judge to report to her residence. When he asked her why, she said, "Be here within the hour or face contempt charges." She gave him her address and abruptly disconnected. Preferring to remain out of the slammer, the sergeant drove to her home. He was met at the front door by the judge. She was wearing a robe, but instead of being black it was pink and very short. She handed him a glass of wine and told him the hot tub was in the back of the house by the pool, and that she would be there in a minute.

BROKEN BONES

I once spent most of the day in Juvenile court testifying on a child custody issue. Also present in court were a group of law students who were observing courtroom procedures, tactics employed by attorneys and decisions made by the court. The mother was attempting to regain unsupervised custody of her four-year-old son. She had been convicted of child abuse; x-rays revealed her son had a number of broken bones in his arms and legs.

The mother was also a licensed chiropractor. Testimony was introduced in her criminal trial indicating she boasted to friends that she could break bones and not leave any evidence of an injury.

After hearing the case, the judge ruled the mother would be granted unsupervised custody of her son with a few stipulations. All the principals in the case cleared the courtroom and only the law students and I remained behind. She discussed the case with the students and decided to take a straw vote to determine how many of them, including myself, agreed with her decision. I don't recall the exact number of students in court, but let's say there were ten. The ballot results showed ten votes agreed with the judge with one dissenting vote, mine. It wasn't hard for everyone in the courtroom to figure out who disagreed with the judge.

The sad part of this decision, at least to me, was that all the students—many of them potential future judges—agreed with the judge and gave this poor four-year-old child back to his mother without supervision. Unfortunately, that decision is fairly typical of a California judge.

I NEED A HAIRCUT

The next incident involves a judge whose grooming was far more important than a criminal case.

I had two criminal cases on the same day in the same court house. And that's not unusual for an officer working a busy division like Newton. It's not uncommon for an officer to work all night and make an appearance in court the next morning and continue with this same routine for the entire work week. My first appearance was in a courtroom that was virtually empty except for me, the judge, his clerk and the bailiff. I overheard the judge telling the clerk to cancel all the cases that had been scheduled for that morning. The clerk asked the judge if there was a problem. The judge told her no, there was not a problem, but he had an appointment for a haircut at 10:00 a.m. He added that he had to drive across town and not to expect him back at court until after lunch, around 2:00 p.m.

I was a little upset when I heard the judge make that statement to his clerk, but there was not much I could do about it. I made my second appearance that day in a different courtroom on a case that had been trailing for months for a variety of reasons. However, on this particular day everyone was ready to go to trial. The defense ran out of excuses to extend the trial date, and the prosecutor was ready to go. When it was formally announced that both sides were ready to proceed, the judge asked his clerk to schedule the matter for another courtroom but for that day, if possible. The clerk made a phone call and informed the judge that not one courtroom was currently available. The case was reset for the following week.

Now I was more than upset. The courts were packed with cases, but a matter that was ready to go to trial had to be postponed because a judge would spend the entire morning getting his haircut.

The next day I explained what had occurred in court to my supervisor, and he discussed the incident with the captain. The captain directed me to write a lengthy report and include as many details and names as possible. I submitted the report and assumed nothing would be done. A month or so later, I was told to report to the captain's office. I had no idea why the captain wanted to see me, but I assumed I was in big trouble for something.

I was elated when I learned from the captain that the judge, who had wasted half a day getting his haircut, had been reprimanded by his supervisor. I guessed, however, that the supervising judge told the offending judge to keep his mouth shut the next time he goes for a haircut.

HIDING OUT IN THE WOMEN'S RESTROOM

I was almost late for court, and the judge in this particular courtroom would go ballistic if officers or attorneys were late. I also desperately had to locate a men's room. I had been working morning watch so I was still in uniform. On my way to the courtroom I passed the bathrooms in the hallway and made a quick mental note of their location. I made it to the courtroom on time, quickly checked in with the prosecutor and immediately bolted for the head. I went inside, found an empty stall and made myself comfortable. Seconds later I heard someone else enter the bathroom followed by two women talking. At first I thought the cleaning lady entered the men's room, but why would there be two of them. I heard a third person enter the facility and strike up a conversation with the first two. Now there were three women in the men's room. Or I had made a big mistake? It took me a few moments but I soon realized I had screwed up.

I tucked in my feet as close to the toilet bowl as possible and remained quiet. I sat there for about ten minutes until the room was empty. When all was quiet, I jumped up, fastened my pants and nearly sprinted out of the stall heading for the exit. As I pushed open the door leading to the hallway, I ran into a woman who was now entering the bathroom. And she just happened to be the defendant in my criminal case. She said, "What are *you* doing in here?" I mumbled "Police business," and I tried my best to disappear, but at six-two and two hundred and twenty pounds it was impossible to go unnoticed, especially in uniform.

This had to be a firing offense for a probationer. I was sure the defendant would bring it up in court and I would be met by Internal Affairs on my way out of the courtroom. Now what do I do? "Never cop out" ran through my mind, but the hallway was full of witnesses. There was just no way I could deny being in the women's bathroom, especially in uniform.

I approached one of the female sheriff's deputies stationed behind the information counter in the hallway, and explained to her in detail what had just happened. She immediately burst out in laughter. I, of course, failed to see the humor in the incident. I explained one more time that this could be a serious issue and it was a complete mistake on my part, and I really didn't think it was *that* funny. Once she stopped laughing and smirking, she said she would document the incident and clearly state that I had initiated the report.

I returned to the courtroom and testified against the defendant. I could see the defendant and her attorney whispering to each other, and I knew exactly what they were talking about. Fortunately for me, her lawyer wouldn't allow her on the stand. After testifying, I was excused by the prosecutor and got out of there as fast as I could.

I was a nervous wreck for the next week; I was certain Internal Affairs would be interviewing me about some perverse allegation—like the guy under the outhouse. No complaint was ever initiated, but to this day, I carefully scrutinize the outside of every public restroom door I enter. I'm especially cautious if I see terms like *Cowboy's* and *Cowgirl's* or ambiguous stick figures. The incident has clearly scarred me for life.

SUICIDE—ALMOST

Every division seemed to have at least one officer who was not very stable. And Newton was no exception.

Years ago the only type of handgun authorized for LAPD patrol officers was the revolver; semiautomatics were not permitted except for a few SWAT officers. All of LAPD's revolvers had been modified—some referred to them as being castrated—so they could not be cocked. Most modern revolvers are designed to be fired by pulling the trigger through its entire range of motion. Pulling the trigger rotates the cylinder which contains the bullets, draws the hammer back into the firing position, and releases the hammer that discharges the bullet (commonly referred to as double-action firing).

Most revolvers, however, can also be fired by manually pulling the hammer back into a locked position (usually with one's thumb), which cocks the gun. When manually cocked, the trigger is far more sensitive, and it only needs to be pulled a short distance before the gun will discharge. Some believe a revolver fired from a cocked position (commonly referred to as single-action firing) is more accurate than a revolver that has not been cocked. That sounds reasonable, but I don't know if it's true. I do know, however, that a cocked handgun is far more prone to an accidental discharge, and that's why LAPD revolvers had been modified so that they could not be manually cocked as in single-action. Consequently, these modified revolvers were safer weapons.

The hammer of a modified LAPD revolver can be manually pulled back until it stops, but it will not remain in the cocked position. In fact, if the hammer is manually pulled back and released, it will fly forward, but it will *not* discharge the round as the firing pin will not contact the primer at the base of bullet. I don't know how this was accomplished, but it works. The hammer on a loaded LAPD revolver can be pulled back and released all day long and it will not fire a bullet. It was supposed to be physically impossible to cock a modified weapon.

Almost every officer who was issued a revolver would take it to the range and make sure it could not be cocked. And during this checking-out process, I'm sure nearly everyone would pull the hammer back and release it on a live round to make sure the gun would not fire. If for no other reason, it satisfied your curiosity.

One Newton officer, however, had his own way of checking to make sure the gun would not fire by pulling and releasing the hammer. In front of other officers, he would put the end of the barrel against the side of his head—as if committing suicide—pull the hammer back and release it. There was always a click and the gun never fired, but why take such a foolish chance? From that point on, everyone had some serious doubts about this officer's judgment.

WHERE'S MY GUN

LAPD definitely had a double standard for judging regular police officers compared to high ranking officers, captains and above. Not surprisingly, many rules were ignored or excused for a few chosen, senior leaders. And what follows is a good example: Two of the three captains assigned to Newton were engaged in a conversation about guns. One of the captains mentioned to the other one that he could not find his handgun. The second captain stated he too could not locate his weapon. Frankly, captains had very little use for weapons as they spent most of their days stuck behind a desk. Both captains, however, had lost their guns and neither one could remember the last time he had it in his possession.

It was unusual to see a captain in civilian clothes walking around the station with a sidearm tucked away in a holster. Most of the captains stored their weapon under the front seat of their take-home police car, using it or seeing it once a month when they had to qualify on the range. The captains didn't want to tell anyone they had lost their weapons, but they suspected the guns had been taken by local gangbangers hired by Newton's Community Relations section to wash police cars. A stakeout was established on the roof of the station using supervisors. Had officers been used, everyone would have known the captains screwed up and they would not have been able to conceal their careless behavior.

As expected the local gang members, brought in to wash cars, were ripping off the handguns left under the front seat of the captains' cars. When an unmarked car was given to a gang member to be washed, the first thing he did was check under the front seat for a hand gun. Somehow both captains got their guns back and neither one was disciplined. However, had uniformed line officers lost their handguns to local gangbangers, it would have made the front page of the LA Times and they would have been suspended from duty without pay.

DECENT CITIZENS

The overwhelming majority of the people living and working in Newton were decent, hardworking citizens. Many of them didn't care for the police, but they were good folks who, like almost everyone else, worked very hard to maintain a decent lifestyle and to accumulate the good things in life. And when these folks were burglarized or robbed, the suspect was generally someone from their own community, one of their own brothers or sisters.

I have a very good recollection of taking a burglary report from a single mother who lived in Newton. Like almost everyone else she went to work in the morning, put in a long, hard eight hours, and returned home at night to take care of her children. On this day, however, she came home to a residence that had been almost completely stripped of everything of value—even some items of very little value. The suspects had taken her TV, her jewelry, most of her furniture, the rug on her floor, and even the hot water heater.

A lot of victims create their own problems and, in general, I have very little sympathy for them. This woman, however, was different. Everything for which she had worked so hard had been stolen. When I met her at the front door, she and her young children had been crying and were almost hysterical. She didn't blame me for the burglary, and she wasn't upset that it took us so long to arrive at her house, but she and her family had been devastated. It's likely that all of her hard work went out the front door because a hype—heroin addict—needed heroin.

I printed everything in the house that had a suitable surface for latent prints, and I actually obtained several good ones from the refrigerator and the point of entry. Later on I followed up on the report and the prints with the Newton's burglary detectives and learned they actually had a named suspect, an address, and a warrant for his arrest. I had clearly taken an interest in this case, and they asked me if I wanted to join them for the arrest. You bet.

I wish I could report that the guy resisted arrest and we were able to get a pound of flesh, but like most hypes he was not violent and was arrested without incident—well, maybe the cuffs were a little tight. We recovered a few items that had been listed on the original burglary report, but almost everything of value had already gone into his arm. He was convicted of burglary and sent to the slammer, and he would eventually get released and probably start all over again. However, we did our job; the system actually worked, and we probably prevented another hard working citizen from becoming a victim.

Aside from a paycheck, there were some lasting rewards for doing a good job. And once again, there was no sound like the slamming of a jail door on someone who belongs in custody.

NAZIS IN NEWTON

Why a small group of Nazis would establish a club house in Newton Division is completely beyond my comprehension, but they did. Unfortunately, my memory of the following incident is not as clear as other incidents, probably because I had no direct involvement in it. Everything I'm about to relate is second-hand information, but the essence of the story is not too far off the mark.

Many of the coppers who worked the South-end simply did not like the citizens who lived there. And far more of the citizens who lived there absolutely hated coppers, especially white coppers. Was there open contempt between the two groups, you bet. I hope the situation today has changed or is changing. However, in 2013, I drove by Newton Station and it had been completely remodeled. It now looks like an armed fortress: high block walls with no windows, huge steel rolling gates and no welcoming entrance for members of the community. It was so intimidating in appearance that even I would have been somewhat reluctant to enter the station from the street.

The Nazi club house was located in the extreme northeast corner of the division, an area, perhaps, with the fewest number of blacks and Hispanics. One afternoon someone from inside the clubhouse began shooting at kids walking by the location, black and Hispanic children. No one was hit, but the shooter was fairly close to the kids, so it appeared that whoever was doing the shooting simply wanted to frighten them. Openly shooting at anyone, of course, on the streets of LA was not tolerated. Officers were called to the scene and eventually made entry into the clubhouse. I don't recall if anyone was located or if anyone was arrested, but officers now had access to the interior of the facility. Guys reported seeing an amazing amount of Nazi propaganda, photos of Hitler, Hermann Goring and Adolf Eichmann were on the walls along with an abundance of Nazi flags and photos of concentration camps with emaciated prisoners. The concentration-camp photos were on display as if they were proud of the imprisoned Jews.

The coppers who entered the facility were outraged at these Nazis. Not so much because of the contents of the building, although that was abhorrent to all the guys, but because they were indiscriminately shooting at very young, very innocent school children. The coppers and the citizens clearly did not get along, but when serious and important issues confronted the officers, all of them, without exception, supported these kids and their parents. The officers were concerned for the kids and unbelievably angry at these neo-Nazis.

I heard the building caught fire and burned down, but I don't know that for a fact. I was hopeful, however, that relations between the police and the community would eventually improve.

CHAPTER THREE: COMMUNICATIONS DIVISION

After successfully completing a one-year probationary period, officers were transferred out of the patrol division to which they had been assigned and into a support division. New assignments could be Jail Division, Parking and Intersection Control (PIC, directing traffic at a busy downtown intersection) or Communications Division. I was assigned to Communications.

There were two types of officers assigned to these three divisions: young guys, just off probation, who were eager to be on the streets, and the old-timers who had little or no job interest and were about to retire—guys just collecting their pay checks.

The involuntary reassignments for those officers just off probation lasted six months, and at the end of that period they were generally allowed to transfer to any patrol division of their choice.

A Communications assignment meant you were destined to sit at the complaint board along with twenty or so other officers to answer emergency phone calls. The department wanted sworn officers answering the calls so they could evaluate the nature of the call to determine if a police officer was, in fact, needed. LAPD had a huge demand for "called for services": citizens demanding that a police officer be dispatched to a location. However, many of these requests were frivolous, non-emergency calls and did not require the presence of sworn personnel. It was the complaint board operators' responsibility to determine if a black-and-white was needed and would be dispatched. A conscientious officer working the board could easily reduce the demand for "called for services" freeing up officers to respond to real emergencies.

NO "POKE" CHOPS

I received a few memorable calls while assigned to Communications. On one particular evening an older gentleman called the emergency number and demanded we dispatch a car to his house. When I asked him why he needed a car, he stated his wife would not prepare him any "poke" chops. I tried to explain to him that not having pork chops did not constitute an emergency and we would not dispatch a car. He remained upset and continued to demand the presence of a policeman. Normally I would have simply hung up on the man, but that usually meant he would just call back and continue his demand for a car. In this case, I told him to put his wife on the phone.

His wife took the phone and meekly said, "Yes, officer." I asked her if it was true that she would not prepare him any pork chops. She told me that it was true; she was tired and didn't want to prepare pork chops for dinner. I asked her if her husband worked that day. She said yes, he worked *every day* (which is a phrase that is heard a great deal in the African-American community). I quickly launched into a short lecture about taking care of her man—very politically incorrect, but she admitted that he was a good provider. She eventually agreed to cook the pork chops, and her husband told me it wasn't necessary to send a policeman.

The watch commander had been monitoring this particular phone call. I was called into his office expecting to be reprimanded for taking a long time to complete this call. I was surprised when he told me that I had done a good job. He explained that most of the complaint board operators, especially the old-timers, would have automatically dispatched a car, which would have been a complete waste of manpower. I was often chided, in a friendly way, by my fellow complaint board operators for answering the fewest number of calls per shift; however, I almost always dispatched the fewest number of black-and-whites, which was the reason for having a sworn officer answer the phone. I was not happy working Communications, but I was pleased the boss thought I was doing a good job.

A TRULY HOT CALL

The Complaint Board was a long table with officers sitting across from one another. These officers answered all the emergency phone calls made to LAPD except for the Valley divisions.

Down the middle of the table was a conveyor belt that would transport a card from the complaint board operator to the dispatcher and ultimately to the RTO (Radio Telephone Operator). The card contained all the pertinent information about the call: the address, the nature of the call and the reporting district. The RTO would then assign the call via the radio to a black-and-white.

Most of the calls were routine and were not considered a priority. A family dispute, a burglary report, a minor traffic accident were all nonemergency calls. A shooting in progress, a bank robbery, or a homicide were all priority calls, and a patrol car was usually dispatched code-3. Code-3 calls were referred to as hotshots. When the operators were bored or wanted to liven up the atmosphere in Communications, they would place the card containing all the information about the hotshot call on the conveyor belt and set it on fire. A flaming, smoking card quickly traveled from the operator's position all the way to the dispatcher. This usually pissed off the dispatcher but it always got his attention and was good for a laugh.

OFFICER, THIS IS A LITTLE EMBARRASSING

As mentioned previously, it's very common for officers working morning watch and night watch to get very little sleep, especially in busy divisions. Daily appearances in court and overtime are the rule rather than the exception. It's not at all uncommon for a morning watch officer to fall asleep while his partner is driving the patrol car. Occasionally, if both officers have had little sleep, they will find a secluded and safe location to shut down for a few minutes. Generally, the radio is turned up so that no radio calls are missed.

The department made no allowances for officers working excessive overtime. Sometimes, however, exhaustion took its toll and officers were simply unable to remain awake.

A good example of complete exhaustion was brought to my attention while working the complaint board during one morning-watch shift. I received a phone call from a concerned citizen who stated, "Officer, this is a little embarrassing, but one of your patrol cars is stopped at a red light and both officers appear to be asleep." The caller assured me that both officers were sleeping and were not injured. I thanked him for the call, and advised him that I would take care of the matter.

The complaint-board officers were expected to call the divisional watch commander and advise him of any misconduct reported by a citizen. A supervisor would have been dispatched and the officers would have been disciplined for sleeping on duty. Having been in that situation myself, I thought there might have been a different way to solve the problem without notifying a supervisor. I called the divisional desk officer and asked him if there was a unit inside the station that *he* could quietly dispatch to the location of the sleeping officers. He too had probably been in that same situation and told me that he would wake the officers.

He called back a few minutes later and explained that both officers had been in court all week and were exhausted. About three in the morning they had stopped at a red light and quickly fell asleep. The engine was running, the transmission was in drive, but the driver had somehow managed to keep his foot on the brake. He also said they really appreciated my efforts to keep them out of trouble.

It was always a little surprising and disappointing to me when the department severely disciplined officers for acting like humans. The department expected you to work sixteen hours a day for a solid week, but would give you days off—a type of suspension—if you happened to fall asleep on duty. And if some asshole spit in your face and you knocked him on his ass, it's likely that you were going to be investigated and disciplined. I suppose there are people who would not physically react to someone spitting in their face, but very few of them were LA cops.

HI CHIEF

The Chief of Police, Ed Davis, a man I respected a great deal, urged me to apply to become an LA cop when I was in college. He taught Police Science at Cal State LA, and I was one of his *unremarkable* students. I was flattered by his encouragement but at the time I wanted to be an FBI agent. (I always thought FBI stood for Federal Bureau of Investigation, while on the department I learned that it probably stood for Fan Belt Inspector.)

The chief would occasionally use the men's room that was adjacent to Communications Division. In order to reach the men's room, he had to walk through a war room that was set up for disaster control. It was common for complaint-board operators to use this usually empty room to catch some sleep during their lunch period.

On one occasion I was in the room sitting in a chair, sound asleep, with my feet up on a desk; my legs were blocking the way to the bathroom. I heard someone say, "excuse me, officer" as he stepped over my outstretched legs. I looked up, saw Ed Davis, and sheepishly said, "Hi Chief." I was sure I was in big trouble and I dearly hoped that he didn't recognize me as one of his former students. Fortunately, he didn't. He said nothing to my boss about sleeping, even though I was on my lunch break. I had a feeling that he understood that at times officers could act like humans and not be judged or disciplined for their humanity. He was a good chief. I learned from his classes that he loved being a cop, and he even liked the term *cop*. It was not a pejorative to him and that's why I use it so often.

OFFICER, THERE'S A MAN OUTSIDE MY HOUSE WITH A GUN

The citizens of South-Central Los Angeles were not dummies. They understood that the department was understaffed and at times extremely busy. It was not uncommon to be assigned a low-priority radio call, sometimes even a high-priority call, and actually arrive at the scene an hour after the call was placed. The citizens also knew that the quickest way to get an officer to respond was to report that a gun was involved in the call, even if no gun was seen. If you wanted the police now, the magic word was *gun*.

Sworn officers acting as complaint-board operators earned their money when they were able to determine that a caller reported a gun was involved just to get the police to respond quicker. It was always a difficult call for the officer to make; mistakes could be deadly. Unfortunately, guns were nearly always present and were used frequently in South-Central LA.

One busy evening I received a call from a woman who was reporting there was a man outside her house with a gun. I asked her questions about the man in an effort to determine the validity of the call. She was, naturally, a little annoyed with me when I didn't immediately indicate we would dispatch a car. She insisted the man had a gun, but I continued to ask her questions about the incident. I could hear the frustration in her voice and began to believe there really was a man with a gun.

Seconds later, there was no doubt about the man with a gun. I heard over the phone the sound of a weapon being discharged rapidly. The firing sequence was so quick and loud that it could easily have been a fully-automatic assault rifle. I was convinced. I designated the call a code-3 hotshot, warned the responding officers that a fully-automatic weapon may have been involved, lighted the card on fire and sent it down the conveyor belt in flames, directly to a royally pissed-off dispatcher.

OFFICER, I'LL CALL YOU RIGHT BACK

This incident did not happen to me and I'm not sure if it is true. I suspect, however, that it could be. A young officer was recently assigned to Communications and was not at all familiar with South-Central Los Angeles. It was a busy weekend night with hundreds of calls flooding into the Complaint Board. He went to his assigned position, put on his headphones, plugged into the system and started answering emergency calls. One of his first calls was from a man who had found a dead body. Probably a homicide. The citizen making the call told the officer that he had discovered the body just outside the phone booth from which he was calling. He told the officer what he had discovered and asked him to dispatch a black-and-white, no need for an ambulance. The officer asked the man several questions, one of which was the location of the dead body. The citizen told the officer he was on Figueroa, but he was unsure of the cross street. The caller was difficult to understand and the officer was not familiar with downtown Los Angeles as he had previously been assigned to Harbor Division. The officer asked the caller to spell "Figueroa" for him. The citizen, who may have been under the influence of alcohol or drugs, was confused by the question. His response went something like this: *Whatuch you mean, spell it?* The officer probably responded by asking the citizen to *spell* the name of the street. For example, *cat* is spelled *c-a-t*. The citizen told the officer he was not sure how to spell Figueroa but he would try.

He started with the letter *f* followed by the letter *i*. Not a bad start, but he was lost after *i*. He stumbled through about half the alphabet and was clearly frustrated. The officer finally provided the letter *g* and the caller said he thought that was correct. After the *g* was established and with a bit of a delay, the caller continued with the letters *y-o-u* and then *r-o-w*. The officer stopped the man and told him, "No, no that's not possible."

Out of extreme frustration the citizen told the copper he was going to hang up and call him back. The officer said, "Wait; don't hang up the phone." Followed by, "What are you going to do?" The citizen told the officer, "I'm gonna drag this dead motherfucker to First and Adams and call you back!"

He could spell First and Adams, but Figueroa was not in his dictionary.

After my six months were up, it was time to go back to patrol. I could hardly wait to get out of Communications and return to real cop work. To my surprise, I received an outstanding rating report at the end of my tour. My lieutenant told me he almost never issued an outstanding rating to board operators, but my refusal to dispatch a car over the pork chops and still keep the caller relatively happy was the deciding factor. If I didn't make it as a street cop, I apparently had a home in Communications. No thanks.

CHAPTER FOUR: HARBOR DIVISION

I always wanted to work Harbor Division, probably because of my attachment to the ocean. After working Communications, I was given my choice of patrol divisions, and Harbor was the obvious choice. I discovered, however, that there was a huge difference between my first patrol division, Newton, and Harbor. The waterfront division had a much lower crime rate, fewer homicides and far fewer gang members. And the local gang members seemed to be somewhat less violent.

My father lived in San Pedro on Beacon Street during World War II. He once told me there were fights and stabbings almost every night. Life in San Pedro had changed; it was now a fairly quiet bedroom community.

There was also a big difference between the officers. Newton officers were hard chargers, seemed to enjoy working patrol and were more conscious of their personal safety. By comparison, more than a few—but not a majority—of the Harbor coppers seemed to view the division as a final home until retirement. Many of them were simply lazy and content working a slow division. The locker rooms were also very different. There was not a lot of complaining and harping among the officers of Newton. Harbor coppers, however, seemed to complain about everything. I know it's the nature of the beast to complain, but there was a clear difference between the officers who made up each division.

I enjoyed working Harbor, but if you were young and eager, the South-Central divisions were the only place to work. The pace was much quicker, the camaraderie was stronger, you learned a great deal more and my feeling of accomplishment was greater in South-Central than Harbor.

FRIED CHICKEN

My first noteworthy incident at Harbor occurred during night watch while patrolling 6th Street in San Pedro. I was the passenger officer and we were driving slowly down the street, windows down, looking and listening for bad guys. Our watch was about over and the radio had been fairly quiet all night long. There was a fine Greek restaurant on 6th Street not too far from the court house. The owner had played football at USC and was a well-known figure in the community. As we approached the restaurant—we were driving close to the curb at about five m.p.h—the front door suddenly opened and an African-American male flew out of the entrance, stumbled over the sidewalk and crashed into the side of our black-and-white. The man was uninjured and our car wasn't damaged, but he had been knocked out by the collision with our car.

We stopped the car, detained the suspect, who appeared to be drunk, and interviewed the young and rather muscular restaurant owner. He advised us that the suspect had walked into his restaurant, which only served traditional Greek food, and demanded that he be served Southern fried chicken. The owner explained to him that he only served Greek cuisine and was unable to fry any chicken. The drunk continued his demand for fried chicken, and once again, the owner explained to him that he did not serve fried chicken. The big Greek owner finally told the man to leave the restaurant. The drunk, however, was not budging—he was going to stay until he got his chicken—and he continued to cause problems.

The drunk was now disrupting his business so the owner decided to take the matter—literally—into his own hands. He grabbed the man by the back of his shirt collar, walked him to the front door, opened the door (fortunately) and rather unceremoniously tossed the guy out onto the sidewalk where he stumbled and eventually collided with the side of our car. The collision startled me and my partner. We weren't sure exactly what had happened until we interviewed the owner and a few witnesses. We learned the suspect was causing a problem inside the restaurant and was eventually tossed out by the owner.

The guy was drunk in public and no real harm had been done. We advised the owner that we would transport the suspect to the nearest Colonel Sanders or the Harbor Jail, depending on which one was the closest. He thanked us and invited us to eat at his restaurant with our wives.

MOTOR COPS

Harbor station was also home to South Traffic Division. Traffic divisions are responsible for taking traffic accident reports, writing as many tickets as possible— yes, there really is a quota system but the word *quota* is never used—and booking "deuces" (drunk drivers).

South Traffic Division motorcycle officers used Harbor station as their home base, which is where roll call and inspections took place. There was a suspicion among most LAPD officers that motor cops were not very bright. This erroneous belief probably began at the academy. Academy instructors were constantly making fun of—and joking about—dimwitted motor cops, often referring to their motorcycles as ball bearing jackasses. Ironically, the instructor who was primarily responsible for this misconception was a former motor cop.

Motor cops, of course, were not generally liked by the public. As previously mentioned, their primary function was to write tickets and book DUIs. Most of the public believed that the motor cops should be focusing on putting bad guys in jail and not writing them a ticket, a position with which I do not disagree. (The city, of course, could not afford to give up the lucrative source of income provided by citations.) A well-known and likeable motor cop, a Greek named Tony (naturally), was assigned to South Traffic Division and generally worked the Harbor area. A help call was broadcast during day watch at one of the hospitals in San Pedro. The responding officers found Tony—who was an ER patient—in uniform on the floor of the emergency room *fighting* with a hospital employee. Order was restored and Tony related the following story: While on his "motor," he had been involved in a traffic accident with another vehicle. He sustained a few minor injuries to his body but he had a severely broken leg. He was transported to the hospital by an RA unit and delivered to the ER. Tony was lying on a gurney in uniform waiting to be seen by the ER doctor. One of the attendants, a hospital employee, walked by his gurney and recognized Tony as the cop who had given him a ticket several days before.

The attendant, who obviously didn't have any warm, fuzzy feelings for Tony, decided it was time to get even. He asked Tony if he remembered him. Tony, who was in a lot of pain, said no and even apologized for not recognizing the guy. The attendant said, "You're the asshole who gave me a ticket last week." Following that statement, he pushed Tony off the gurney onto the floor. Tony, who was now in excruciating pain, was not about to let this jerk get away. He grabbed him by the leg and wouldn't let go. I think I would have been tempted to shoot the son-of-a-bitch, but as I said before, Tony was a real decent guy.

Another hospital employee saw and heard the two fighting in the small cubicle and called the police. The arriving officers placed the attendant under arrest for battery on a police officer and transported him to jail. Tony made a full recovery and continued riding his "motor" and writing tickets.

THE MOTOR COP AND THE JUDGE

As I mentioned before, some folks question the judgment of motor cops. The following story, if true, would suggest that at least one of them had questionable judgment. The hero of this story worked South Traffic

Division. I would like to think the incident is accurate, but I have no personal knowledge of the facts.

It seems that a motor cop was on-duty but parked at an intersection looking for violators. A passing vehicle, driven by a young man, rolled down his window, extended his left arm and flipped-off the motor cop. This was a clear "contempt of cop" violation. You won't, however, find the section in the Vehicle Code. The motor cop fired up his ball-bearing jackass, pursued and eventually stopped the young man and gave him a citation. I'm not sure of the exact violation but I suspect it may have been one of the lesser known sections of the code: *no wind on the windshield* or *no gloves in the glove box* are two good examples. Regardless of the section cited, the violator was issued a ticket by a pissed-off motor cop.

Several weeks later the motor cop received a subpoena to appear in traffic court. The motor cop testified to the facts of the violation, including the display of the "finger" by the defendant. This, of course, was a mistake. After the motor cop testified, the judge decided it was time to explain the law to the officer. The judge began his lecture by admonishing the cop that he needed probable cause to stop a violator and that giving the "finger" was not probable cause. The judge went on to explain that it was perfectly acceptable for the young man to extend his middle finger at the cop, and there was absolutely no justification for the traffic stop and the citation. This officious judge explained that the violator was merely exercising his right to free speech, and he promptly dismissed the case.

The motor cop left the stand and walked to the doors leading out of the court room. However, just before he left, he turned to the judge and said, "Excuse me your honor, but did you mean to say that it was perfectly acceptable for the defendant to "flip me off?" From the bench, the judge said that there was nothing wrong with the defendant giving the "finger" to the cop, and that it was not probable cause for a traffic stop and citation. The officer acknowledged that he understood the judge's comment.

Just before leaving the court room, the motor cop raised his arm and extended his middle finger in a classic display of the "international gesture of contempt." He said, "this is for you judge" and he walked out of the courtroom. The judge, of course, went ballistic. He ordered the officer to return to his courtroom for a blistering reprimand. I don't know the outcome of this event, but if it was true I'm sure the department suspended the motor cop for conduct unbecoming an officer. True or not, it's a good story.

WAY TOO MUCH HAIR

All uniform officers are subject to routine inspections, usually unannounced. The inspecting supervisor, a sergeant or a lieutenant, will scrutinize each officer to determine if his hair, including his mustache, meets departmental standards. The supervisor will also determine if his uniform is pressed and clean, are his shoes highly shined, is his badge polished and is his hand gun clean and loaded? (I once worked with an officer who worked the entire shift with an empty gun.)

LAPD had very strict standards for the length of an officer's hair, especially his mustache, and of course, almost every officer in uniform wore a mustache. I started growing mine the day I got off probation, and thirty-seven years later it's still in place. The section of the department manual that defines the size and shape of a mustache and the length of an officer's hair must be several pages in length (the section was probably written by some pencil-necked geek who worked the street for about a month). A few supervisors have actually used rulers to determine if a 'stash was in compliance with the manual. Some mustaches were too long, they extended below the bottom of the upper lip; some were too uneven, the very bottom of the mustache did not have a razor edge indicating that it hadn't been trimmed recently; and some were too wide, they extended beyond the width of the mouth. It always gave me a warm and fuzzy feeling knowing that our supervisors were so concerned about the size and shape of a mustache and the length of hair.

Inspections were almost always interesting. Guys would do some silly things to turn a formal inspection into a good laugh. And supervisors generally went along with the jokes. One officer kept a long-haired wig in his locker that he would quickly don just before we lined up for inspection. Another guy would switch his boots: right boot on his left foot, and left boot on his right foot. I once got a royal ass chewing from a lieutenant, who had been a marine gunnery sergeant, because my gun and bullets were covered in rust. (I had been hosed down by a fireman the day before and hadn't checked my gun.)

It was inspection time and a squad of South Traffic motor cops was lined up in the parking lot as a sergeant walked by each officer and scrutinized his appearance. The sergeant stopped at one officer in particular and studied his mustache. He didn't use a ruler, but he quickly formed the opinion that the mustache was not within departmental standards. In fact it was huge, black and stood out like a preacher in a whore house. The sergeant advised the officer his mustache was so beyond the standards that by tomorrow he wanted to see about half as much hair.

The next day the motor cop reported to the sergeant with exactly half as much hair as he had on the day of the inspection. He had shaved off one-half of his mustache, the right side. The left side was still completely intact and had not been touched by a razor. Every officer in the station cracked up over the mustache. The sergeant, however, failed to see the humor of half a mustache and wanted to give the motor cop some days off (a form of suspension).

OFFICERS SMITH AND JONES

As previously mentioned, a few officers would occasionally fall asleep on-duty when assigned to morning watch. Most of them were sleep-deprived after working all night and then spending all day in court. And it was not unusual for a hard-working officer to work all week on morning watch and be in court each day after work, compounding the problem of not enough sleep. The radio was usually very quiet from about three in the morning until sunup. Most of the time the driver would continue driving the patrol car and the passenger officer would slump down in the seat and try to sleep for a few minutes. Occasionally, if both officers were exhausted, they would find a secluded spot where a parked black-and-white wouldn't be noticed and try to catch-up on sleep. However, it was always necessary to listen to the radio so that any radio call assigned to the sleeping officers would not be missed. A few officers, dedicated morning watch coppers, became extremely adept at falling asleep but still picking up a radio call assigned to their unit. One Harbor officer, an old-timer who worked morning watch for years, was famous for his ability to be sound asleep and still pick up a radio call.

Two officers took sleeping on-duty to an extreme; I'll call them Officers Smith and Jones. Most of the guys in the division wouldn't have been surprised if pillows and blankets were routinely carried in their car. One early morning, around three, a group of Harbor officers found themselves in a big fight with a clan of Samoans. The "blue-suiters" were outnumbered and losing the fight. A help call was eventually broadcast to all units within the area. A flood of black-and-whites and even officers from the south end of 77th Division responded to the call.

Once everyone had gathered together at the scene of the call, a sergeant organized the officers for an assault on the front porch of the residence. The sergeant, who knew all the officers within the division, noticed two of his men were in effect out of uniform. It seems that Officer Jones was wearing Officer Smith's uniform shirt—all uniform shirts have name tags—and Officer Smith had on Officer Jones' shirt. What happened? It was suspected that both Smith and Jones had been sleeping in their concealed black-and-white but still listening to the radio. In order to avoid wrinkling their uniform shirts, they removed them and placed them in the back seat of their car. When the help call was broadcast, both officers grabbed a shirt, quickly put it on and responded to the call. It was obvious that both men were sleeping comfortably. The sergeant, who was actually a good supervisor, called them on the shirts, but they were hard-pressed to explain the mix-up. I'm sure they had to do fast talking to stay out of trouble.

FIGHTING SAMOANS

There were a fair number of Samoans in Harbor Division; most of them resided in the community of Wilmington. Wilmington, often referred to as "Wilmas" by local gang members and the police, also had a large population of Hispanics. Samoans were generally very decent, law abiding citizens. And that's reason to be thankful as many of the men and a few of the women hit the scales at over four-hundred pounds. Fighting a Samoan or a group of Samoans—a more likely scenario—is never any fun. I was involved in two separate altercations with them; the first incident involved a single individual who was drunk and causing a problem. He was uncooperative and I foolishly tried to choke him out. His neck was probably over thirty inches in circumference and there was no way I was going to control this guy—who was the size of a sumo wrestler—by choking him out. Unfortunately, I was working with a reserve officer who was fairly useless as a dependable partner (most reserves, however, performed reasonably well).

As I was rolling around on the ground with the suspect, my partner, the reservist, was literally running around in circles (the Samoan and I were in the middle of the circle) and yelling, "What do we do, what do we do?"

I was finally able to tell my partner to put out an *officer needs assistance* call as we needed a lot more humanity to control this guy. I had no delusions that I was going to be able to handcuff this suspect by myself. I was hoping I could hold on long enough for more troops to arrive and to avoid being thrown around like a rag doll. Fortunately the man was not extremely aggressive toward me. Had he decided to hit me with one of his paws, the fight would have been over and I would have lost. However, other than shooting this giant, it was impossible for me to control him by myself and my partner, the observer, was no help.

The cavalry finally arrived; we cuffed the guy (we needed two sets of cuffs because his wrists were so far apart) and almost had to call for a B-wagon to transport him to the station. He was nearly too big for the back seat of our cruiser. I retrieved my uniform hat and discovered it had been crushed by my four-hundred pound friend. The cloth top of the hat was torn and the shiny bill had been scratched badly, it was hardly recognizable as a hat. I also noticed that my badge had been torn from my shirt and was hanging by a thread and my pants were torn and ripped. A nice cool breeze told me I had also ripped out the seat of my pants. I was uninjured but a complete mess. My partner, however, was ready for inspection: not a hair out of place, and his uniform was immaculate. After I collected all my gear (my baton, hat and flashlight were scattered all over the man's front yard), he told me, "I guess we kicked his ass!" I said, "Ya, *we* sure did. It only took about half of the watch just to cuff the guy."

A UNIQUE BATON

The unique baton incident is actually a continuation of the Smith and Jones switched-shirts story. A Harbor patrol unit was assigned to a call concerning a 415 party at a house located at the north end of San Pedro. It was later determined that several complaints regarding the party had been received earlier in the evening. When the morning-watch unit arrived they were met by an unruly crowd in front of the house. The crowd gathered on the large front porch that was above street level by about ten feet. In other words, they had the high ground. The initial responding car quickly realized they were seriously outnumbered and the crowd was growing more and more hostile. Before any action was taken, the primary unit decided to request back-up units to help with crowd control. The officers wisely remained in their car, which was parked about one hundred feet from the party house, until additional units arrived.

As the officers sat in their black-and-white, rocks, bottles, and just about anything that could be thrown was hurled at their car. A large rock finally made contact with the front windshield and nearly smashed it out of the frame. The incident was quickly getting out of control and the officers decided it was time to put out an *officer needs help* call. Almost every morning-watch unit arrived at the location, including Smith and Jones, as well as a field sergeant. The sergeant decided the party was over; he gathered a squad of eight to ten officers to mount an assault on the raised porch and end the party. I was one of men who had gathered at the base of the steps that led to the porch. The crowd became more and more hostile, and the rocks and bottles had not stopped. As we were planning our tactics, a radio about the size of a loaf of bread was thrown from the top of the porch and struck me in the arm. No serious damage was done, but everyone, including our sergeant, was now royally pissed-off.

The sergeant was a real leader, not to be confused with an administrator. He was the type of man who led from the front not the rear. He instinctively knew we had to quickly disperse this crowd or the rocks and bottles would begin again and we'd have a full-scale riot on our hands. With little regard for his own personal safety, the sergeant announced, "Come on boys, follow me!" And he charged up the steps leading to the top of the porch followed by all his "blue-suiters." Of course, once we got to the top of the stairs, the fights began.

I had a pretty good idea who had thrown the radio and I made a beeline for the guy. As I got to the porch and approached my suspect, I struck him in the right shoulder with the heel of my right hand to spin him around so that I could choke him out. The tactic worked and I found myself behind the suspect with my right arm across his throat and my left hand applying pressure to my right arm to effect the choke-out. However, before I could render the suspect unconscious, another Harbor copper, Sal, struck my guy in the head with an elongated object. At the time I couldn't tell exactly what it was, but it was effective. My suspect went down like a home-sick brick, and I could feel a warm, wet and sticky substance on my arm. I cuffed my guy and went to the next suspect. However, the crowd apparently realized that the party was definitely over—watching one of their friends collapse into a bloody heap didn't hurt—and everyone quickly dispersed. After a few minutes all was quiet and the suspects taken into custody were transported to the station or the hospital. My guy needed a few stitches.

While at the station and writing arrest reports, I casually asked Sal if he used his heavy, aluminum flashlight called a Kel-lite (some people called it a "kill-light") to strike the suspect. Sal stated, "No, I used my baton." I said, "Bullshit, a baton wouldn't knock this guy to his knees with one shot." Was Sal not telling me the truth? Some officers who hadn't yet developed a sense of trust, were reluctant to cop out to their partners when they had violated department procedures (striking a suspect on the head with a metal flashlight was a violation of department policy). I was a little hurt that Sal apparently felt he couldn't trust me with the truth. I didn't believe for an instant that he had used his baton. One blow from a baton, even to the head, will do very little to subdue someone who really wants to fight. At the time, batons were made of hardwood, but they were still fairly light and ineffective. There was just no way that Sal could have used a light, wooden baton so effectively.

Sal displayed one of his big grins and said that he would be right back. When he returned, he was carrying his baton. Sal looked around to make sure no one was watching and then removed his baton and tossed it to me. Expecting it to be fairly light, I nearly dropped it on the floor. Sal's baton was almost twice as heavy as a normal baton. And most of the additional weight was located near the top of his stick. I said, "Jesus, where did you get this?" He told me he made it himself. He'd cut off the end of the baton, drilled out the inside of the wood and filled it with lead. He then glued the top back in place, sanded it carefully and repainted it black. It looked like a normal baton, but was much more effective. Sal's baton ended the fight on the front porch and quickly put an end to the party and near-riot.

Several years later the department began authorizing the use of a heavier, fiberglass baton that came with a handle that was mounted perpendicular to the main shaft. It was far more effective than the lighter, wooden sticks used in the past. I guess Sal was ahead of his time.

THE MAN FROM THE ICE HOUSE

Terminal Island is a small manmade island that is between Los Angeles and Long Beach Harbors. It's probably best known for housing a federal prison, but it was also the location of several canneries and a commercial fishing fleet. One night we received a code-30 radio call for a structure located on TI. A code-30 meant a burglary alarm had been activated and officers were directed to investigate the structure for signs of a burglary. I can't provide the exact stats, but something like ninety-five percent of all code-30s in the city were false alarms. When responding to code-30s, officers usually inspected the exterior of the structure; if all the doors and windows were secure, we assumed it was a false alarm. As you might expect, code-30s were low priority calls and most guys were in no hurry to respond.

The structure was on Terminal Island and we happened to be close to the location when the call was broadcast. My partner and I thought that if this was a legitimate call—which was unlikely—we had a good chance of catching the suspect. When we arrived, we discovered the building was an ice house that supplied ice to the commercial fishing boats. We also noticed a man, wearing a heavy coat, was walking away from the ice house. It was late at night and except for a bar across the street, no one was around. A person walking away from a code-30 was an obvious suspect. Tony, my partner that night, and I wanted to talk to this guy. We drove our black-and-white close to him and yelled for him to stop. He turned his head in our direction, made eye contact with Tony but continued walking away. We now thought there was a very good chance this guy had been involved in a burglary. Tony yelled again for him to stop. And once again, he looked directly at us but continued on his way. He didn't run, he didn't speed up his walk, he simply ignored us. If the guy was really good for a burglary, he probably would have run and we would have pursued him on foot.

We stopped the car, got out, and quickly walked toward the guy to catch up with him, and for the third time we ordered him to stop walking. He looked over his right shoulder, directly at us, but continued on his way. Tony and I thought this guy had to be dirty for something or he would have stopped when we first made contact. There was, however, something unusual about this suspect but we weren't sure what it was. We were about to find out.

Walking quickly we finally caught up to him and again told him to stop, and he continued to casually walk away. It was time for some physical intervention. I reached the guy first, grabbed him by his right arm and attempted to stop him. He pulled away from my grip, rather effortlessly, and continued to ignore us without saying a word. Okay, I'd had enough; it was time for the old bar-arm control hold. I was in a good position to apply the hold. I was behind the suspect and he couldn't see what I was about to do, or, in this case, attempt to do. I placed my right arm around his neck, grabbed my right wrist with my left hand, buried my head into the back of his neck and began to apply pressure around his throat. I was taller and probably heavier than the suspect and didn't think the choke-out would be a problem. However, he continued walking, which was a little unusual as most suspects fall to the ground once the weight of the officer is on their back. He reached up with one of his hands and pulled my right arm away from his throat. And once again, he did it without much effort. This was a fairly common reaction from a suspect. To counter this reaction, officers were trained to let the suspect have your right arm, but to place your left arm around his neck and apply the hold again, but with opposite arms and hands. For the third time, the suspect continued walking and effortlessly pulled my left arm away from his throat. This guy was beginning to piss me off!

What the hell was going on here? The suspect, who didn't look very big, was as strong as a bull, and my choke hold wasn't working. I was unable to keep an arm around his throat and I couldn't stop him from walking. Tony, who was also a little surprised by this guy's actions, finally got in front of him and tried to hold his hands so that he couldn't pull down my arm. This had some effect on him as it forced him to the ground.

I had my baton with me but it was still in the ring that secures the baton to the Sam Browne. As I went down to the ground with the suspect, I saw the bottom of my baton make contact with the pavement. As I continued toward the ground, my baton appeared to magically float up and fall out of the ring. I watched the baton slowly roll away from me as we were on a slight incline. I couldn't reach for the baton as I would have lost my hold on the suspect. Damn, this was clearly not working out very well.

A few of the bar patrons from across the street gathered in front of the bar and started yelling "police brutality" and a few more silly comments. That was to be expected and we didn't think too much of it. Fortunately, no one from the bar was interfering with us, and at this point the guy didn't *need* any help as he was controlling us.

The suspect was now on his hands and knees and I was literally riding on his back as he was attempting to crawl away. Tony didn't want to leave me alone with the suspect, so he was unable to return to the police car and put out a request for a back-up unit. I was still trying to choke this guy out, and Tony was still trying to prevent him from pulling my arm away from his throat. We were unable to control the guy as he continued to crawl on his hands and knees with me on his back. The cat calls and yelling from the bar patrons continued, and we began to hear a familiar chant: "police brutality, police brutality!" Tony and I looked at each other and both of us thought *police brutality* my ass, we were the ones getting our butts' kicked. We had absolutely no control over this guy. To be perfectly honest, however, he was not trying to hurt us. He was just trying to get away; he never once swung at us or tried to kick us.

We weren't able to get to the radio to put out a call for more officers, the crowd clearly was not going to help, and we were losing the battle with this guy. It was time for a little more force. Tony was not wearing his baton and my baton was still rolling down the hill. In place of his baton, Tony was carrying a long, aluminum flashlight, a Kel-lite. He used the flashlight to strike the suspect in the arm, but it had absolutely no effect. Shit! Now what do we do? A blow to the head with a heavy flashlight could do some serious, even fatal damage; however, we were out of options. Tony whacked the guy in the head with the light, but used as little force as possible. That didn't seem to work, but it did slow him down a bit. One more shot was enough, and we were able to cuff him and get him in the back seat of our car.

The suspect's injuries didn't seem to be too bad, but he had a few cuts that needed to be stitched up. We thought he was probably good for a burglary, so we weren't too concerned about justifying our actions.

However, a check of the building indicated all the doors and windows were secure and it was unlikely a burglary had occurred, and who would steal ice? So it was off to the hospital and a visit to the ER.

Once at the hospital we asked the guy a few questions, but he refused to talk to us. He wouldn't even tell us his name. We eventually found his wallet and somehow managed to talk with his mother. We asked her to meet us at the hospital. While in the ER, the doctor asked us to remove his cuffs so he could be examined and treated. Both Tony and I were reluctant to remove the cuffs as we were not up to another round with the guy in the ER. The suspect, who wouldn't talk to us, told the doctor he wouldn't cause any problems in the hospital. Reluctantly, we removed the cuffs and took off his heavy jacket and shirt. This guy looked like a young Arnold Schwarzenegger; he had muscles on top of muscles and no body fat. With his jacket on he looked fairly normal; with it off he looked like a freak. It was now no surprise why we couldn't control him; we were thankful he wasn't violent toward us. The doctor stitched him up and his mother finally arrived at the ER.

His mother, who was not outwardly hostile toward the police, told us that her son worked and lived at the ice house and spent his working days loading fishing boats with one-hundred pound blocks of ice. She said that it was an old-fashioned facility with no automation; all the ice had to be moved by hand. She went on to explain that her son simply did not like the police, and he always tried to avoid any contact with them. It was fairly clear the young man had some mental disorder, and we felt sorry for him and his mother, but because of his injuries we had to book him for a criminal violation. There was no burglary, so that was out of the question. We booked him for battery on a police officer, which, unfortunately, was a felony, but it was the only section the watch commander would approve.

The next day we contacted the detective who was responsible for filing the case against the young man and explained to him that it was perfectly fine with us if the DA declined to prosecute this guy. We filled him in on the details and explained that we were not injured. The work load for most prosecutors in LA is exhaustive, so they were not opposed to dropping the charges.

There is generally a weight room at every station so that officers can work out when they are off- duty. The next day before roll call and without any prior planning between us, Tony and I found ourselves together in the weight room pumping iron and laughing at each other.

A LITTLE-KNOWN MUNICIPAL CODE SECTION

The following incident is supposed to be true. Two veteran Harbor coppers were involved with a nasty suspect who belonged in jail. He apparently had struck his wife but she didn't want him arrested. The officers checked to see if the suspect had any outstanding warrants and found none. Both officers, however, felt this guy needed to go to jail, and they could tell that his wife was intimidated and afraid to have him arrested. He had no identification so he was transported to the station where his fingerprints were checked against the name he had given the officers. They matched, still no warrants.

The incident had taken place in the parking lot of Cabrillo Beach, which was adjacent to a sand beach not far from the beginning of the rock breakwater. As this guy had just left the beach, there was an unusual amount of sand in the cuffs of his pants—enough to fill a tablespoon. The officers started to scrutinize every California criminal code they could find that might provide a reason for a booking. They looked at the Fish and Game Code, the Business and Professions Code, the Health and Safety Code, the Vehicle Code and of course the Penal Code. No luck, they could not find a criminal violation that applied to this guy's behavior. Finally, one of the coppers picked up a Los Angeles City Municipal Code and went through it page by page. He discovered it was a violation to remove or transport sand from a Los Angeles city beach. No amount of sand was specified.

Bingo! The suspect was booked for removing sand from a city beach, problem solved.

BOOK HER

One evening while leaving the Harbor station I noticed what appeared to be a civilian female cruising the parking lot reserved for black-and-whites. I stopped her, remained inside my car and advised her that the civilian parking lot was in front of the station. She looked directly at me, nodded her head as if she understood what I had said, and continued to drive around rather aimlessly in the restricted parking lot. I pulled in behind her and hit the red lights. She stopped her car almost immediately and I approached the driver's side of the car. Once I was close enough, I could smell alcohol on her breath and determined she had been drinking. I asked her to get out of the car and showed her how to perform the field sobriety test, which she failed. I was never fond of booking deuces—although I once booked a deuce who was sitting in her car in her own driveway—but I really didn't have a choice in this particular case. It didn't take a lot of good cop work to arrest a drunk driver in the parking lot of the police station, though I had to admit it was a bit unusual.

I escorted the woman, who was fairly attractive and seemed to be a bit of a tease, into the station and asked for her identification. She fumbled through her purse and eventually came up with a driver's license. As I was writing down her name and address, she asked me if she was in trouble. I advised her I was going to book her for drunk driving. She smiled just a bit, said okay and then advised me that her husband was a Los Angeles County deputy sheriff, a sergeant. I had the feeling that this was not going to end well.

I asked her for his name and his phone number. She told me she wasn't going to give me his name. She was making it very difficult for me to be helpful. I had a lot of admiration for LA County deputy sheriffs, and I really didn't want to book this woman. I didn't want to be responsible for poor relations between LAPD and the sheriffs. After repeated requests, she flatly refused to give me any information about her husband.

I had her last name and assumed she was using her married name on her license. I made a series of phone calls and eventually located the sergeant at work. He was a supervisor assigned to the jail. I called the jail and discovered he was on duty. I asked to be connected with him and when he came on the line I explained what happened. When I finished my little story, I asked him if he could come down to the station and pick her up—I made it clear I wasn't going to book her. There was a long pause and he said, "No, book her!" I said, "You mean you want me to arrest and book her for deuce?" He said, "Yes, book her." It turns out they were going through a divorce and the sergeant was not happy about it. He thanked me for making the call, said that he appreciated it and hung up.

I advised the watch commander what happened and he said fine, book her. And I did.

FAMILY DISPUTES AND FLYING FLOWER POTS

Most coppers have very little interest in handling family disputes. A twenty-five year-old officer can do very little to solve a bad relationship. He can keep the peace, but that's about it. If a crime has occurred, he can arrest the suspect, usually the male, but once the cuffs are on the guy you can expect his wife or girlfriend to do everything she can to prevent him from going to jail. It's not uncommon for the male to get booked for assaulting his wife, and the wife gets booked for battery on a police officer. Family disputes are rarely fun, and frequently dangerous.

My partner and I received a radio call about a 415 family dispute in Wilmington. We arrived in the midst of a major argument between a man and his wife. He came home drunk with no money; she yelled at him and he kicked her in the stomach. She was pregnant. We decided to book the guy for ADW (Assault with a Deadly, or dangerous, Weapon). Once the cuffs were in place she did an about-face and started yelling at *us*. She apparently didn't want this soon-to-be father, carted off to jail. She called me a blond-haired, blue-eyed devil (a phrase I grew to like), and she referred to my partner, who was black, as an Uncle Tom. And these were the nice things she said about us. The guy had committed a serious felony and he was going to jail, but his wife was clearly not happy with us.

As the three of us walked out the front door, I looked over my shoulder and saw the wife picking up a large flower pot. As she cocked her arm, I pushed my partner and the suspect out the door and quickly slammed it shut. I heard the flower pot crash against the just-closed door. Wow, a scene out of the movies. Now the wife had committed a felony. My partner and I looked at each other and silently decided that one felony per family dispute was enough. Some family disputes can be entertaining, but we really didn't want to mess with this woman.

TRANSFERRED TO 77TH DIVISION

I took the Policeman-three (P-three) examination after completing the minimum time requirements to qualify for the job—three years. P-threes were responsible for training new policemen fresh from the academy. With three years on the job I really didn't have the experience to train young officers, but I passed the written and oral portion of the test and was placed in the outstanding pool (not a difficult accomplishment). There were no openings for training officers at Harbor, but there was an open slot for a P-three at 77th Division. I applied for the job and was accepted. I'm pretty sure I was the only applicant.

I still had doubts about not only becoming a good policeman, but would I be a good training officer. I sincerely believed that a P-three assignment, as a training officer, is one of the most important jobs on the department. Was I really qualified to train young policemen? I had three years less experience than the least experienced of my training officers at Newton. The harsh reality: they were much better and far more experienced than I was.

In spite of that realization, I was still excited about returning to a busy division. Looking back at my truncated career, working 77th Division was the best job I've ever had; even better than the "Elite Metropolitan Division." With just a few exceptions, we had good supervisors, and outstanding coppers. It was a great place to learn the art and science of becoming a policeman. And I still had a lot to learn.

CHAPTER FIVE: 77TH DIVISION

I have to admit I was a little intimidated when I attended my first roll call at 77th. In front of the assembled group, the watch commander asked me the location of my last assignment. I told him Harbor Division. Unless I'm trying to project my voice, I usually speak in low, quiet tones. One "old-timer," Buck, who probably had a grand total of five years on the job, announced in a loud voice, "Speak-up like you got a set of balls!" His comment instantly pissed me off. The guy probably weighed one hundred and fifty pounds, had buggy-whip arms and he's questioning the size of my cashews? But I understood the underlying question: Could a brand-new P-three straight from Harbor cut it at 77th. I didn't mention that I also had worked Newton, a South-end Division. Clearly, I had to perform before these guys would accept me as one of them. In time, I learned that the laconic and outspoken

Buck was an outstanding officer, a guy I eventually admired.

Things progressed normally for the next month or so, and I seemed to be accepted by my fellow officers and supervisors. But I had yet to be tested. I had been assigned to PM watch, which usually started around 3:00 p.m., and lasted until midnight. It was common, almost mandatory, to have a drink after watch, but bars started to shut down around 1:30 a.m., and by the time you changed clothes and drove to the local watering hole, the place was already on "last call." Rather than stop at a local bar, a lot of the guys grabbed a six-pack and we'd meet at an isolated location somewhere in the southern part of the division, usually next to a few producing oil wells.

One night after a particularly busy evening and with a few beers under my belt, I scaled the fence that surrounds the pumping unit of an oil well. The pumping unit is the horsehead-like piece of machinery that is seen going up and down at the well site. The up and down motion is activating an elongated pump located at the bottom of the well. I worked in the oil fields during high school and college and was familiar with production wells and oil-field equipment. After climbing over the fence, I located the ladder that provides access to the top of the pumping unit and climbed aboard the top beam as if I were riding a horse. It was really a stupid and dangerous stunt—the heavy, slowly spinning counterbalance could easily crush a person—but liquid courage did that to guys. Years later I learned from Dave Reynolds, another outstanding South-end copper, that when the group I was drinking with saw me on top of the well, they thought I was probably just a bit unstable and would fit in just fine at my new division.

I have a tremendous amount of respect for the men and women assigned to 77th Division. As I mentioned before, women were not permitted to work patrol during the seventies, but they were assigned to the divisional Detective Bureau. The women were hardworking dedicated officers who were probably more productive than most of their male counterparts. The officers, both men and women, who worked the division were special people, and I admired and trusted nearly every one of them. If your personal safety was endangered—and it's not an exaggeration to say that it frequently was—you could always depend on a 77th copper to be there.

My long-time partner, Danny Rockwell (Rocky), once pushed me aside—to a position of safety—after I had fired at an armed suspect. His actions placed him directly in the suspect's line of fire. The suspect's wounds prevented him from firing at Rocky, but Rocky didn't know that at the time. Sorry if this sounds overly dramatic, but Rocky was one of many South-end coppers who could be trusted with your life.

Hang on to your hats! This is 77th Division.

GOOD COP WORK

I had been working 77th about a week when my lieutenant, Art Melendres, asked me if I had made any arrests that evening. I proudly said, "Yes sir, two warrant suspects." Art shook his head and said, "That's not police work in this division. Half of the citizens walking the streets have warrants for their arrest." Art said he wanted to know how many arrests I had made as a result of my own observations, arrests that I had initiated. To Art, an arrest based on a warrant or a radio call was not real cop work, anyone could do it. That was a seminal moment for me. I learned from the lieutenant that good cop work was not answering radio calls or booking warrant suspects.

Good cop work was based on associating behavior or circumstances with criminal activity and then making a good arrest that takes a bad guy off the street. A few examples: a copper sees a man wearing a coat on a warm day and walking with a flaccid gait. Is this guy a hype under the influence? Two identical cars—same make, model and year—traveling on the same street and in the same direction. Is one of the cars stolen? Three or four gangbangers in a car wearing clothing that is not consistent with local gangbangers. Are they armed and looking for someone to shoot? An alarm technician who spends too much time at a premises where an alarm has been activated. Is he involved in a burglary?

MULTIPLE HOMICIDES

To say the division was a high crime rate neighborhood is like saying the sun occasionally gets warm. For a number of years the homicide count exceeded one hundred per year. Many were gang related, many were drug related and more than a few of them were simply disputes that were settled with guns. Two kids living next door to one another get into an argument that quickly escalates into a fight. The mothers get involved, one of them picks up a hand gun and another homicide is recorded. This scenario is not at all unusual; it didn't happen every day, but it did happen far too frequently.

COLDEN AVENUE

One afternoon while assigned to 12 A 23, a shooting-in-progress radio call—a hotshot—was broadcast for a residence on Colden Avenue. Colden was just north of Century Boulevard and this particular address was close to the Harbor Freeway. A shooting-in-progress call always draws a crowd of patrol units. It's not unusual to see six or eight black-and-whites jamming the street at the call site. We weren't assigned the call, but we were one of the first responding units to arrive. We parked about two houses from the residence where the shooting was supposed to have occurred, about mid-block.

An ambulance was present at our location, but we noticed that another ambulance had just arrived at a residence two blocks west of us. None of this was too surprising. We assumed a wrong address had been given to the paramedics. Moments later, a *third* ambulance arrived, but it responded to an address about two blocks east of the original call. Three ambulances were now present on Colden, spaced about two blocks apart. What the hell was going on?

We were a little confused, but continued to focus on our call. We were out of the car and did not hear any details about the second and third calls, but still assumed the other units, including the ambulances, were given an incorrect address.

We entered the first crime scene and confirmed that a shooting occurred and it was, in fact, a homicide. We helped the assigned unit to secure the premises and maintain crowd control. While we were outside dealing with the crowd, we noticed there was lots of activity around the second and third ambulances. Far too much activity for a wrong address.

I don't think I have ever seen this many police cars on one block. Confusion and chaos reigned over three solid blocks of Colden Avenue. Twenty black-and-whites, three ambulances, five or six unmarked detective cars and at least two fire trucks clogged the entire street.

Nothing coming out of the radio—the lifeline for every policeman—was clear.

Because of all the activity, a make-shift Command Center was established by one of the black-and-whites parked on the street. A sergeant was trying to gather information about the crime or crimes and obtain descriptions of suspects and vehicles. The sergeant was finally able to determine not one, but three homicides had occurred on Colden that afternoon. Multiple homicides at one crime scene are not that rare, so we assumed all three killings were related, probably involved drugs or gangs. The next day we learned the homicides were, in fact, *unrelated*. Three homicides occurred on one street, Colden Avenue, within a distance of about four-hundred yards, and within a time span of about twenty minutes. What are the odds of that happening? Better than you would expect if you lived in 77th.

Cruelty is often associated with a high crime- rate area, and our homicide was a perfect example of cruel and insensitive behavior by someone in the crowd. A young teenager, who was not originally at the scene of our homicide, was observed walking toward the crowd that had gathered in front of his house. As he neared the crowd and was recognized, someone within the group of gawkers yelled out, "Hey, they killed your mama!" The young man, of course, immediately tried to enter the house to see if his mother was the victim. I could not allow him to enter his own home; entering the house would have contaminated the crime scene. The teenager was undeterred when I told him he had to remain outside, and he attempted to walk around me. I stopped him by grabbing his arm, but he pushed my arm away and continued to try to enter. Unfortunately, I had to use the bar-arm control hold to stop him. The crowd, of course, went ballistic as they observed a blond-haired, blue-eyed devil choking out someone from the 'hood who had just lost his mother. To the crowd I was the cruel one, not the jerk who took delight in the death of this kid's mother. I felt bad about the incident, but the rules were set in cement: No one, even the chief of police, is allowed to contaminate a crime scene. If you weren't needed at the scene, you weren't allowed in. It was not unheard of for a low-ranking officer to inform a deputy chief that he couldn't enter a structure because he might contaminate the scene. To their credit, the "brass" almost always willingly complied with the officer's request.

BULLETS

When I returned to work after a few regular days off, my unit was assigned a shots-fired radio call. It was not a hotshot, so I assumed the complaint board operator didn't have a lot of confidence in the person who reported the incident. The location of the call was an apartment complex on one of the major north-south streets in the division. Two apartment buildings were separated by a common courtyard. We appeared to be the first unit to arrive on the scene. As we approached the courtyard, we immediately observed a man lying on the ground in a pool of blood. He had been shot several times in the upper body. A quick check of his pulse and pupils indicated that he was dead.

After checking the body, I noticed one of the inside walls on the south apartment had several bullet holes that had already been chalked-off. At about the same time another black-and-white arrived on the scene to offer their assistance. I asked the officers if they had arrived before us, chalked-off the bullet holes and then departed in pursuit of a suspect. Both officers indicated they had just arrived, but they knew about the circled bullet holes. They explained to me that the rounds in the wall were from a homicide that occurred the day before at the same location. I never learned if the two homicides were related; however, two homicides at one location—two days in a row—should be extremely rare, but not at 77th.

"BUT OFFICER…"

One of my favorite incidents did not involve a homicide, although it could easily have been one. Once again my partner and I received a hotshot radio call about a shooting in progress. As is typically the case, the incident had ended before the police arrived, but all the evidence, the suspect and the victim were still at the scene. The first thing I observed was the victim's car. I don't recall the make or model, but it looked like it had been through a war. The front window was shot out, there were bullet holes in the fenders, bullet holes in the hood, a tire was blown out—and, again, contrary to Hollywood, it's very difficult to shoot out a tire—and hissing steam was pouring from under the hood. My first thought was the suspect probably reloaded the gun in order to do so much damage. I later discovered she used a nine-shot .22 caliber handgun for this handy display of marksmanship.

When we arrived, the victim, who was the suspect's husband, was shaking like the leaves of an aspen tree in forty knots of wind. He was a skinny guy who was so nervous he could barely talk, and who could blame him: his wife had just fired nine rounds at him, at very close range, but missed him completely (she did, however, kill the car).

We discovered later that he had been fooling around on his wife and she found out about it. After her discovery, she grabbed a hand gun—I'm guessing that about ninety percent of the houses in South-Central Los Angeles have guns—and chased him back to his car. On the way, she emptied the gun into the car as he tried to make his getaway. The car, of course, was DOA, but she managed, somehow, to miss her husband.

I interviewed both the husband and his wife and their stories were almost identical. He, however, denied fooling around on his wife, but like most criminal acts, motive is not a necessary element of the crime. It's the actions that are significant to law enforcement. She admitted that she had emptied her gun at her husband, but she told me that she was certain he had been fooling around with another woman. After interviewing witnesses, the victim and the suspect, I advised the woman that she had committed a serious felony, and I had to arrest her and transport her to the station. She told me she understood and was actually very polite and friendly. As I walked her to my car, I explained to her that I had to handcuff her before I could transport her to the station. Again, I had no choice in the matter, almost everyone who was under arrest and being transported in a black-and-white had to be handcuffed. This was departmental policy and was strictly enforced.

She looked me directly in the eyes and said, "But officer, I'm not a violent person!" I thought about what she had said—and the nine rounds she had fired at her husband—and burst out in laughter. I could not stop laughing. She completely failed to see the incongruity of her statement, and didn't appreciate my reaction. I doubt, however, she would have caused me any harm. She admitted that she shot at her husband, but I'm certain she felt perfectly justified in her actions. And the two of us got along very well throughout the booking process. She didn't call me any names and was never hostile toward me. I was never subpoenaed and assumed the case was never filed. It was just another family dispute, but this one had a happy ending, no one was shot and killed.

ALEX AND THE CIA

I worked patrol with Alex at 77^{th,} and he too was on the Underwater Dive Unit (UDU). Alex was somewhat disgruntled, but he was an outstanding policeman. He eventually left LAPD and worked for the CIA. He was great at making bombs. I don't believe he had any formal training, but acquired his expertise from books augmented by an inquisitive and sharp mind. The Underwater Dive Unit had a joint training day with LAPD's bomb-squad divers. A simulated bomb was placed on a boat in Los Angeles Harbor. Alex volunteered to construct and hide the bomb. The UDU was responsible for locating the bomb, describing how it was made and how it was attached to the vessel. Once located, we would report this information to the bomb squad, and the bomb-squad divers would disarm the device.

The UDU divers searched for and found the bomb. Once it was discovered, the crime scene was turned over to the bomb squad. After inspecting the bomb and determining how it was made, the bomb-squad divers reported that it was impossible to disarm Alex's device without detonating it. Right away they wanted to know who made it—as if we had committed a crime. No one, of course, hesitated to say that Alex did it. He was a bright guy and I respected him a great deal. If I had to go to war, I'd want Alex in my foxhole.

Alex and I had worked patrol together on a fairly uneventful night. It was end of watch and I had changed into my off-duty uniform: white T-shirt and Levis. Alex was still in uniform and we were talking in front of the watch commander's office, which was located across the hall from the jail. We were approached by one of the jailers, civilian employees who spend all their working hours with officers and arrestees, who asked if we could help with a potentially combative arrestee. We said sure. And because Alex was still in uniform, he said he would help out. He gave me his gun to hold while he went into an area of the jail that was not visible from the hallway. A few minutes passed and Alex had not returned. I had a feeling there may have been a problem with the suspect. I stashed Alex's gun in the gun locker and quickly entered the jail. I found Alex in front of one of the cells along with the civilian jailer and our recalcitrant guest, a big Hispanic guy. Just as I walked up to the three of them, the arrestee said, "I ain't goin' inside." He reached over and slammed the jail door shut as he remained outside the cell. That, of course, was the signal for the fight to begin.

We were in a confined area and Alex wasn't able to get behind the suspect. His only approach was from the front. Alex immediately and forcefully struck the guy in the nose with the palm of his hand. This quickly resulted in a broken and very bloody nose, but it didn't take the fight out of the man. Alex was finally able to get behind the guy and attempt to use a bar-arm control hold. However, the broken nose and the buckets of blood made it almost impossible for Alex to effectively apply the choke hold. The two of them were rolling around on the floor, but because of all the slippery blood Alex was unable to control the guy.

Alex was in great physical shape, much better shape than I, and he had some expertise in the martial arts, but he was covered in blood and could not put a good lock on the guy's neck. We decided to switch places and I would attempt the choke-out. A dry arm made a huge difference, and I was finally able to render the guy unconscious.

While I was rolling around on the floor with our friend, the jailer placed a handcuff on *one* of the suspect's wrists. One handcuff on a suspect who is fighting with the police is worse than no handcuff at all. A loose handcuff makes a great weapon. Once the guy was unconscious, the jailer was able to open the jail cell door and we dragged the suspect into the cell and quickly locked the door. Unfortunately, we forgot to remove the handcuff. It didn't matter that much as our guy was safely in custody and we could catch our breath.

Both Alex and I thought we had better report the incident to the watch commander, a Greek who was a good, dependable supervisor and truly cared about the troops. As we walked into his office he looked up and saw that I was covered in blood. The front of my white T-shirt was now blood red.

The sergeant looked at me and said, "Jesus Christ, what happened to you? Are you OK?" I told him I was fine and the blood wasn't mine; I went on to explain what happened in the jail. I was certain there was going to be an excessive force complaint over the incident. The watch commander probably felt the same way.

The sergeant said, "OK, let's go back and talk to this guy and see if we can get our cuffs back." All of us returned to the jail. We found the arrestee standing up in the cell with one handcuff on his wrist. He didn't say a word as he stood behind the bars looking out at the four of us. The watch commander asked the man to extend his cuffed arm through the bars of the cell so we could remove the cuffs. We were all shocked when he said sure; he stuck out his arm and we removed the cuffs. The sergeant told the arrestee that he was the watch supervisor and quietly said, "Okay son, do you mind telling me what happened?" This somewhat battered, bloody pulp of a man—who had just spent ten very unpleasant minutes with two LA coppers and had every reason to be pissed off—said, "Well sergeant, I must have fallen out of my bunk."

None of us could believe what we had heard. We were expecting to hear that we beat this guy for no reason, and we were certain Internal Affairs Division (IAD) would soon be involved. We had no idea why this guy went from being extremely combative to almost friendly. He wasn't drunk, he wasn't under the influence of drugs and he seemed to be perfectly normal. I think he understood that he was completely wrong and we were just doing our job. He never lodged a complaint and we heard no more of the incident. We finally met a suspect who took responsibility for his own stupid actions.

LOYALTY

I learned early as a policeman that officers take care of one another, but I didn't fully appreciate that concept until I was involved in a single-car traffic accident while responding to an *officer needs help* radio call. I was not assigned the call so I was not authorized to respond code-3, with red lights and siren. I was driving a brand-new Matador, made by American Motors. I always thought these rather unpopular cars made pretty good police cars. They were fast, handled corners reasonably well, and had "stop on a dime" brakes.

I was traveling southbound on Broadway, approaching Manchester when a help call was broadcast. The location of the call was south of my position, close to Century Boulevard. I was working with a new probationer named Tim—a good guy and an accomplished artist. I was driving the Matador flat out, just as fast as it would go. The siren was blaring and the red lights were flashing—a clear violation of department policy. Broadway is, in fact, quite broad. There is a raised center divider planted with small trees, bushes, grass and a few small pipes sticking out of the earth. As I was approaching 98th Street, in the number one lane (the lane closest to the center of the street) a car, traveling eastbound on 98th turned southbound on Broadway into my lane. He was driving at a very low speed. I immediately slammed on the brakes and swerved the Matador to the left to avoid the fast- approaching rear end of the slow car. The left front wheel of my brand-new police car struck the raised, concrete center divider. The car bounced up and continued to slide on the grass for a very long distance. I killed a few plants and completely severed a small pipe, which, fortunately, was not full of pressurized water. The right-side front and back tires remained in contact with the pavement and did not jump the curb; the left side of the car was on the center divider.

When the dust settled and we climbed out of the car, the left front wheel was turned all the way to the left and the right front wheel was turned all the way to the right—I don't think I had ever seen that before. Clearly there was no way I could move the car under its own power. And it was imperative I move the car away from the damage I had caused and the very long set of skid-marks I left behind during my four-wheel locked slide down Broadway.

I really don't know how fast I was traveling when I hit the divider—at the time I thought I was probably in the mid-eighties—but I knew the skid marks, when measured and analyzed, would accurately establish my speed at the time of the collision, which was way beyond the posted speed limit. The skid marks, of course, would establish two issues: I was traveling too fast and I was at fault.

My first thought was to contact a private tow truck and have the car towed away from the center divider and the skid marks. I told Tim to remain with the car while I used the phone at a nearby liquor store. I was just beginning to run through the Yellow Pages when a sergeant's car pulled up behind our unit. That killed my plan to tow the car to another location. Fortunately I got to the sergeant before Tim had an opportunity to explain the accident. The sergeant, who was well-liked by the troops, asked me what happened. About half way through my cock-'n-bull story—I didn't mention that I was responding code-3 to a help call—the sergeant stopped me and asked if the car was a white Chevy with the rear trunk up (so there was no way for me to see the license plate). I can be a little slow at times, but I immediately understood what he was doing. I told him yes, that was the car that drove in front of me. He told me that just before he arrived at our scene, he noticed the same car driving in the area. He told me he would complete a fifteen-seven (a supplemental report) to support my version of the story. Looking back on the incident, I'm sure he knew exactly what had happened and had a pretty good idea that I was driving way too fast on my way to a help call.

A traffic unit was called to complete the traffic accident report but none was available. Patrol officers absolutely hate to complete T/A reports, so I was surprised when a patrol unit volunteered to write the report and complete the investigation. Fortunately one of the officers in the patrol unit had just left Traffic Division, so a T/A report was no big deal to him. I noticed him measuring the length of my skid marks and I immediately started to worry. I asked him if he knew how fast I was driving based on the marks. He looked at me and said about twenty-five m.p.h. I said, "No, really, how fast was I going?" He told me the report would show I was traveling between twenty-five and thirty; however, my speed, based on the evidence, was closer to one hundred m.p.h. It was hard to believe my ears; how could he possibly establish such a low speed. He told me he was one of only four officers on the department who was a court qualified expert in skid marks and estimated speed.

We returned to the station where I began to complete the paper work associated with the T/A. While there I was approached by my lieutenant (he was an administrator not a leader) who asked me if I knew the speed limit on Broadway at the location of the accident. I told him I thought it was thirty-five, but I wasn't sure. He advised me he would check it out for me, as if he were doing me a big favor.

A few minutes later I was ordered to meet the lieutenant at the scene of the T/A. When I got there I noticed a regular traffic unit was now present and the officers were measuring my skid marks with a two-wheeled measuring device. This time the lieutenant asked me how fast I was traveling at the time of the incident. I had a lot of faith in the officer who took the initial report, so I stuck to my story and indicated I was only going about thirty. He clearly didn't believe me and said he estimated that over one-hundred feet of skid marks were laid down just before I hit the curb. I shrugged my shoulders but didn't say anything. About that time the regular traffic unit approached us and told the lieutenant the skid marks would have to be measured during the daylight hours as they were too indistinct to accurately measure at night. They also reported that part of the pavement had recently been repaired or resurfaced so the coefficient of friction would not be consistent for the entire length of the marks. Clearly I had won a reprieve, but I knew it wouldn't last very long.

The word apparently had gotten out to all the officers on watch that the incriminating skid marks would be re-measured during daylight hours.

Later in the evening I returned to the scene and discovered that about twenty sets of skid marks had been laid down at 98th and Broadway. There were skid marks on top of my marks, beside my marks, and across my marks. I couldn't believe it. I hadn't asked anyone to help out, and I hadn't thought of adding additional marks to the pavement.

A very good sergeant and some extremely loyal officers prevented me from being disciplined for a clearly preventable accident. And I learned a good lesson: better to arrive at a help call a second or two later than not arrive at all. By the way, the help call was a hoax, no one needed help.

THE NATIONAL RIFLE ASSOCIATION

I really don't know how most coppers feel about the NRA, but I'm no fan. In late 1973, a small company was producing a handgun round that could penetrate body armor. It was a Teflon-coated bullet that was designed to minimize the internal wear on the lands and groves found inside gun barrels but could also penetrate Kevlar. Was there a need to prevent this type of wear? Probably not.

I suspect that thousands and thousands of rounds would have to pass through a barrel before any noticeable wear occurred. Why allow a round—capable of penetrating body armor and possibly killing a police officer—to be marketed and sold in California? Ask the NRA.

Who wore body armor in 1973? Street cops. The State of California decided that a handgun bullet, capable of piercing body armor, was probably a bad thing and was working on legislation that would prohibit the round from being sold in California. Other than terrorists, bank robbers and militant Black Muslims, who would oppose this legislation? The National Rifle Association, that's who. I was incredulous over their opposition to this proposed law, it made no sense to me. How could any organization misconstrue—so badly—the meaning of the second amendment? I quickly parted ways with the NRA and formed the opinion the organization was bad for the country.

To clarify my point, I'm opposed to legal gun ownership for anyone convicted—and in some cases arrested—for a violent crime. I'm also opposed to anyone who is unstable, has a tendency for violence or is mentally ill to own a gun. These are not insurmountable issues. We simply need politicians who are not afraid to buck the NRA or the mental health professionals.

MY OWN FORM OF GUN CONTROL

Depending on the nature of a radio call—usually a family dispute—many South-end coppers would ask the PR if a gun was in the residence or available to a potential suspect. The answer was usually yes. Many of these heated disputes had the potential for gun violence. This was almost always a judgment call for the involved officer. If the potential for a future shooting—involving other officers, family members or neighbors—was high, and a gun was clearly present, a few officers would exercise their own form of gun control. My favorite method was to moisten the insides of the gun and pour as much table salt as possible into the barrel and the internal moving parts of the weapon. Most of these guns were cheaply-made Saturday Night Specials, and it wouldn't take long for the corrosive effects of the salt to disable the weapon. If our actions prevented a shooting, this obvious violation of department policy and complete disregard for the second amendment was worth the risk and effort.

An NRA supporter might argue that we effectively removed a gun from the hands of a citizen and prevented that person from using the gun in self-defense. And it's a decent argument, but I've never seen this scenario play out in a positive way for anyone. Using a gun in self-defense simply did not happen that often, especially in South-Central LA.

COCKROACHES, COOKIES AND CAKE

Almost all arrestees were thoroughly searched before being turned over to jailers. Part of the search included removing the suspect's shoes and socks. And nothing smells as bad as a pair of socks that had not been changed in a very long time.

I arrested a man for a drug charge and was in the process of booking him into the jail at 77th. He was tall, very thin and I doubt he had bathed in weeks. I asked him to remove his shoes and socks; he complied without complaint as he probably had gone through this process a number of times. The fact that he was thin was significant, as you will see in a moment. For some reason almost all suspects remove their socks and then whip them up and down in the air as if they were trying to flog a junk-yard dog. A fairly low, concentrated odor now becomes airborne and permeates the entire booking cage. Sensory overload affects almost all cops. Sometimes it's what you see, sometimes it's what you hear and feel, and just as often it can be what you smell: a rotting dead body, an unwashed homeless person and even dirty socks.

Just after my suspect's shoes were removed and placed on the floor, a rather large, live cockroach climbed out of his shoe. Because my guy was so thin, the cockroach apparently had plenty of room and air to survive. I've heard that if there is ever a nuclear war the cockroach may be the only survivor—I can believe it.

There was a hallway separating the booking cage from the jail at 77th. The cockroach calmly walked out of the booking cage, crossed the hall and strolled into the jail. It paused for a moment just before it crossed into the entrance. After pausing, it turned slightly and looked back into the booking cage where I continued to process the arrestee. I had an eerie sensation there was some kind of silent communication between my suspect and the cockroach. I had an unshakable notion that the cockroach was telling his companion that everything was cool and they'd meet up again, in the jail, after he'd been processed.

There were a lot of cockroaches in some areas of the Division, but to be fair, we also had a few cockroaches in Lakewood, where I lived.

About once a month, day-watch officers assigned to the local "A" unit had to attend a block captain's meeting. This was a community relations affair where complaints were voiced by local citizens. As a general rule the citizens involved in these meeting were fairly pro-police and decent folks. Coffee and cookies were often served to the officers as a gesture of good will. On one occasion my partner and I were seated on a couch discussing some problem with the attendees. A very large plate of warm, chocolate-chip cookies was placed directly in front of us—now this was a smell I could get into. Not wanting to appear too eager to dive into the cookies, I continued to engage in a conversation with these folks, and I'm sure my attention was, at some point, drawn away from the plate. When coffee was served I quickly started munching on these very delicious cookies. Strangely, my partner, who probably a bigger chowhound than I, didn't touch them. I kept telling him how good they were and was shocked when he still refused to eat any.

After the meeting, while seated in our patrol car, I asked him why he didn't eat the cookies. He told me that while I was yakking away at the meeting, a rather large, live cockroach calmly climbed down from the plate of cookies and made its way back into the kitchen. It would have been embarrassing for everyone if he had warned me about the cockroach in the cookies. Thanks partner.

Later on I was able to add chocolate cake to my list of fine dining experiences within 77th. A community service award was being presented to several officers. Food, of course, was provided by members of the community who were supposed to be pro-police. A nice, three-layer chocolate cake with chocolate icing was presented to the officers working the front desk. I happen to walk by the desk, saw the cake and assumed it was provided by the Community Relations folks who supported the presentation. I sliced a big piece, put it on a paper plate, grabbed a plastic fork and dug in. Pretty good stuff until I got around to the third or fourth bite. I bit down on a solid steel object that had been buried in the cake. I spat out an inch-long sheet-metal screw. This nice piece of hardware chipped a tooth and cut the inside of my mouth. I later found out that the cake mysteriously appeared at the front desk from an unknown citizen; it had not been provided by the pro-police organization. Screw you, I guess, was the message.

ROLL CALL

Roll call can be quiet and informative or raucous and loud. At 77th it was usually the latter, especially PM watch. PM watch or the night shift was usually the loudest and certainly the busiest. If you really enjoyed cop work, PM watch was the place to be.

A new sergeant recently assigned to the division was generally in for a bad time. The roll-call room had a dais in the front of the room where the watch commander and sometimes one additional sergeant would conduct roll call. The watch commander could be a sergeant or a lieutenant. A table sat on the dais and the supervisors usually sat behind the table. When it was determined that a new sergeant was going to be present at roll call, the guys were almost always up for some kind of trouble. One of the old-timers would come in early and set up the table for a fall. The trailing edges of the front legs of the table were carefully placed at the very edge of the dais.

The slightest touch or bump to the table meant that it would fall off the raised platform and onto the floor. Papers and anything else on the table went flying as the table crashed and burned. And the face of the new sergeant was about as red as a traffic light.

About once a year, around the Fourth of July, someone would invariably collect a firecracker to be used at roll call. Before the watch commander appeared, one of the guys would insert the fuse of the firecracker into the end of a lighted cigarette. The cigarette and the firecracker were usually placed in an ashtray on top of a filing cabinet behind the supervisors. People could smoke in buildings in those days so it wasn't too unusual to smell a burning cigarette. About half way through roll call the firecracker would detonate. Any officer who wasn't aware of the firecracker, would usually jump up, pull his gun or at least reach for the grips, and start looking for someone to shoot. To my knowledge, there were never any shots fired during one of these incidents, but who really knows.

Surprise inspections were generally held during roll call. One of our lieutenants was a retired marine gunnery sergeant; he was a real *spit-and-polish* guy, but he was always out to protect his troops. And he loved inspections.

Part of the inspection process required the officers to remove the ammo from their guns, hold it in an open palm and display the gun for cleanliness. The order is called Inspection Arms. During one inspection, I was shocked to look down and see that all six of my bullets and the cylinder of my gun were rusty. I wasn't particularly fastidious about a spotless gun, but I was surprised about all the rust. Then I remembered the day before a fireman had squirted me with a small, hand-activated water pump. He was getting even for a water balloon that another copper had thrown at him and his fellow firefighters. When the lieutenant stood in front of me and looked at my gun and ammo, I knew I was in for a good ass-chewing. I really admired the lieutenant and I was sure he'd be disappointed in me for having such a dirty weapon. He asked what happened and I told him the truth. He just shook his head and said, "Son, never get into a water-fight with a fireman; it's what they do!" It sounded like he spoke from experience.

LIVE SHARKS

Coppers love to mess with other coppers; the officers of 77th were certainly no different. I've been hit with water balloons thrown from the roof, I've had carbon paper applied to the inside of my hat so that I would have a blue band of carbon around my forehead during an inspection, I've had the zipper on my pants sewn closed—I may have deserved that one—and I've had the muffler on my patrol car rigged to blow up, not with an explosive but from a build-up of gases. However, the shark incidents

I'm about to relate really surprised me. I was, and still am, an avid spear fisherman and free diver. Most everyone in the division knew I liked to dive and a few of my partners would always give me a hard time about the possibility of confronting a shark. I always explained that the danger from sharks was grossly exaggerated and almost nonexistent—several years later I had two separate encounters with great white sharks. I suppose I was engaged in wishful thinking.

The land-shark incident occurred on a hot day in the middle of summer. I was working PM watch and everything at roll call was fairly normal: no exploding fire crackers, falling desks or inspections. Roll call ended and everyone slowly made their way downstairs to check out their shotgun, ammo and patrol car. My partner and I were the last officers to check out equipment. For some reason my partner, Danny Rockwell, was dragging his feet. Seventy-seventh is so busy, especially on PM watch, that officers were encouraged to hit the streets and clear as soon as possible. Once you cleared—clearing is simply advising communications that you are ready to go to work—it was very common to receive three radio calls right out of the gate. Occasionally, on a very busy day, a clearing unit might receive as many as five radio assignments. Many of them could be code-2 calls, calls that should be handled right away. We knew we'd have lots of work to do and Danny was taking too much time to prepare for patrol.

We finally made it out to the parking lot and things seemed a little odd. It felt like every officer on the watch was standing by their cars looking directly at me. I wasn't sure what was going on so I continued the ritual of checking out the car that was assigned to Danny and me. Part of that process includes walking around the car to make sure there were no unreported dents, dings or scratches in the paint. We also had to remove the backseat and search under it to make sure that no suspects, who may have been transported by the previous watch, had disposed of any contraband or weapons. The backseat search was performed at the beginning of the watch and after anyone had been transported in a police car.

I quickly threw open the rear door and pulled the rear bench seat up and away from its mounting. I immediately jumped back about five feet as a still-alive and very bloody blue shark was quivering under the backseat of my black-and-white. My mind must have registered some degree of danger as I reached for my gun and apparently thought about shooting the shark. All the guys were now laughing hysterically about this poor blue shark and my reaction to its presence. I understand that the shark eventually ended up in the locker of a motor cop who was not too pleased.

We eventually cleared from the station after disposing of the shark and probably received our usual three or four radio calls. On the way to our first call, I received a radio call from another unit to meet him on Tac-2. Tactical frequency two was used for communicating between cars without going through Communications. After switching the radio to Tac-2, the calling unit advised me he had driven the car I was in on the previous day and he wondered if his ticket book was still in the glove box. I opened the glove compartment to check and the bloody head of a large blue shark rolled out and fell into my lap. Two sharks, twice in one day! It had to be a record.

I eventually found out who had been on a fishing trip that morning and got my pound of flesh, but it was hard to top the sharks.

ABALONE STAMPEDE

Homicide detectives were generally pretty sharp officers, not easily fooled and certainly not naïve or uninformed. A friend of mine, who was recently assigned to work homicides at 77th, turned out to be more than a little uninformed about sea life.

An abalone is a tasty shell fish—a marine gastropod related to a snail—that spends its time underwater attached to a rock. It generally spends its entire life clinging to the same rock formation. It's capable of movement; it may move from one rock to an adjacent rock, but it does so at a pace much slower than its cousin, the land snail.

Bud Arce, the homicide dick, was interested in learning how to scuba dive, and we were talking about the hazards of the sport. He asked the usual questions about sharks, killer whales and other dangerous marine critters. I told him they were almost never a problem. I did, however, tell him about a little known event that could pose a serious risk to scuba divers in California: Once a year, the abalone population would stampede through a kelp bed. The exact time of the stampede would vary from area to area and scientists were currently studying the phenomenon to determine what triggered the mad rush of these gastropods. Preliminary results indicated that it related to reproduction, but it would take years before the answers were revealed. If a diver happened to be diving in a kelp bed and was caught in a stampede, it's likely he or she would be seriously injured or even drowned. I told him there had been several documented incidents of divers drowning as a result of a major abalone stampede.

He, of course, was incredulous. An underwater stampede, who would have known? I told him to give it some thought and if he was seriously interested in learning how to scuba dive, I'd sign him up for my next class.

A day or two later, he approached me and said, "You asshole!" and he walked away, shaking his head. That was the extent of our conversation. In a cop bar that night, he apparently had told several of his close friends about stampeding abalone. He had been "punked" and was laughed out of the bar. He never signed up for my class.

FOLLOWING THE LIEUTENANT

One of our lieutenants had a bad leg and walked with a limp. I was told he was hit by a car on the freeway while engaged in a traffic stop. He probably could have retired on a medical disability, but chose to continue to work. One night while searching on foot for an armed suspect, I noticed the lieutenant was by himself. Supervisors usually drove one-man cars and didn't have partners; patrol officers were almost always assigned to two-man cars.

The suspect we were looking for was a clear threat to the safety of everyone, and I didn't feel the lieutenant should be by himself on this search. I was also pretty sure he wouldn't tolerate someone looking out for his safety; he was a typical marine gunny. I quietly started to follow him throughout the search. I couldn't get too close, but I had to be close enough to help out if he needed assistance. After a few minutes of this cat-and-mouse routine, the lieutenant had figured out what I was doing. He abruptly stopped, looked directly at me and said, "Officer, you're not following me, are you?" I was caught. I said, "No sir, I'm just behind you." He sent me on my way and continued to search by himself—typical gunny.

"OFFICERS, THEY'RE ROBBIN' TAMS!"

It was not unusual to see people running in the ghetto. They're usually not working out, they are just… running. One afternoon my partner, Kirk, and I were driving eastbound on Manchester when we observed a guy running like he was trying out for the Olympics. That *was* unusual. In a full stride with both arms pumping, he looked at us as we drove next to him and said, "Officers, they're robbin' Tams!" We had just passed Tams, a Greek hamburger joint that served great pastrami sandwiches and hot, crisp fries. Normally we might ask this witness a few questions, but we knew he was telling the truth; no one runs that fast in the ghetto without a reason.

I hung a U-turn in the middle of Manchester as Kirk requested a back-up for an armed robbery in progress at Tams. I only had to travel about a half-block so we arrived in seconds. As we entered the parking lot, we both saw a white guy, probably Greek, run out the side door with a gun in one hand and a cash drawer in the other. He looked directly at us, turned and ran down the alley that was behind the hamburger stand. There was no need for us to get out of the car in a foot pursuit; we simply followed him in the car. This particular alley had very high fences on one side and the back of buildings on the other side. Normally this type of suspect would jump a fence and try to get away, but he was trapped until he got to the end of the alley where he could have gone left or right.

As we were traveling down the alley, Kirk leaned out of the car and fired one round from his gun. He didn't hit the suspect, fortunately, but the shot stopped him in his tracks. I'll never forget what Kirk did next: he leaned back in and said to me, "I didn't do that!" Firing the round and not reporting it were clear violations of the department's shooting policy. The escaping suspect was not a threat to our safety, and his gun was never pointed at us. The suspect wasn't hit but I was concerned about collateral damage. Fortunately, as a background, there was a large, stucco building with very few windows at the end of the alley. It didn't look like we had done any damage but we never found where the round hit the wall.

The suspect was cuffed and placed in the back seat of our car, and we began collecting evidence, mostly money, and photographing the scene. I was somewhat preoccupied with these duties when I heard someone being smacked around accompanied by yelling and screams. I looked up and saw the victim of the robbery, the worker behind the counter, slapping and hitting the cuffed suspect sitting in our black-and-white. I gave the scene a little bit of thought—no serious damage had been inflicted on the suspect—and continued collecting evidence. A moment later I heard the gunny, our lieutenant, say, "Officer, don't you think you should stop that?" I sheepishly said, "Yes sir, right away".

We had a few problems at the trial, something about an unreported officer involved shooting and missing photographs—Kirk knows what I'm talking about—but the guy was eventually convicted and we "dodged a bullet."

"12 A 17, I'M IN PURSUIT!"

Twelve A 17 was in pursuit of a stolen motorcycle. He was northbound on Central Avenue approaching Century Boulevard. The crotch-rocket was traveling at very high speeds and wasn't stopping for red lights. The motorcycle driver could easily outrun the black-and-white and seemed to be having fun at the officers' expense. He would let them get fairly close, turn around and flip them off as he accelerated away. He did this several times before he ran into trouble. As he approached a busy, controlled intersection—one with red lights—he turned around on the motorcycle, looked directly at the officers, smiled broadly and extended his middle finger (must have been some kind of friendly greeting).

What he didn't see was a Datsun 240Z that was crossing Central Avenue, west bound, on the green light. The motorcycle center-punched the Z on the driver's side of the car. I'm not sure of his exact speed—there were no skid marks at the scene, which meant he never applied his brakes—however, he was accelerating and had to be traveling in excess of eighty m.p.h. The violent collision threw the driver forward and easterly into a chain-link fence set back about twenty feet from Central Avenue.

As near as we could figure, the chain-link fence acted like a vertical trampoline. The driver flew through the air, hit the fence, and it bounced him back into the center of Central. I was the second or third car to arrive at the scene, and when I got to the suspect I could see that he was not going to have a good day: He was lying prone on the pavement; his right leg pointing south and his left leg pointing north. His left foot, however, was above his head. This had to hurt, and I could tell it hurt by the moaning, groaning and string of expletives coming from the suspect.

In addition to the rather unusual extension of his left leg, he was also pretty proficient at The Twist—the old sixties Rock and Roll song by Chubby Checker. I suppose we should call this the one-legged Twist. In addition to his left leg being completely out of its socket, his left foot was now facing backward. The leg had rotated about ninety degrees to the left. Instead of moaning and groaning into the *inside* of his left knee (his head was also turned to the left), the driver was talking into the *back* of his left knee cap. This *really* had to hurt.

The suspect was scooped up by an RA unit and transported to Killer-King. This was the name given to Martin Luther King Memorial Hospital by the local residents as well as the coppers. An injured policeman was almost never transported to MLK by RA units. And fellow officers would never transport another cop to this county facility. I've actually heard one officer say that if anyone tried to take him to MLK, he would pull his gun. I don't think he would have shot anyone, but who knows. I've also heard citizens breakdown and cry when advised by an RA unit that they were transporting a loved-one to MLK.

My unit was assigned to remain with the suspect until he was stabilized enough to be transported to the Jail Ward of Big County (LA County General Hospital). Our would-be Evel Knievel lasted about four hours and then succumbed to his injuries. The family of our suspect, of course, blamed the police for his death and we nearly had to call for a backup unit at the hospital to prevent a miniriot. When we finally returned to our black-and-white every glass surface on the car, including headlights, taillights and red lights, had been smashed-out or broken. Take me to MLK, no thanks!

SOUNDS OF THE GHETTO

Coppers dread hearing an *officer needs help* call. And the only thing worse is if you are the one putting out the call.

Responding to help calls was never fun. You got there as quickly as possible and you never knew what to expect. I've seen officers shot, officers under the influence of drugs (liquid PCP was thrown into his face), officers with cuts and ripped uniforms, officers seriously injured, officers experiencing a Vietnam flashback and one officer completely soaked after he jumped into a pool to save a suspect under the influence of PCP.

Needing help was always serious and waiting for help to arrive seemed to take forever. I still have a clear memory of putting out a help call when I saw my partner take a serious fall during an altercation. We were in the projects, late at night, involved with multiple suspects and a growing crowd. The big crowd was our own fault. The radio had been left on the PA function and not the Communications frequency. I broadcast a help call over the PA system to the projects known as Nickerson Gardens. Most of these folks didn't care too much for the police and expecting the crowd to help us can safely be placed under "fat chance."

Fortunately, hostile crowds gathering at a police involved altercation or some other criminal incident generally did not join in on the side of the suspects. They usually just watched and yelled at the coppers, and they might toss a beer can or two into the melee just for fun.

Our help call was finally broadcast to Communications and now we had to wait for the cavalry to arrive. The first sign that they were close was the sound of a big V-8, accelerating at wide-open throttle. What a great sound! Most of our black-and-whites were not fuel injected, and I was certain I could hear all four-barrels of their carburetors dumping gas into the cylinders. There is nothing quite like the whine of an American-made V-8, revving to max r.p.m. during a flat-out acceleration—especially when it's coming to save your ass.

The next encouraging event is a four-wheel locked skid. The sound of tires laying down some of Firestone's best rubber clearly means the troops are on the way and close. The sound of slamming car doors followed by running boots hitting the pavement is next, help is close by. You still can't relax, but the anxiety level is beginning to change and you begin to feel as if you might regain some control of the situation.

A help call, a high revving V-8, four-wheel locked skid, doors slamming shut, boots hitting the pavement, most South-end coppers have heard that sequence of events many, many times, and like a jail cell door slamming shut, these are unforgettable sounds that signify needed help has arrived.

A VERY UNPOPULAR CAPTAIN

I think I'm a good judge of leadership; in fact, I think most coppers have a good handle on who is and who isn't a good leader. We received a new captain at 77th who had very poor leadership qualities. He was black and seemed to show favoritism to black officers. This was only a perception on my part, but it was based on watching the captain walking down the hallway and saying hello to black officers and ignoring the white ones. I learned later that many of the black officers didn't care that much for him either. Was he being unfair, or was he simply a poor leader, who knows. I did something, however, that no one else had done: I sued him in Small Claims Court.

It all began as Rocky, my regular partner, and I were traveling westbound on Century Boulevard east of the Harbor Freeway. It was early afternoon with plenty of daylight. We noticed a car that was being driven erratically. In fact, its maneuvers were so dangerous that we were being hailed by other drivers to do something about the car. After a lot of quick and sudden lane changes, we finally managed to stop the vehicle in front of an apartment building. Because of this unusual behavior, we felt that it was likely the driver would try to escape and this traffic stop would end in a pursuit. Afternoon traffic, however, was so heavy on Century that the car eventually stopped.

The car was being driven by a white female and the passenger was a white male. Rocky was driving, so after the stop he approached the driver's side of the car, and I focused on the passenger. Before the passenger door was opened I noticed Rocky was having some difficulty controlling the female driver. She was trying to get away from him and managed, somehow, to run into the middle of Century Boulevard. Rocky grabbed her by the arm and dragged her back to the trunk of our black-and-white. Moments before we made this traffic stop, we had assisted another unit with the arrest of three or four suspects. Rocky had given his only set of handcuffs to the other officers.

The male passenger, who appeared to be drunk, decided it was time to come to the aid of the driver—chivalry, apparently, wasn't dead. Drunks are usually easy to control and I had no difficulty choking out this guy. I was, however, now on his back and he was lying face down on the ground. The female driver tried to rise up and escape from Rocky's grasp. Rocky forced her down again on the trunk and wanted to cuff her but he didn't have any cuffs. I threw him my cuffs as my guy was still out or just plain drunk and wasn't a problem. Rocky missed catching the cuffs and they landed on the ground. He grabbed the girl by her wrists and forced her to the ground next to the cuffs. We eventually got everybody cuffed and into the car. My guy was uninjured, but the driver had a lot of cuts and bruises on her arms, a cut on her forehead, a broken nose and a broken wrist. The injuries were understandable as she was trying desperately to escape Rocky's grasp and she was very difficult to control. A small number of people were hanging out of the windows of the apartment building and yelling at us for arresting the suspects and using force to do so, pretty typical actually.

When we returned to the station with the suspects, we were met by a sergeant who advised us to prepare for a serious personal complaint. We booked the suspects, completed the paperwork and were interviewed by Internal Affairs that night.

Personal complaints for excessive force, referred to as a one-eighty-one, (which was the number on the form designating a complaint against an officer) were common at 77th. This one, however, was a little more significant because of the large number of people who were willing to come forward as witnesses.

After the investigation, the department alleged that Rocky had used excessive force. He was forced to take a Trial Board, a hearing by three captains to determine guilt, innocence or the degree of culpability. If an officer was *forced* to take a trial board, the penalty could be termination or even the possibility of criminal prosecution.

This was serious for Rocky. The allegation against me was fairly minor. I was offered a five-day suspension or the option of taking a trial board. If you were innocent, a trial board would appear to be the best option. However, once you decided to accept the hearing, you were immediately suspended—without pay—for a period of one to two months until the board convened. Rocky didn't have an option and was immediately suspended.

If you were found innocent at the trial board, you were returned to duty with all your back pay. If your penalty was a suspension of five days, you would be paid for your time off, thirty to sixty days, minus the salary for five working days, your penalty.

Was this a fair process? No, not really. I could afford a five-day loss of pay, but I could not afford to go thirty days without being paid, even if I was later reimbursed for twenty-five of those days. A lengthy trial board would have been a real hardship. The reason this was unfair is because the department counted on this system to avoid trial boards. In many cases, mine included, it was simply easier to accept the five-day suspension rather than go unpaid for a month or more.

The allegation against me was that I observed excessive force being used by Rocky and failed to report it. So here's the problem I faced: If I accepted the five-day suspension, the acceptance would be tantamount to an admission that Rocky used excessive force. Rocky was a close friend and a great partner; it was unconscionable for me to put him in that position, even indirectly. However, my advocate, a respected investigator who worked Homicide, advised me that if we both took a trial board—Rocky didn't have a choice, I did—he would do everything possible to exonerate me at Rocky's expense. He convinced me that if we both went before the board, Rocky and I would be pitted against each other and he would suffer. I reluctantly accepted the five-day suspension.

There were a number of specific complaints against Rocky, and many of the witnesses lied about what occurred and what they observed—I know, I too am shocked. However, the trial board did a good job of separating the "wheat from the chaff" and exonerated him of most of the allegations. One of the charges of which he was found innocent involved the use of excessive force that I supposedly observed and failed to report. In other words, the trial board indirectly found me innocent. However, it doesn't work that way. I accepted the five-day suspension and other than going to superior court, I had no recourse. Going to superior court meant hiring an attorney, which would have been far too expensive to recover five day's pay.

Rocky was suspended, I'm not sure of the exact number of days, for using excessive force and a few other policy violations, but he was returned to duty.

I had a strong dislike for our captain. I was hoping I could get my five-day suspension back and embarrass him at the same time. I thought I might be able to sue him in small claims court for the five-day loss of pay. I filed the suit, obtained a trial date and had the marshal's office serve the captain with a notice to appear in small claims court as the defendant. If nothing else, serving him with a notice to appear, at the station, might cause him some discomfort or embarrassment, and there was an outside chance that I might get some back pay.

The trial date was set for several months after the incident. On the day of the trial, I was called to present my case; however, the captain was not present. Somehow he managed to get the city attorney to represent him. I mistakenly thought attorneys were not allowed to represent either party in small claims court; apparently I was wrong.

I presented my case as the plaintiff and did fairly well, I thought. The city attorney, the lawyer for the defendant, stated that the facts as I had outlined them were accurate—I really thought I had won—but there was a jurisdictional issue to be addressed. The city referred to some statute of which I was not aware, that mandated the issue be heard by the Superior Court of Los Angeles County, not small claims court. The judge was apparently familiar with that part of the law and sided with the defendant. I lost. But it was still worth all the effort.

You might think the department or the captain would try to punish me, in some way, for going to court against them, especially small claims court. But that never happened. I was subsequently transferred to two sought-after assignments and the department made no effort to block those transfers. It's a bit hard for me to say these words, but the department was reasonable and fair to me following the suspension.

About five-years after the incident, I was called to testify for the city in a civil trial filed against the city by the female driver. She was seeking damages in excess of $100,000 for her injuries. It was my time to pay the city back. I testified that during the intervening years I had become a court-qualified expert on PCP, Angel Dust. I testified that in my professional opinion the driver of the car had been under the influence of this dangerous and violent drug at the time of the incident. We did recover some marijuana from the car, but no hard evidence of PCP. However, my testimony was absolutely accurate. Neither Rocky nor I had much experience with PCP when she was initially arrested, but we did gain a considerable amount of expertise during the next five years.

By the way, the city won the civil case and she was not paid one cent for her injuries.

TONY MITCHELL

Tony was, and still is, a very good friend. He was about the only friend I had that was not on the department. And that's fairly typical of most coppers: You have lots of friends who are not officers before you join the force and then within a few years most of your close friends are cops.

Tony drove through 77th twice a day while commuting back and forth to work. He took Century

Boulevard, and if I was working PM watch, I would be on-duty when he was driving home. One afternoon, while working with a brand-new recruit—I was his training officer—I found myself behind Tony's car. I explained to the recruit that Tony was a friend of mine and I wanted to play a trick on him. As I mentioned before, a recruit will do almost anything you tell him to do. I told the new officer that I was going to fire-up the red lights and do a traffic stop on Tony's car. I explained to the recruit that I would remain behind the wheel of our car, with my hat down low, while he approached the driver—really poor tactics, but obviously not a problem with Tony. I told the recruit to rip into Tony for driving with his head up his ass and committing numerous violations. I told him to use the most obscene language he was capable of while slapping his baton against the palm of his hand. The recruit was clearly in a panic. He was fresh out of the academy and was just told to violate almost every rule that was drummed into him during his six months of training. He was clearly torn: should he do as he was told by his God-like training officer or follow the rules. He kept asking me if I was positive this would be okay. I, of course, told him not to worry, Tony was a close friend and it would be a great joke. I'm sure the helpless recruit was certain that we'd be met by Internal Affairs as soon as we returned to the station and this would be his last day on the job.

The plan worked to perfection. After being confronted by the probationer, I could see Tony shaking his head back and forth, and throwing his hands up in the air. The recruit had replaced his baton with a ticket book and, per my instructions, was explaining each made-up violation, in detail, to him. Tony, who was usually polite and respectful, was obviously pleading his case; he has always been a little tight with a buck and I could almost see him counting out money to pay the fine. Before actually citing any real violation, the recruit returned to our car to find out how to end the traffic stop. As he leaned into the driver's window of our car, I told him I had made a mistake and this was not my friend. I could almost see the blood draining from his face after I made this admission. He said, "What are we going to do?" I said, "What's this *we* shit! You're the one who talked to him!"

I finally got out of the car, removed my hat and sunglasses and had a good laugh at Tony's expense. This was clearly a two-fer, I punked a good friend and a probationer with one traffic stop.

SCRAP IRON

Most LA coppers wouldn't take shit from anyone and would never back down from an asshole regardless of how big and tough he appeared to be. One night I made an exception to that unwritten rule. My partner and I observed a fairly new Cadillac speeding westbound on Century toward LAX. It was about two in the morning and traffic was light. The vehicle was traveling in excess of eighty m.p.h. and weaving in and out of traffic. We didn't think the suspect was a deuce (driving under the influence) as he appeared to be a skillful driver. We eventually caught up to him, hit him with the red lights and made the stop. He quickly and carefully pulled to the curb. Except for the Cadillac, I'm now thinking this guy must be a cop, maybe a deputy chief or some other honcho.

I ordered the driver out of the car while remaining behind our open driver's door, which was fairly typical of most traffic stops. If possible, we always tried to avoid walking up to a car during a stop. Per our request, the suspect got out of the car, and then continued to get out of the car, and continued; he was huge. He was tall, muscular and had a broken nose. He was about as intimidating a guy as I have ever met. I almost put out a backup call before I had even talked to the guy. However, he was extremely polite—what a pleasant surprise that was. He told us his name was Scrap Iron Johnson. He was a professional heavyweight boxer whose name I recognized. He also said that he was extremely sorry for driving so fast, but he was trying to catch a red-eye out of LAX.

My response was somewhat atypical for an LA cop: "Mr. Johnson, if you don't mind, would you *please* slow down." And I added with a smile, "But if you don't want to, that's perfectly okay." A big grin told me he knew I was trying to be funny. We sent him on his way without a ticket—most South-end patrol coppers don't write many tickets. He thanked us, waved and was on his way, and he did slow down.

TIM

Tim had worked 77th for a number of years. He was a seasoned and respected veteran officer. Not much got him upset and he had seen almost everything. With one exception: We had been deluged with heavy rain storms for a solid week; records were being set almost daily because of these torrential rains. Tim and his partner were driving slowly on one of the many residential streets within the division. (Tim later told me there must have been at least six inches of water covering the streets. There was so much water present that it was not unusual to see water pouring *out* of manhole covers. The drainage system in LA was totally overwhelmed.) All of a sudden the car stopped, floated for a second and sank into a huge hole that was not visible because of all the water on the street. Tim and his partner were completely taken by surprise. When the car finally came to rest, the water level had covered the hood and trunk of the black-and-white; they were now seated in a *white* only patrol car. The only visible parts of the car were the white top, windows, red lights and siren.

Tim grabbed the mike and started to broadcast a radio call for some form of assistance. He didn't want to use the word "help" because of all the problems it might create. And he didn't really need a backup, no point in more cars sinking; and requesting assistance was real close to a help call. It really didn't matter, however, because the water had shorted out the battery and his radio was useless. Tim and his partner climbed out the windows and perched themselves on top of the car and waited. Tim thought it was safer to remain on top of the car until someone came along. There was, however, a problem: no one came along. Finally, an elderly woman opened her front door and asked Tim if he needed any help. Tim said yes, and asked her to call the station and tell the desk officer that he and his partner were trapped on top of their patrol car that was slowly sinking into a gigantic hole. She said she'd be happy to help. Tim felt much better knowing that he would soon be rescued. It didn't matter that he would be the brunt of jokes; he needed to get onto dry land or at least solid ground.

Five minutes passed, then ten minutes passed and no officers or firemen showed up to help. After yelling as loud as he could, he finally got the attention of the woman who offered to call. When she opened the front door, Tim asked her what happened. She said she called the station, just like he asked, and she told the desk officer two uniformed officers were trapped on top of their car, just like he asked, but she said they weren't going to send any officers or firemen to help. Tim was generally a very patient guy, but the situation and this woman, who was trying to be helpful, was almost a little more than he could take. He finally yelled, "Why aren't they sending anyone?" She said the desk officer, an irascible character who should have retired years ago, didn't believe two uniformed officers would be trapped on top of their car in the middle of LA during a rain storm. The desk officer was sure this was a made-up, bullshit call and he had no intentions of dispatching another car.

Tim and his partner eventually made it back to the station and confronted the desk officer. He was an old guy who simply didn't care about other coppers. Shortly thereafter he retired.

EVERYBODY LIKES TO GO CODE-3

An unrelated incident showed how sensible Tim was about police work. It was also a pretty good window into his grasp of what was important and what wasn't. First off, almost everyone I knew loved to drive code-3 to a hot call; everyone, that is, but Tim. An assigned, code-3 call meant that red lights and siren had to be used. Unlike most coppers, Tim did not like to drive fast. He almost always drove sensibly, even to hot calls; help calls were probably the exception.

One afternoon, after stopping for coffee at a donut shop—where else—we received a code-3 call. I don't remember the exact nature of this call, but we both knew that it was not serious. It could have been the location of the call or any number of reasons, but we were in no hurry to get to the address. And, of course, the main reason we were taking our time was because Tim had not finished his cup of coffee. When we finally responded to the call, Tim continued to be his usual unhurried self. Picture this: One black-and-white police car traveling southbound on Broadway with red light flashing and the siren blasting—traveling about twenty m.p.h.! A single black-and-white traveling under these conditions probably would not have seemed too unusual. However, when I looked to our rear, I noticed about six additional black-and-whites, all of them had their red lights activated, driving single file behind us. None of them was traveling faster than we were. We were the assigned car and no one wanted to get to this bogus call before we did.

A GAME OF DOMINOS

Tim was the most non-confrontational LA copper I had ever worked with. He was not weak, he was not afraid; he just tried really hard to keep minor problems from escalating into major ones. It actually made cop work a lot easier. I learned this one day after we received a radio call about a family dispute. We arrived at the house and determined that the husband, who had been drinking, had assaulted his wife. Unless the wife was injured, we'd usually tell the husband that he had to leave. We generally would explain to him that once he sobered up, and if he promised not to do it again, he could return in a few hours. We made a similar notification to the suspect, but he didn't want to leave. Normally when this happened, we would throw him physically off the premises and tell him not to return. About half the time we'd end up choking the guy out and booking him for interfering or some other minor section of the Penal Code. But Tim had a better idea; he noticed a set of dominos on the kitchen table and told the husband he would like to play a game with him. There were some unusual rules, however: If Tim won the game, the guy would agree to leave. If the husband won, we would leave. The husband agreed to Tim's rules. Fortunately, Tim kicked his ass in dominos and the guy willingly left. No altercation, no arrest reports and no one was injured. Tim probably saved the city a ton of money.

FIRECRACKERS

As I mentioned before, Tim was fairly straight-laced and professional, but he was not without a sense of humor. It was the fourth of July and Tim and I were assigned to different cars. Tim confiscated some firecrackers and decided that it would be a good idea to light one off and throw it into my car as he sped by. He caught me and my partner completely by surprise and scared the devil out of us. I, of course, had to retaliate.

Somehow I managed to get my own supply of cherry bombs and planned a reprisal. I listened for Tim's unit to be assigned a radio call. I planned to drive by the location and toss a lighted cherry bomb into Tim's car. Tim's call came out as "See the woman, 415 juveniles." When I drove by I noticed that Tim was talking with an elderly white woman. She was quite animated and was obviously giving him a hard time about something, probably this group of unruly juveniles. Tim saw us approaching his location and quickly determined what I planned to do. He looked at me very seriously and he yelled, "No, not here!" By that time I had already lighted the cherry bomb and had no choice but to throw it out the window of our car. The cherry bomb blew up and we drove from the location as quickly as we could.

We found out later that Tim's call concerned some kids who had been throwing firecrackers in the neighborhood and causing all kind s of problems for this poor woman. The police were worse than the local kids; I'm still not sure what Tim told this very upset citizen, but knowing Tim, he was probably able to sooth her ruffled feathers.

AN OUTSTANDING OFFICER DIED AND THE CROWD CHEERS

This is an event that I did not observe and, in fact, know very little about, but it's entirely possible—even likely—that the following incident is true.

Jim was a hard-working, dedicated officer and a Vietnam veteran. A likeable guy with a mustache that must have driven supervisors nuts because it was significantly wider than departmental standards allowed. I'm not certain what type of detail he was working at the time of his death, but I believe he was on some type of drug related stakeout. Typically, an officer would be assigned to a hidden observation post (OP) watching for a drug deal or some other observable crime. A second team of officers, usually sitting nearby in a car, was the chase car. This team would stop the suspect, either on foot or in a car, and make the arrest.

The dope deal or crime was witnessed by the OP, and Jim was given the go-ahead to make the stop and the arrest. He would have been given a description of the vehicle or the suspects and their direction of travel. I'm assuming this was how the incident unfolded, but I could easily be wrong about the details. It doesn't really matter, however, as they are not that important.

The pursuing chase car generally has to catch up with the suspect's vehicle, which means, of course, that it is being driven quickly. My recollection is witnesses indicated Jim was speeding through an intersection on the *green* light and should have been given the right-of-way. The other driver failed to stop for his red light and collided with Jim's car, killing him instantly. Other officers have advised me that Jim entered the intersection on the red, it doesn't matter as it is not relevant to the story. The incident occurred near one of the Projects and it was reported that an open container of alcohol was found inside the violator's vehicle.

Jim's body was not quickly removed from the wrecked police car. He had died in the accident and it usually took an hour or so for the coroner's van to arrive on the scene. During this interminable wait, a large crowd had gathered at the site of the accident, close to the Projects. Crowds that gather in these areas are almost always hostile to the police.

Jim's uniformed body was finally removed from the car, covered and placed in the coroner's van. At a critical moment during this process—when it was clear and unmistakable that Jim had died—it was alleged the crowd happily cheered when they understood that an LA copper had been killed. I wasn't present and I haven't talked to anyone who was at the scene, but this type of behavior would have been typical for a gathering crowd from the Projects. Over thirty years have passed since the incident, but I still harbor feelings of anger and disgust towards these individuals. I hope the environment in South-Central LA has changed, but I suspect it has not.

Senior management knew exactly how explosive this incident could have been to street coppers once the word had spread throughout the South-end divisions. They quickly mounted a counter-attack that attempted to discredit the "rumors" of a cheering, elated crowd at the scene of a dead officer. They actually sent some captains or deputy chiefs to roll calls to explain or convince officers that the incident never took place. In general, LAPD management didn't have a lot of credibility with hard-working coppers, and like the conflict between officers and citizens, I seriously doubt that has changed.

CHOKE THAT FOOL OUT!

This is one of my favorite stories. It actually took place in Hollywood Division, but the involved officer had been transferred to 77th when it was told to me.

There was a 415 party at a house in Hollywood. Officers had been called to the party at least twice because of loud music and a drunken fight. On both occasions a retired—Hall of Fame—NFL running back told the responding officers to leave and get the fuck off his porch. The first time, in the interest of good community relations, the officers let it slide. They had enough, however, after the second call and an old-timer decided on a game plan: He located one of the smallest coppers in the division and assigned him the task of returning to the party and telling the two hundred and thirty-five pound running back to shut the fuck up and turn the music off! The senior officer also requested the presence of a fairly young officer who was a dedicated weightlifter. This guy was as strong as an ox and had biceps the size of my thighs.

The weightlifter was briefed on the plan and was overjoyed that he was going to be a part of it. He was assigned to stand beside the front door—completely out of sight—as our munchkin-sized officer knocked on the door and made the announcement to quiet down. The former player, a real knuckle-dragging philistine, stepped out of the house and onto the front porch to confront the short officer. And the moment he did so, the weightlifter placed a bar-arm control hold around the former player's 19-inch neck and choked his ass out. To the amusement of everyone present, our NFL hero did the "chicken" on the front porch and pissed his pants. I don't know if the guy was arrested, but the story did have a happy ending.

A PUBLIC DEFENDER...REALLY

Our suspect was arrested for possession of an illegal drug with the intent to sell. The quantity and the nature of the packaging was enough to establish intent. At the time of his arrest he was driving a new Cadillac and he had over $5,000 in cash in his socks. It's not easy to cram five grand into your socks, but he did.

It apparently was a good arrest as I received a subpoena to attend the preliminary hearing. I appeared, testified to the facts of the arrest and waited to hear if the case would go forward. It apparently did as the defendant requested that a public defender be assigned to his defense. The tax payers of LA County, of course, would be paying for the services of the public defender. For some reason the type of car he was driving and the amount of cash in his possession was not addressed during my testimony. The judge considered the request and decided to grant it. I was seated as a spectator in the court room but decided to "object" to the judge's decision. This, of course, was almost never done, but there was an atmosphere of informality with this particular judge and I thought he would listen to me without any repercussions.

I stood up and explained to the judge that the defendant was driving a new Cadillac, with a clear title, and he had over $5,000 in his socks at the time of the arrest. The judge looked a little surprised, but advised me that the defendant would be referred to the PD's office and they would make the decision based on an outline established by the County of Los Angeles.

I shouldn't have been surprised, however, when a month later the dope dealer appeared in Superior Court with a public defender. What a great system we have.

CIGARETTES AND JELLY DONUTS

Coppers have been accused of being pretty callous when it comes to tragedies that affect crime victims. I suppose shrinks have a good explanation for this behavior, and it probably relates to self-preservation, or at the very least, the idea that there is a limit to the amount of empathy one can display. A callous reaction, or no reaction whatsoever, to a tragedy may be a way for the officer to bank his emotions and save them for a worthy victim.

My partner and I were assigned to guard the dead body of a gang member who had been killed in a drive-by shooting. We were in a small, no smoking room at Morningside Hospital. The room was not located in the ER, and it was not a regular hospital room full of doctors or visitors. I was not a smoker, so I was probably more sensitive to tobacco smoke than a regular tobacco user.

While sitting in the room and paying little attention to my surroundings, I began to notice a strong odor of burning tobacco. I could see my partner and he clearly did not have a cigarette in his hand and, except for the dead guy, we were the only ones in the room. How strange. I quickly glanced at the deceased gangbanger and noticed that a burning cigarette was sticking out of his mouth, and smoke was beginning to fill the room. My partner began lecturing the stiff about the dangers of smoking—and the lecture sounded suspiciously like comments I had made to him about his smoking habits.

No one deserves to be the victim of a homicide, but it's hard to generate any emotions or feeling for these cretins, even when they are victims.

The second incident involves a shootout between two individuals involved in a drug transaction. One of the victims died at the scene and the suspect managed to escape. The shooting took place inside a house, so the crime scene was contained and under our control. We were waiting for the arrival of the homicide investigators who had been delayed for some reason, probably another homicide. My partner, who was complaining about being hungry, managed to get another unit to make a run to a donut shop and return with some jelly donuts. When the donuts arrived, we sat down in front of the TV and began watching a late-night program and munching on donuts that were oozing red jelly. The jelly had a pretty strong resemblance to the blood that had pooled under the victim. After an hour or so, the detectives arrived and noticed that we were quite relaxed sitting in front of the TV and eating donuts. While seated in an overstuffed chair, my partner extended his legs over the victim as if he were using the victim as an ottoman; he made sure, however, not to touch the victim with his shoes. I don't think anything really shocks an LAPD homicide detective, but these guys seemed to be surprised, almost shocked. One of them, I think, saw the red jelly on my partner's face and may have assumed, for a brief moment, that we had turned to cannibalism. Even today it's difficult for me to generate any sympathy for these young gang members. A stray bullet that kills an innocent child, of course, is an entirely different story.

SORRY SERGEANT, I CAN'T DO THAT

I can still clearly see a twelve year-old boy lying on the ground with a hole in his stomach. The wound was caused by a shotgun blast fired at fairly close range and that's why the tissue damage was confined to an area about the size of a silver dollar. The wound was not large, but very fatal. There was a great deal of blood on the ground, which suggested that it took him a few minutes to die. To die from a gunshot wound to the body is always painful, but this young man's death was not quick and most certainly painful. The boy appeared quite normal from the chest up and from the waist down, but his stomach was a bloody, open mess.

He was a handsome kid. He had short hair and was dressed just like my kids, conservatively. He wore no gang-type clothing and except for all the blood, his clothes were clean and fairly new.

He had been shot outside his house which was located in the heart of gang territory, and it was alleged he was shot by a gang member. Based on a preliminary investigation and a review of gang records, he apparently had absolutely no gang affiliation. His mother indicated he was a great kid, no arrests, a good student and fun to be with. I know that most mothers feel their kids can do no wrong, but I believed her and had a feeling that he really *was* a good kid.

While at the scene the mother sat down next to her son and held his head in her arms. I tried to discourage her from touching the boy as we didn't want the crime scene to be contaminated. I could tell, however, that she needed to be with her son, even in death.

A uniformed sergeant was at the scene and gave me an order to transport the mother to the station. I felt uncomfortable asking her to leave the scene, but an order is an order. I approached her while she was sitting on the ground holding her son, and told her that we had to take her to the station to be interviewed by the detectives. She very calmly looked me in the eye and said she would not leave the scene until her son had been removed. I asked her again, but she said, "Sorry, I'm not leaving my son." Unfortunately it could take hours for the coroner to arrive and move the body. The only way I could comply with the sergeant's order was to use physical force to move her.

I was standing over the mother and her son when I was approached by the sergeant, a gruff, no-nonsense supervisor who expected his orders to be obeyed. He was also one of the good guys who took care of his troops but he also expected them to perform. The sergeant was not accustomed to telling his officers, more than once, to do their job. He told me a second time to take her to the station. When this incident occurred I didn't have a lot of time on the job and it took me a few seconds to work up the nerve to tell him no, I couldn't transport her. I explained why I thought it was not a good idea and hoped that it was a logical explanation. The sergeant clearly had good judgment, and quickly understood how this situation could easily turn into a nightmare.

He finally said, "Okay, she can stay, but I want you to remain with her until the body is removed." Someone called the coroner's office and managed to get the victim removed from the scene in a reasonable amount of time.

It wasn't easy and it doesn't happen very often, but LA cops and supervisors are capable of compassion; but we tend to ration it carefully, preferring to use it for deserving victims.

DRUNK ON A HORSE

Sometimes officers had contact with a guy or a gal who had to go to jail because of some outrageous behavior but no obvious criminal violation (the guy who was booked for removing sand from a city beach is a good example). No crime, no booking number—a real bummer. A morning-watch officer once booked a man for driving under the influence of alcohol. Nothing unusual about that except in this case the vehicle was a horse. It seems that the California Vehicle Code section (at that time) for driving under the influence of alcohol read *conveyance*, and not *motor* vehicle. And a horse met the CVC definition of a conveyance—I always wondered if that anomaly also applied to horses without brake lights. I don't know the circumstances of the incident, but it seems likely that the drunk on the horse was causing a serious problem and a "deuce" arrest was the best solution.

THEFT OF ELECTRICITY

I once booked a guy for theft of electricity. The suspect drove to a city school, climbed over the fence and plugged in a long extension cord. The school's electricity was charging eight car batteries housed in the trunk of his car. The batteries powered the hydraulic pumps that raised and lowered his car with the flick of a switch. With this many batteries in the trunk, he could drive down the street and bounce his car up and down, nearly becoming airborne. He couldn't believe he was going to jail. He seemed to feel that if he couldn't see it, touch it or remove it, how could he steal it? I couldn't find a section that applied to the theft of electricity so he was booked for simple theft, section 484 of the Penal Code.

The electricity thief was a member of a group of car enthusiasts within the division who had modified their vehicles—using multiple batteries and hydraulic pumps—so they could raise and lower them while driving on the road. Why anyone would do that is a little hard for me to understand, but they did.

BIG STEVE vs. LAPD'S SHOOTING POLICY

Before he became an LA cop, Big Steve was a school teacher from one of the mid-western states. He was a bright guy who stood six-six and weighed over two hundred and sixty pounds. After a few years on the streets he became a little disgruntled and eventually left the department. On this particular night we had two New Zealand coppers riding with us as observers. They were on vacation and wanted to see what it was like to be a big-city policeman.

New Zealand had strict gun control laws that effectively kept guns, especially hand guns, away from their citizens. If New Zealand officers needed a gun, they would contact a sergeant, explain the circumstances and he would make the final decision about being armed. If a gun was necessary, the sergeant would drive to the station and check out a weapon. I guess this system worked in New Zealand, but I think it's foolish. Most of the time, when you need a gun, you need it right now.

About half of our calls on this busy night used the word "gun". The two Kiwi officers, at first, would not get out of the back seat of our police car when we responded to these calls. There were simply too many guns around and they were unarmed. Sounds like good judgment to me. I had an enormous amount of respect for these guys. They worked in a different world, one with very few hand guns. They weren't being cowardly or even afraid; they simply thought it was smarter to remain in the police car. I later found out these two guys, like most New Zealand coppers, were expert ass-kickers and were very adept with a baton and sap.

We finally convinced the New Zealand officers that it was perfectly okay to get out of the car and accompany us on a radio call. I facetiously offered them the use of our shotgun, but they declined.

On this particular night one of our patrol officers—involved in a stakeout—was shot by a drug dealer. The officers observed what appeared to be a drug transaction. Money was exchanged for an unknown substance that was wrapped in a way that was nearly the same as packaged drugs. The officers followed the suspect's car and stopped it not far from where the transaction took place. As one of the suspects exited his vehicle, he removed a handgun from his waistband and fired at the officers. (We later learned he had just been released from prison and told his accomplice he was not going back.) A number of shots were exchanged between the officers and one of the suspects. After the shooting, the clear-thinking wounded officer had the presence of mind to broadcast a help call and request an ambulance. We, and almost every black-and-white on the entire planet, immediately responded to the scene of the shooting. When the sound of four-wheel locked skids finally stopped, and the smoke settled—we could actually detect an odor of gun powder in the air—we observed one suspect and one officer down. The suspect appeared to be dead, and the officer was badly wounded. The injured officer took a round in the stomach about an inch below his body armor. All of our efforts to convince the New Zealanders that shootings were fairly rare immediately went out the window.

After the wounded suspect was handcuffed—yes, we almost always cuff a wounded suspect, especially if he is the shooter—everyone pretty much ignored him as he was motionless and *may* have been dead. A sergeant finally arrived, took charge and advised Big Steve, who was one of the responding officers, to guard the injured dope dealer. His exact words to Steve were, "Don't let *anyone* near the suspect." Steve's response was, "Okay sergeant, I won't."

The first RA unit arrived and immediately went to the fallen officer. They scooped him up and transported him to Daniel Freeman Hospital. It was not the closest hospital but they had a great ER. A second ambulance arrived and approached the badly wounded suspect. Big Steve stepped in front of them and said something that we could not hear. After their brief conversation, the paramedics returned to their ambulance and left the scene. I thought that was a little odd as neither one of the firemen attended to the suspect.

About five minutes later a fire department battalion chief arrived at the scene. He had been driving code-3. I thought to myself, why the red lights and siren, everything was now pretty quiet. The chief located the sergeant who advised Big Steve to keep everyone away from the suspect, and proceeded to chew on his ass. Fire and police supervisors rarely have conflicts, so I was genuinely surprised to see such an animated discussion. I could not hear what was being said, but the body language and gesticulating displayed by the chief was pretty clear. Our sergeant, who was normally tough, aggressive and wouldn't take an ass-chewing from anyone, looked like a whipped puppy that had been spanked for peeing on the floor. He was clearly embarrassed and more than a little pissed off.

After the ass-chewing, a second ambulance returned to the scene, examined the suspect, declared him to be dead and then left. I don't know exactly when the suspect died, but the delay in receiving medical attention could not have helped. No one, however, shed any tears for this asshole. He tried to kill a cop and paid the ultimate price. Fortunately, the LA Times didn't get any details about the ambulance fiasco and a community relations disaster was avoided.

Our sergeant finally located Big Steve and asked him why he didn't let the paramedics examine the suspect. And Steve, of course, said, "Sergeant, you said not to let *anyone* near the suspect, and I didn't." That was Big Steve.

The wounded officer had a full recovery and ultimately returned to the job. The two vacationing New Zealand officers decided not to immigrate to Los Angeles, and returned to New Zealand.

Big Steve was also involved in a questionable shooting. I have few details about the shooting, except that the suspect was unarmed. Shooting an unarmed suspect is almost always problematic and that was certainly the case with Steve. Every officer-involved shooting is thoroughly investigated by a small team of detectives whose only function is to investigate officer-involved shootings. The detectives were generally well-respected and very good at what they did.

When an officer shoots a suspect, he is quickly removed from the scene, separated from his partner and returned to the station. He was generally placed in a small office and not allowed to talk to anyone until he was interviewed by the Officer-Involved Shooting Team. The lieutenant conducting the interview wants all the unvarnished facts, no bullshit. Almost all of our shootings were justified. No copper I knew wanted to get into a bad shooting. There is too much at stake and it is clearly not worth the risk. That is not to say, however, that some shootings could have been handled differently, without the use of deadly force. Steve's shooting was probably a good example of a shooting that was justified—one of his arms was broken by the suspect—but could have been handled differently.

The interview with the Officer-Involved Shooting Team was extremely important and more or less set the tone for the inquiry and the nature of the questions that followed.

Lieutenant Charles Higbie, the detective conducting the investigation, was admired by nearly everyone on the department. He sat Steve down in the captain's office and made the following statement, "Steve, we need to get something straight right from the beginning: this is no *Medal of Valor* shooting." And it wasn't.

Steve didn't face any criminal charges and he wasn't fired, but the department was not happy with the incident. An officer-involved shooting investigation usually had one of three possible results: The shooting was In Policy, which meant the officer would not be disciplined or even criticized for his actions. If the shooting was Out of Policy, the officer would probably face some disciplinary action by the department, perhaps even criminal charges.

The third possible outcome was, In Policy, Review Tactics. It's hard to imagine that the shooting of an unarmed suspect could actually be In Policy, but it happens all the time. I don't know the actual outcome of Steve's shooting, but I suspect the incident—and the criticism of his actions—was one of the reasons he eventually left the department.

"PUT OUT A HELP CALL AND GET AN AMBULANCE!"

I was working with a seasoned officer and there was absolutely no reason for me to tell him we needed help. He had already figured that out. We also had a probationer who was still assigned to the academy riding along as a third officer, an observer, actually. We were working PM watch and had been assigned a "shots fired" radio call. As I've mentioned before, it was pretty common for South-end coppers to receive this type of call. We were never complacent when responding to a potentially serious call but we were almost always doubtful.

We arrived at the scene and we immediately noticed the glass in the front window of the house had been shot out. I was never a detective, but even I could figure out that this could be a good call, someone had apparently used a gun, but how recently? My partner and I carefully approached the front of the house with heightened awareness, forgetting about the rookie we had in the back seat. I removed my handgun while my partner exited our car with the shotgun. As I walked toward the front door I heard a round go off, and then I smelled gunpowder. It's pretty common to hear rounds being fired in the ghetto, but to hear a round and then smell it was a clear indication that the shooter was close, real close.

Seconds later a woman stumbled out of the front door. She was bleeding from a wound in her neck and was holding a bloody towel. We've already established that I was not a detective, but hey, this was a good call. About that same time I turned around and noticed that my rookie was flat on his back. I thought to myself, "Shit, my recruit's been shot!" That's when I told my partner to get some help and call for an ambulance. My partner rushed to the recruit, who was now standing up (he apparently wasn't seriously shot), while I grabbed the wounded woman, slung her over my shoulder and tried to find a place to hide that put us out of the line of fire.

About that time every black-and-white in the country was beginning to roll into the scene: CHP units, Housing Authority officers, sheriff's units and LAPD black-and-whites from all over the city. I was trying to talk to the wounded woman and get some information about the suspect. I was certain he was still inside the house. At the same time, I was trying to make sure we had officers in the back of the residence so the suspect could not escape. The woman, who was not badly injured, kept insisting there was no one else inside. I didn't believe her. I was certain she was trying to cover for someone.

No one likes to turn over a scene to SWAT, but I was beginning to think maybe that was a good idea. There was a good chance that our guy could have escaped out the back door, but just as good a chance that he was still inside the house. About that time, another officer from PM watch casually walked up to me and said, "Code-4, your rookie fired the round." My response was, "Are you serious?" I couldn't believe what I was just told. He eventually convinced me our shooter was the recruit.

Here's what happened: We arrived at the location and after viewing the shot-out windows, my partner and I commented about the possibility that this could be a good call. All three of us exited our car and I removed my hand gun. When our recruit saw me unholster my weapon, he did the same thing and continued to follow me toward the house. There was a patch of ivy growing on the parkway in front of the location. I went around it but my recruit walked through it. He got his feet tangled up in the vines and fell flat on his face, discharging his weapon as he hit the deck. His round went through the front window shattering the already broken glass. The woman was standing behind the window and the exploding glass shards cut her face and neck. These were facial cuts that bled quite a bit, but they were all minor. There had been a shooting at the house moments before we arrived, which accounted for the bullet holes in the window, but the suspect had already left the scene.

Once we figured out what happened, I was really pissed at my recruit. We had needlessly broadcast a help call endangering the lives of responding officers. I asked him why he didn't tell me that he was the one who fired the round. He told me he assumed that a help call was always made whenever shots were fired, even when it was an accidental discharge. I was not happy with this guy.

Someone made a quick calculation of the trajectory of the round from the location of the recruit to the glass window. The round missed the back of my head by inches. Now I was really pissed.

Several days after the incident, I drove to the academy on my own time and talked with the academy instructors about the recruit. I had some serious doubts about the guy and wasn't convinced he'd make a good officer. I also had a lot of respect for the academy staff. These were all seasoned, dedicated officers whose judgment was generally pretty sound. When they erred it was usually on the side of the department not the recruit. Everyone I talked to had good things to report about this probationer. He was a good recruit and they all thought he'd make a good policeman. For the next year or two I checked up on this guy to make sure no one had made a mistake. No one had, he was a fine officer.

ANOTHER ACCIDENTAL SHOOTING

Guns were everywhere in the ghetto. It was just a fact of life. And, with so many guns being displayed by officers and suspects, accidental discharges were bound to happen. I would guess that almost every copper in the South-end unholstered his weapon—or removed the shotgun from its rack in the car—every day they worked the street. We've all heard stories about officers who have worked through an entire career without pulling a gun. That's always a nice feel-good story, but my guess is these officers were incompetent or just foolish.

On the afternoon of my accidental discharge, I was working with a reserve officer who was an heir to a wealthy family that made their money distilling a good brand of Scotch (no wonder he was so popular). Seriously, he was a good guy, competent and fun to work with. We were southbound on Figueroa somewhere near Century Boulevard. I observed a guy looking into the front window of a liquor store. He was concentrating on the inside, but would quickly look up and down Figueroa every few seconds. I thought there was a good chance an armed robbery was going down and this guy may have been involved. I stopped the car north of the entrance, but away from the front window so that no one inside knew the police were present. I grabbed the shotgun, jacked-in a shell, took the safety off and carefully approached the front of the store, still out of sight. However, as soon as I jacked-in the shell, our suspect immediately walked away from the store and made a right turn on 97th Street. I called for him to stop, but that wasn't happening. We quickly looked inside and determined that no one except the clerk behind the counter was present.

We picked up our pace and followed our suspect. The moment we rounded 97th Street, it was apparent that aliens had abducted him. He was gone, GOA, no dust, no barking dogs, the guy simply disappeared within about five seconds. There was, however, a stairwell that led up to a second story apartment. The guy had to be inside the apartment. We carefully walked up the stairs and approached the front door. There was a hasp and a lock on the *outside* of the front door. There was no way the guy could be inside with the front door locked from the outside, no way. Shit, he really did disappear.

We didn't have enough information on this guy to bother putting out a broadcast. He hadn't done anything wrong, he just looked and acted dirty. He probably had a warrant for his arrest or he just didn't want to be bothered by the police. As we returned to the car I remembered I had chambered a shell and taken the safety off. The barrel was pointed toward the ground and my finger was on the trigger or at least through the trigger guard. I rotated my right thumb off the stock of the gun so I could push the safety button—making the gun safe to handle—with my right index finger. As I did so, the weight of the shotgun fell against my index finger, which was on the trigger, and I killed the cement sidewalk. It was a quick and startling death. At first I couldn't believe I actually fired the weapon, but as soon as I saw smoke swirling from the end of the barrel I knew I had done a really stupid thing.

My partner, who was walking next to me at the time of the incident, jumped in the air about fifteen feet straight up, and when he came down he sprained his ankle. I had two bloody, round impressions just above the outside of my right ankle, about the size of double-ought shotgun pellets. I had actually shot myself. I couldn't believe it, I shot myself in the leg. Unbelievable!

I knew that if I reported the incident I would be given some days off. My injury just needed to be cleaned and covered with two Band-Aids, but my partner's ankle probably had to be x-rayed. I thought, screw it, I messed up, I had better not make things worse by failing to report the incident. I called for a supervisor and fessed up to the incident.

A week or so later I was told to report to the captain's office. I did and we had a brief discussion. He advised me the incident was serious and we were lucky no one was badly hurt. He told me that he was giving me four days off as punishment. The captain, a guy I admired and respected, asked me if I had anything to say. This is when guys would usually argue their case or try to explain their actions. I said, "No sir, I was at fault and I'm really quite embarrassed about the incident. I deserve the days off." He appeared to be surprised by my attitude and said, "OK, that's all."

IN POLICY

It was Valentine's Day and I was working with Rocky, my regular partner. We were working PM watch. Roll call was uneventful and it was my turn to "keep books" and Rocky would be driving. "Keep books" meant that it was my responsibility to complete the Daily Log and write most of the crime and arrest reports. The officer who was driving was responsible for getting the car keys and checking out the shotgun. I was a little late collecting forms and whatever else we needed for the shift. Rocky was already sitting in the car by the time I left the station for the parking lot. When I got into the car I noticed there was no shotgun in our black-and-white. I asked Rocky, "Where's the shotgun?" He said, "Ah, we won't need it." Did he know something I didn't? Rocky and I were of the same rank, but he was senior to me in time on the job. I would usually acquiesce to him if we had a disagreement, which was very rare. However, I was not going to work without a shotgun. I returned to the station, checked out the 12-gauge and we were off.

Later that evening we received a radio call about suspects shooting at kids in an alley. There was nothing too unusual about the call; it was designated as a code-2 which meant the operator at the complaint board didn't take it too seriously. We were close to the location when the call was broadcast, so we arrived quickly and were the first officers on the scene. We approached the front of the house cautiously. I was leading the way as I had the shotgun. Rocky, of course, was behind me. As we walked by the large, bay window I noticed someone was inside and had just pulled the curtains back to get a better view. I assumed everyone inside the house knew the police had arrived. Another unit responded to the location and we asked them to watch the front of the house as we checked out the back.

We walked down the long driveway toward the garage that was located near the rear of the house. The opening between the corner of the house and the corner of the garage was only fourteen inches. Because of this layout it was difficult to look into the opening without stepping completely into the gap. We were concerned the suspects would escape out the back door as they must have known we were present. As I stepped into the gap, I saw two men crouched down next to the back porch. One of the men had a rifle pointed at my head and was looking in my direction. I was not sure what the other guy was doing. Under the circumstances you tend to focus on the most immediate threat and that was the guy with the rifle. His rifle is pointed at me and the barrel of my shotgun was about three feet from the suspect's center mass. I yelled, "Police! Freeze!" I actually meant to say "drop the gun" but freeze came out first. To be perfectly honest, the suspect complied with my request. He didn't move a muscle. This is when time really did slow down. It seemed to take me forever to chamber a shell, release the safety and pull the trigger on the shotgun.

Training takes over whenever someone points a gun at you. Your mind goes on autopilot and you simply react to the circumstances. The rifle was a clear threat to my safety and deadly force was used to end the threat. It was very dark and the shotgun blast effectively destroyed my night vision. I was blind for several seconds after the shot was fired.

Because the gap between the house and garage was so narrow, Rocky had no idea what I was looking at when I fired. Over three decades after the incident, I still have a vivid memory of Rocky pushing me aside and lighting up the suspects with his flashlight. I really expected to see a big hole in the chest of the guy holding the rifle. However, my shotgun blast was off by a few inches. I was focused on the rifle and that's what I hit. The double-ought buckshot pellets, however, hit both of his hands, the one holding the forward section of the

233

stock and the one holding the trigger mechanism. The shot also damaged a small part of his right bicep. The blast took off one of the fingers of his left hand and removed a big chunk of skin from the back of his right hand. The wooden stock of the rifle was also damaged by the blast.

Rocky pushed me away from the gap, stepped through it and handcuffed the suspect. I don't think I have ever heard anyone yell and scream as loud as this guy as Rocky cuffed him. At the time nothing was said about Rocky's actions, but I think it took a big set of balls to push me away from the gap and step directly into what was a very narrow line of fire. Rocky, of course, had no idea what I had just shot at.

The detectives conducting the investigation discovered several interesting items after the shooting. About eight shell casings were located next to a fence that bordered the alley. The casings matched the caliber of the rifle that was in the possession of the suspect who had been shot. So it appeared the radio call was accurate and someone had been firing at kids in the alley. One report indicated the "kids" were actually local gang members, but we were never able to make that connection.

The detectives questioned me extensively about what I saw as I fired at the suspect. I told them I was only focused on the end of the rifle pointed at my body and didn't see anything else. They wanted to know if I saw a muzzle flash from the rifle or heard a round being fired about the time I fired. I told them I was blinded by the muzzle flash of my shotgun and was a little deaf from the shotgun blast.

The reason they wanted to know this information was because they also discovered one shell casing on the ground next to the location of the suspect who pointed the rifle at me. The caliber of the casing also matched his rifle.

The detectives wanted to establish that the suspect knowingly fired a round at a police officer, but here's what we think happened: The suspect was holding the rifle in both hands and had it pointed in my direction. The finger on his right hand was on the trigger and grip, and his left hand was holding the wooden forestock of the rifle. When I fired the shotgun, pellets struck both hands and the wooden stock. The blast from the shotgun probably forced his trigger finger back against the trigger with enough force to fire the rifle. I don't know why I wasn't hit by the round—Guardian Angel is the only explanation I can think of—or maybe the suspect was a worse shot than I. In any event he missed and I didn't.

At court his attorney tried to argue that the rifle was never pointed directly at me. This was not the O.J. trial, so no forensics, expert opinion or extensive analysis was performed. It was just me against the defense attorney. When I testified I was very clear about the position of the rifle. I was looking right down the barrel of his .22 caliber rifle. A .22 is a fairly small bore, but I testified that the hole in the end of the rifle appeared to me—at the time—to be about the size of a small cannon. I also established that the scratches on the wooden stock were probably caused by my shotgun pellets. The defendant was convicted or "copped," I don't remember which, at the criminal trial and there was no civil trial.

Well over a year after the shooting, I was approached by one of the divisional dicks and asked if I remembered the name of the suspect involved in my shooting. I told him of course and I even remembered the name of the street he lived on. He told me that he had a warrant for his arrest, burglary I think, and asked me if I wanted to pick him up. Once again the answer was sure.

We drove to his house, knocked on the door and he answered it with a lighted joint in his badly mangled hand. We advised him to step out onto the porch and put his hands behind his back. He did so and I cuffed him. I asked him what happened to his hand and he said he was shot by the police. The entire back of his right hand was a mass of scar tissue. Clearly, no Beverly Hills plastic surgeon had touched this guy. What remained of the fingers on his left hand, however, had healed nicely and looked pretty good.

My partner drove us to the station and I rode in the back seat with the arrestee. After staring at me for a few minutes he finally said, "Hey, you're the dude who shot my ass!" I told him, "Yeah, that was me." He didn't flip-out and was not especially upset; he did say, however, "You really fucked up my hands!" I think we were both pretty lucky.

THROW HIM DOWN!

We received a radio call about burglary suspects at a local store. Four-five-nine was the Penal Code section for burglary. The location of the call was a market on Figueroa Street. My partner and I received the call but we were the second unit to arrive at the location. Two old-timers had arrived before us and advised me (I was still fairly new to the division) that in the past burglary suspects had made entry into the market from the roof. There was no sign of entry to the front or back of the store so if there was a burglary in progress, the point of entry had to be the roof.

My partner and I climbed to the roof while the old-timers stayed in the parking lot. As we approached a large vent on the roof, we were met by a young man trying to make his way out of the market by this same vent. We cuffed him and walked him over to the edge of the roof. The two old-timers were patiently waiting in the parking lot for the arrival of our suspect. It was about the easiest burglary arrest I had ever made, or so I thought. When we got him to the edge of the building, and he could be seen by the officers in the parking lot, the two old-timers began yelling, "Throw him down! Throw him down!" And they sounded serious to me. He was cuffed at the time and I was sure he'd probably break his neck if I actually threw him off the roof. We made our way to a lower level overhang, a portico, supported by several poles, and slowly lowered him to the disappointed officers waiting below. I asked them to watch my guy while we returned to the vent to see if any more suspects were inside.

We spent about ten minutes on the roof checking the point of entry and looking for burglary tools. When I finally returned to ground level I was overwhelmed by what I saw: My suspect was handcuffed with his hands behind his back to one of the poles that supported the portico. The old-timers had quickly left the scene, burning rubber as they departed. None of that was too surprising, but what really got my attention was watching the suspect trying to jump up, multiple times, while his hands were cuffed behind his back. Why was he jumping up? There was a small bonfire at the base of the pole! All I could see were knee-high flames licking at his heels as he tried to escape the fire. If there had been an Olympic event for pole jumping straight up while cuffed to a pole, this guy would have been a gold medal winner.

My first thought was how are we going to explain the burns to the suspect's feet and lower legs? It turned out not to be a problem as the fire at the base of the pole was fueled with trash found in the parking lot and it quickly burned out. Being fairly new to the division, I thought, "Holy shit, what did I get myself into?"

The two officers that cuffed my suspect to the pole had worked together on morning watch for many years and were well thought of by everyone in the division. Shortly after this incident, while off-duty, one of the officers was killed by a gunshot when he was asked to intercede in a family dispute at his apartment building.

HANDCUFFED TO A POLE

Dave Reynolds reminded me of another incident involving a suspect handcuffed to a pole. Two suspects had committed a crime, a robbery I believe, and ran from the scene of the crime as soon as the police arrived. One of the officers went in foot pursuit of the two suspects while the other officer attempted to pursue them in their black-and-white.

The officer on foot eventually caught the slower-footed suspect and, as he was by himself, quickly cuffed him to a pole and continued the chase. As the officer raced from the scene in pursuit of the second suspect, a "citizen" approached the cuffed robber, searched him and removed everything of value on his person. He took his money, his wallet, rings and an expensive watch, which was probably stolen.

This was a case of a suspect being arrested for robbery and at the same time a crime report was taken showing him as the victim of a robbery. Was this an oddity? Not really, I soon learned that nothing involving crime would surprise me when 77th Division was involved.

THE SUSPECT WAS SHOT ELEVEN TIMES

At some point, circa 1980, the department decided the .38 caliber ammunition we were required to use was not effective. The ammunition was a simple 158 grain, lead-ball bullet with a low muzzle velocity. It only took decades for the department administrators to come to this conclusion. One shooting was instrumental in making the change.

Two officers assigned to a traffic unit had stopped a suspect for a traffic violation. My guess is the driver was driving erratically or speeding, but the reason is unimportant. After the suspect stopped his vehicle, he stepped out from the driver's seat with an ax in his hands. Both officers yelled for the suspect to drop the ax. He ignored their orders and continued to close on the duo. One of the traffic officers, Dennis, was a friend of mine. He was a reserve Marine Corps officer who was not especially tall nor was he big, but he was tough as nails. He thought well under pressure and was known for making good decisions in the field. He was smart and had good judgment—a typical Marine Corps officer.

The suspect began swinging the ax at Dennis and his partner. At first they stepped back and away from the suspect to avoid any contact. I believe they found themselves at the rear of the police car as they attempted to maintain some distance between themselves and the suspect. My recollection is that Dennis and his partner attempted to keep their black-and-white between themselves and the ax-wielding suspect. That particular tactic, however, will only work for a short time. While circling their car they talked to the suspect, trying to get him to put down the ax. Clearly the ax-wielding man was not getting the message and continued to close on the officers. At some point in the incident both officers felt their lives were clearly in danger and it was time to escalate their level of force. Using physical force, a choke-out hold, for example, was simply out of the question, they could not afford to get that close to this guy. And the use of batons would still put them way too close. The department would like the use of force to escalate in stages, but at times—and this was a good example—deadly force had to be used almost immediately. We were not trained to shoot to kill; we were trained to shoot to *stop*. And there is a distinction. The targets on the firing range focused on the center mass of the suspect, not the head. Head shots were discouraged.

A shot was fired and probably hit the suspect; however, it had absolutely no affect on this guy. Deadly force was used but it did not stop him. A second shot was fired, a third shot, a fourth shot, but he continued to attempt to close on Dennis and his partner. I have no idea what was going through their minds, but this scenario was not working. You shoot a guy and he usually falls down or at the very least he stops. This didn't happen. If my memory is accurate—sometimes it is, sometimes it isn't—the suspect was fired at seventeen times with .38 caliber rounds. That tells me both officers emptied their six-shot revolvers and one officer probably emptied his five-shot back-up gun. The autopsy revealed the suspect was hit eleven times. Eleven hits out of seventeen shots in a deadly force situation is outstanding shooting. Interestingly, those scores on the firing range probably wouldn't be good enough to qualify for the month. Many of those hits would have been fatal in time, but not one of them "stopped" the suspect immediately. Who knows what would have happened if the suspect had been armed with a gun.

The chief, Ed Davis, made the decision to change the type of rounds his officers could carry, converting to a round that had more stopping power. I know very little about guns, but I've always felt the .38 caliber round was not a good choice. A .45 caliber handgun was a much better weapon. In fact, a short time after I retired, I purchased a Smith and Wesson .45 caliber semi-automatic. Retired officers could carry any type of legal weapon they desired; at the time an active officer could only carry a .38 caliber revolver.

Chief Davis had a good reason, however, for keeping the less effective .38 round: Too many officers were being shot with their own weapons. He apparently felt that fewer officers would die if we used ineffective rounds. That philosophy changed, however, when PCP hit the streets.

The suspect with the ax had been "dusted." He was under the influence of Angel Dust, correctly referred to as phencyclidine. Phencyclidine was, and may still be, a legal drug used by veterinarians as an anesthetic—in other words, it takes away pain. Trying to physically stop a bad guy who feels no pain is just about impossible. The drug is also a hallucinogenic, which simply adds to the problems facing officers.

The department now uses a 9mm semi-automatic hand gun that may hold as many as thirteen rounds, a huge increase. The joke I heard about the new gun is that when the shooting is over the officer can hide behind a mound of empty shell casings. I am clearly not an expert in guns, but a .45 caliber semi-automatic is my handgun of choice. I would avoid any caliber that starts with a three or a nine and stick with the fours. An old saw comes to mind, if you're going to be a bear, be a grizzly bear.

HE ONLY HAD ONE ARM—WHAT'S THE PROBLEM?

"See the woman, 415 man." That's a fairly typical radio call one might receive while working patrol in any division or any police department. My partner and I casually responded to the location without giving much thought to the nature of the call. Almost every call we handled involved a 415 man. When we arrived at the scene, we could not find the PR, but we noticed several articles of male clothing lying on the ground. A little farther from the house we saw several more articles of male clothing, and next door we observed a prosthetic arm lying in the grass. We followed the clothes and plastic arm to the side of the house where we observed a man who was completely naked, covered in sweat and extremely agitated. It was late afternoon but still hot and sticky in Los Angeles. It took us about two seconds to realize this guy was "dusted." He was under the influence of Angel Dust (phencyclidine), a powerful stimulant and hallucinogen. Anyone under the influence of PCP was usually transported to a local hospital, restrained and allowed to "come down" from his or her condition under the supervision of a doctor.

PCP was a drug that was becoming more and more popular in the ghetto, but at that time we didn't know a lot about it.

Our first objective was to handcuff this yahoo so we could safely transport him to the hospital. We were, however, faced with a problem that was never addressed at the academy: How do you handcuff a one-armed man? We didn't have a clue. He was beginning to make more noise and started to show off his Kung Fu moves—his one-armed Kung Fu moves. And a large, noisy crowd was growing by the minute and was enjoying all the excitement and the impending confrontation. We approached the suspect and attempted to talk him into complying with our request to settle down. That safely went under "fat chance." My partner, an officer just off probation, then grabbed the suspect's good arm and attempted to establish some control over the guy. The suspect, however, used his "flipper-arm" to attack my partner. We discovered a guy with one arm can't do a lot of damage with his stump, but can still be difficult to control, especially if he's dusted, sweaty and naked.

I joined the fight and didn't have any better luck controlling the guy than my partner. As the wrestling match continued, the suspect was covered in sweat and was as slippery as a greased pig. And did I mention that he was naked? We now had a sweaty, pissed-off, naked guy who was fully dusted and had only one arm. I have never wrestled a greased pig, but trying to control this guy was probably very similar. Two good-sized policemen were unable to physically control our own one-armed man. It was time for the baton. I hit him as hard as I could on his good arm, but the blow had absolutely no effect. I tried again and had the same result. I was certain I had used enough force to break a bone, but it didn't stop this guy. I gave up on the baton, called for a backup unit and tried to use my body weight to slow this guy down. This type of wrestling around with a suspect is actually very dangerous. It is not difficult at all for an out-of-control suspect to gain control of an officer's hand gun.

The crowd had now increased to about fifty people. They weren't a problem for us, but they were of no help either. They were having a good time watching all the activity. We weren't actually engaged in a fight with this guy. He did not throw any punches at us or try to kick us, we just couldn't control him and couldn't choke him out. He used his good arm very effectively to prevent us from using a bar-arm control hold.

Here are the problems an officer must deal with when fighting or trying to control a suspect who is dusted: The subject is extraordinarily strong; the drug is actually a stimulant and it seems to increase one's physical strength (the flexed muscles in his bicep may have prevented me from breaking the bone in his upper arm). PCP is also a pain killer, so regardless of how many times you whack the guy with your stick, kick him, or try to choke him out, he simply doesn't feel it. And because the drug is a stimulant, the suspect doesn't get fatigued. So, if you are fighting a guy who is super strong, doesn't feel pain and doesn't get tired—a perfect storm—you are in for a very long afternoon (expect to repair or replace one perfectly serviceable uniform).

I was getting tired of this nonsense. I finally went into the crowd, told a spectator to remove his belt and then returned to the match. I put the belt around our guy's waist and was eventually able to cuff his good arm to the belt. It wasn't very effective, but it worked until additional troops arrived. With a few more bodies present, he settled down a bit and we were able to gather his clothes and prosthetic arm and transport him to a local hospital. We stayed with him for several hours until he was fairly normal. He was actually uninjured, but was now extremely fatigued, and he couldn't understand why his arm was so sore. I explained to him that I attempted to break his good arm with my baton, but was unsuccessful. He apparently had no recollection of using PCP or being in an altercation with the police. He actually thanked me for not breaking his one remaining arm. He turned out to be a Vietnam veteran and I felt bad about booking him, but we really didn't have a choice.

WHAT WE HAVE HERE IS YOUR BASIC NARCOTICS MALT

We were on the seventh floor of a flop house that catered to low income people in Central Division, which, of course, included drug users and sellers—the entire building smelled of mold, urine and filth. We received information that one of the occupants had details about the location of a major drug dealer living in 77th.

Our current suspect lived on the top floor of a hotel that would never receive a five-star rating. We knocked on the door and our dealer reluctantly let us in. We advised him that we were there to get information about a dealer he knew and from whom he had purchased drugs. Our suspect denied ever having known this dealer and denied using drugs—quite a surprise.

My partner that night, Tank, started to search the hotel room—yes, it was an illegal search—and almost immediately came up with a large quantity of drugs, most in pill form; however, he also discovered a few grams of a substance that was probably heroin. After we collected a real cornucopia of drugs, I watched Tank open up the refrigerator and remove a carton of sour milk. He poured the milk into a large glass until it was about half full. Tank poured nearly all the pills we had discovered and the heroin into the milk. I wasn't quite sure what he was up to, so I watched—fascinated—as he placed a long-handled wooden spoon into the glass and started to stir the concoction. He did all this in the presence of our confused suspect. He had no idea what Tank was up to, and for that matter, neither did I.

Tank said, "What we have here is your basic narcotics malt." I had never heard of a narcotics malt and I was still confused about Tank's intentions. After this witch's brew of pills and powder was dissolved, Tank grabbed our suspect by the neck and dragged him over to an open window. The suspect was now staring, with eyes the size of saucers, at Tank's narcotics malt. Tank told the suspect he had three options: He could tell us where the dealer was located, he could drink the "malt" or he could jump out of the seventh floor window (with a little bit of help). Tank must have been convincing, as our suspect quickly rolled over on the dealer. I don't think Tank would have thrown the guy out of the window, but I'm glad I didn't have to find out.

HYPES

As you can see illicit drug usage in South-Central Los Angeles was a serious problem. And heroin was at the top of the list in terms of loss of life as a result of an overdose and crimes against property in the form of burglaries and theft. Hypes—people who injected heroin—caused huge problems, either directly or indirectly, for nearly every citizen in Los Angeles.

When a hype was arrested for being under the influence of an opiate, that arrest frequently led to the arrest of drug dealers, burglars, robbery suspects, pimps and almost anyone involved in the theft of property. Putting a hype in jail almost always guaranteed a reduction in some other crime. A hype arrest was a good arrest.

The problem officers had with arresting hypes for being under the influence of an opiate concerns their expertise in drug usage. A hype who is arrested for being "down" (under the influence) usually does not have any heroin in his possession. The heroin is inside their body. How does an officer know the arrestee has used an opiate within the last several hours? Actually, it's not that difficult. The difficulty is convincing a judge that the officer is truly an expert in the use of the drug. This, of course, is not an easy task.

Experts like pathologists, scientists and psychiatrists have *practiced* in their field of expertise. A heroin-using cop, of course, would be—or should be—out of a job. Coppers had to find other ways to gain their expertise. A lesser experienced cop working with a drug expert was the best way to learn and eventually become a court-qualified expert in the use, sales and packaging of drugs.

There were several court-qualified experts working patrol in 77th. And I wanted to be one of them. There was no formal training in how to become a court-qualified expert. If that was your objective, you had to focus on arresting hypes. A hype arrest meant you carefully observed the demeanor of your arrestee: was their speech low, slow and deliberate, or did they slur their words or speak unusually fast? Were body movements flaccid and loose or quick and jerky? Did they frequently scratch a facial itch? Did they nod-off, appearing to be asleep, but still able to respond to a question? Were their pupils dilated or constricted to less than three millimeters? Did their eyes quickly bounce from left to right when following an object held in front of their eyes (nystagmus)?

If puncture wounds were found directly over a vein, were they recent, less than four hours old, or were they older than twenty-four hours? Most of these objective symptoms were fairly easy to identify. The most difficult one to determine was the age of a puncture wound. An officer would have to examine well over a hundred hypes to be able to associate their physical condition with the age of the injection site. Not an impossible task, but one that took a great deal of time. It might take a busy patrol officer several years to become an expert in the age of puncture wounds. I thought there might be an easier, quicker way to make that determination.

When a hype was arrested and a puncture wound—located directly over a vein—was found, the injection site was photographed with a very long, specialized Polaroid camera; one that took extreme close-ups. By the way, locating a puncture wound on a hype could be difficult. Hypes typically injected into the veins located on the inside of their arms, but it wasn't unheard of to find an injection site under the tongue, between the toes (a hype might go weeks without taking a bath, or changing socks) or even in the scrotum. I've checked under tongues and between toes, but I wasn't about to make a hype "drop trou." If he injected in his balls, he was free to go.

I needed access to the Polaroid camera, a syringe needle and about eight hours of free time. The camera was not a problem and I was able to obtain a needle from a friend of mine who worked at one of the local ERs. While assigned to morning watch, I volunteered to work the front desk. I was set.

I placed a rubber tourniquet around my bicep, pumped my fist until the veins inside my arm expanded and carefully stuck the hollow needle into my vein. Bingo, blood emerged from the open end of the needle. I had punctured the vein. I dried the puncture, immediately photographed the wound and noted the date and time of the incident. I photographed the wound every thirty minutes for the next eight hours. When the photos were laid out sequentially, it was easy to determine the relative age of the puncture. The easy part of this learning process was over. Now it was time to test my theory in court.

I arrested as many hypes as I could locate and rather impatiently waited for a subpoena to arrive calling me to testify in court. The big day finally arrived. This was the first time I had testified in court as an expert in the use of heroin. The first time you qualified was the most difficult. The defense attorney goes through a process called voir dire. It's a French term meaning to tell the truth. In practice, the defense was challenging the experience of the witness. It was done to determine if the witness was in fact an expert. It was a difficult process for the officer, especially when he was called upon to determine the age of a fresh puncture wound.

While on the stand, the defense attorney asked me how I knew his client was under the influence of an opiate. I went through the usual symptoms: constricted pupils; low, slow and deliberate speech; on the nod; flaccid demeanor and the big one, a *fresh* puncture wound over a vein. His next question was easy to anticipate, "Officer, how old was the puncture wound on my client's arm?" I testified, with a great deal of certainty, that it was less than an hour old. The attorney asked me a question to which he did not know the answer—he thought he did, but he was wrong. He asked me how I could possibly know that a small, puncture wound was less than an hour old.

At this point in the testimony, the officer usually explains that over the last few years he has arrested, examined and interviewed scores of hypes under the influence of an injected opiate. All the issues of being under the influence were easily challenged, but the age of the wound was the most difficult for the officer to establish. It wasn't unusual for the officer to spend several hours on the stand explaining why he was an expert. And sometimes he failed.

After the question about the age of the wound was asked, I explained how I punctured my own vein with a needle—perfectly legal—and photographed the wound every half hour for eight hours. I placed the photos in an album and studied the difference between a puncture that was an hour old and one that was over four hours old. It was a jaw-dropping moment for the attorney. It took a few seconds for my testimony to sink in, but when it did, the attorney said "No more questions." I had spent less than twenty minutes on the stand and was almost immediately accepted as an expert. The defense must have thought I was absolutely nuts, and he had no intentions of asking me any more questions.

I loved testifying on the stand and always silently gloated when I got the better of a sleazy, criminal defense attorney (Sleazy, criminal defense attorney is, of course, redundant).

"HOW ABOUT A HAIRCUT?"

Tank arrested a suspect for burglary and as a part of the investigation he accompanied the suspect to his place of business, which happened to be a barber shop, to recover some of the stolen property. While there Tank asked the suspect if he was really a barber. The guy said, "Yes, I even went to barber school." Tank said, "We're having an inspection tomorrow, would you mind giving me a haircut?" The suspect said, "Sure, I'll cut it." In the middle of the night Tank sat down in the barber's chair and got his haircut by a guy he was arresting for burglary. Only Tank could pull that off.

A WARRANT

Tank arrested a man for robbery, a serious felony. Tank, as usual, wanted to get information from the suspect about his accomplice and the suspect was not cooperating. Tank was inside the station so his options were somewhat limited: No narcotics malt, and no seventh floor window. The suspect did not appear to be very bright and Tank thought he would take advantage of this fact. He quickly typed up a document that, on its face, appeared to be official and genuine. The document was labeled, "Torture Warrant." Tank told the suspect that if he didn't come forward with the desired information, he would have the warrant signed by a judge and then he would execute the document. It would be very painful.

Tank, as usual, got the information he wanted.

EVERY BLACK-AND-WHITE HAD A BUILT-IN POLYGRAPH

It was a little known "fact" that every black-and-white had a built-in lie detector. Here's how it worked, a potential, dull-witted suspect was handcuffed in the back seat of the car. I used the word "potential" because this was generally used if we weren't convinced of the suspect's innocence. The suspect was advised to watch the red light located on the face of the radio.

The police radio was equipped with a small red light that burns brightly if the mike is keyed. This occurs whenever an officer is broadcasting on the radio. To turn the radio into a polygraph, the radio was switched to Tactical Frequency Two (Tac-2). This is the channel that is normally used to communicate between two police cars and was not typically monitored by Communications.

Just like a legitimate polygraph, the officer would begin by asking questions that didn't relate to the crime and to which the officer knew the answer; for example, what's your name, what's your address, how old are you? The officer would *not* key the mike after each truthful response. The officer would then ask the suspect to tell a lie, any lie would work. As soon as the suspect told the known lie, the officer would key the mike and the red light shone brightly. The mike was held down next to the officer's leg so it couldn't be seen by the suspect in the back seat. The suspect was usually convinced that there was an accurate polygraph in the cruiser. When the suspect was asked if he committed the crime and a negative answer followed, the officer would key the mike and a bright red light would shout, liar,

liar—the suspect could see for himself that he had told a lie.

I suspect any information obtained by this handy, portable polygraph was not admissible, but it did provide us with valuable information.

TAC-2

Tac-2 had another useful function. If arresting officers wanted to obtain information from two suspects, they placed them in the back seat of the black-and-white, handcuffed, and told them they couldn't talk to each other. We'd make a big deal out of this admonition. No talking, don't say anything, keep quiet. This, of course, would usually stimulate all kinds of conversation between the two men. The suspects were alone in the car but were being closely watched, from a distance, by the officers.

Two radio cars were required for this to work properly. The radios in each car would be switched to Tac-2, and a rubber band would be placed around the mike—depressing the key—in the car that held the two suspects. The open mike would then broadcast everything that was said by the suspects to the other black-and-white where the officers were watching and listening. Confessions, names of other suspects, location of stolen property, and all kinds of useful information could be obtained from chatty, nervous suspects who were about to go to jail.

"YOU ARE NOW DIVORCED"

I have never done this myself, but I've heard that it was a common practice among a few old-timers. Common-law marriages were not recognized in the State of California, but many of the folks who lived in the division still thought they were officially married. I believe this was because so many people immigrated to California from states that *did* recognize a common-law marriage, and they simply didn't know the law was different in California.

It was common to return to the same address two or even three times during one shift because of a family dispute. Clearly, husband and wife were not getting along. If it was determined that their relationship was not legal, but they believed they were married, we'd ask them if they wanted a divorce. If both parties agreed, we'd tell each one of them to place their right hand on one of our badges and recite the following phrase: I divorce you, I divorce you, I divorce you. It was only official after the third, I divorce you. Our quickie divorce rarely solved any long-lasting problems, but we generally solved the issue for the day and were not called back.

The most common radio call in Los Angeles was probably "see the woman, 415 family dispute." These calls were especially frequent on the days that welfare checks were dispersed or on paydays if the husband was employed. And they typically involved alcohol. Some of these disputes had been in progress for decades and many of them turned to violence. And the woman was generally the victim. I have, however, seen many cases of a sleeping husband being attacked with a sock full of coins, or a pot of boiling honey—not a pleasant sight. We generally did not make too many arrests for physical fighting between man and wife. A smack or two by either side was normally allowed, but serious injuries generally involved an arrest. Sometimes the best solution to the problem was separating the two combatants. The man of the house was advised to leave and not to come back until the next day. They usually did as we requested, but occasionally someone would balk at our request and refuse to leave. This happened to me several times when the husband asked what gave me the authority to make him leave. A good question, actually, as we clearly did not have that power. My standing answer was: "Because I'm bigger than you," and it worked most of the time.

I can still recall an incident involving a man who refused to leave. I remember grabbing him by the arm and attempting to escort him out the front door. He pulled away from my grasp and after a brief struggle, I placed him in a bar-arm control hold and choked him out.

While he was unconscious, I dragged him out the front door onto his front lawn where he regained consciousness. He looked up at me and said, "Well, I guess you were serious" and he quietly walked away. This was clearly not the best solution, but it worked.

Family disputes were nearly always unpleasant. Officers have been shot, killed, stabbed, battered, cussed out, and generally abused while handling family disputes. And they were a big part of the job in 77th.

THE CENTRAL AFRICAN REPUBLIC

Jean-Bedel Bokassa was the president of The Central African Republic. He was fond of Napoleon and the Los Angeles Police Department. He was so fond of Napoleon that in 1977, he decided to declare himself *Emperor For Life* and change the name of the country to the Central African Empire. He spent 20 million dollars for the coronation and nearly bankrupted the country.

His fondness for the LAPD stemmed from a television series about LA coppers. Apparently there was only one television program, other than news, that played in the entire country: *Adam 12*. For some crazy reason Bokassa absolutely loved LA coppers. He wanted LAPD officers to function as his security team when he transitioned from president to emperor.

I assume that someone from his administration contacted the US State Department to arrange for LA's finest to handle security. If that happened, I'm sure the state department advised him that it would be impossible for LAPD to handle security for the transition and his coronation. Unwilling to accept "no" for an answer, Bokassa's people contacted an unknown individual that knew—or knew of—Lieutenant Danny Bowser, the head of the Special Investigative Section (SIS). SIS was under Detective Support Division (DSD), Captain Tom Ferry was the commanding officer.

We knew very little about Bokassa's liaison man, but it was rumored he was a mercenary who had worked extensively in Africa. The liaison contact asked Danny if he could put together a detail of LA coppers to handle security at the coronation. Danny, who was always ready for an adventure, agreed to head the security detail.

The newly formed Underwater Dive Unit was also under the command of Tom Ferry. A little less than half of the members of the UDU, including Danny Bowser, were assigned to Detective Support Division. The balance of the team was recruited from Patrol. I got to know and admire Captain Ferry and Lieutenant Bowser because I was a member of the Underwater Dive Unit.

Captain Ferry and Lieutenant Bowser, both legendary officers, asked me, and another dive-team officer, Bill Anderson, if we wanted to join their unofficial security detail. Bill was a Vietnam veteran and a Marine Corp fighter pilot whose F-4 was shot down during the Vietnam War. If I had to go to war, I would want Bill, and a few other select partners, to be in my foxhole. Bill was ethical, smart, aggressive, and hardworking, and he had exceptionally good judgment. He was not fond of incompetent supervisors or lazy cops. I admired him a great deal and still do.

We were going to be paid $3,000 each for about three weeks of work. One week in Paris, ostensibly to "prepare and train," and two weeks in Bangus, Africa, the capital of the Central African Republic, performing security duties. We would be staying at a location that was fairly close to a tribe of pygmies—yes, we heard a lot of pygmy jokes. Lieutenant Bowser advised us that our security duties would put us in close contact with Muammar Gaddafi, Idi Amin, and a few other infamous characters. We had to familiarize ourselves with the fully automatic M-16, as they would be provided to us once we were inside the country. How could any young, red-blooded American turn down such an offer? Sign us up!

The team was composed of eight or ten officers and one medical doctor. Almost everyone had a specialty: Bill was a pilot, one or two of the guys were bomb experts—one was later killed when a bomb detonated while he was attempting to disarm it—several of the men were experts in weapons, and all of these guys were seasoned officers or leaders; I was the only exception. I'm still not sure why I was asked to join. I was a competent dive instructor who was comfortable in the water except around sharks, hippos and crocks. I was a good patrol officer but certainly not an old-timer, and my military experience was limited to packing parachutes one weekend a month as an air force reservist. Compared to the rest of the team, I was not a warrior. My heart was there but I didn't have the experience. It didn't matter, if they wanted me, I was going.

We attended one meeting at the Downtown Athletic Club where we met "a guy" who had some contact with the Bokassa administration. I don't think he was introduced by name, but he seemed to have lots of knowledge about the country and the requirements of the detail. He also paid each of us $1,000 cash, up-front. This guy was for real. We made arrangements for time off and started to plan for the big event. As the departure date neared, we got together a second time at the lieutenant's house in Burbank to hash out details, collect airline tickets and review our itinerary. The tickets didn't arrive, but we thought that was a just a hiccup, after all we had already been paid $1,000.

The next day all of our names were on the front page of the LA Times with a story about our proposed security detail. That, of course, killed the trip. There was no way LAPD would allow us to provide security for some third-world emperor. We're still not sure how the Times found out about our trip, but we think the State Department got word of it—didn't want us to go—and dropped a dime to the paper. None of us were ever disciplined. I got a good ass-chewing from my sergeant and was advised that it was illegal for a U.S. citizen to bear arms for a foreign country—I don't recall hearing that at the academy and I'm not sure it is true. None of us, however, was officially reprimanded, and I don't know why. The department was usually quick to discipline low ranking officers; however, the captain and lieutenant were respected by the chief and that's probably why it didn't go any further.

BILL'S TRAFFIC ACCIDENT

As I mentioned before, Bill Anderson was a Marine Corps fighter pilot who flew combat missions over Vietnam from aircraft carriers. I cannot express how impressed I am with Bill and men like him. I think a typical day at work went something like this: you are strapped into an F-4 fighter-bomber that is capable of traveling faster than the speed of sound; you are catapulted off the deck of a pitching, rolling aircraft carrier, traveling at least twenty-five knots and your catapult speed is close to one-hundred and sixty-five knots. I've been told that it was not unusual to experience fifteen-foot seas or greater during flight operations, day or night.

If you think the guys working crab boats on *The Deadliest Catch* is dangerous, try life as a naval aviator. I am *not* speaking from experience, but I suspect taking off from the ship was probably the easy part of your day. Once airborne you head for land where every swinging-dick in the country wants to kill you. The bad guys shoot at you with anything that will hold a bullet; fire deadly, rocket-powered surface-to-air missiles at you and they all hate your guts.

Assuming that you were not shot down while dropping bombs, and did not experience any mechanical difficulties, it was time to return to the ship. The *landing on a postage stamp* analogy is, I think, a poor one. Postage stamps don't travel at thirty knots, they don't roll from port to starboard in a thirty degree arc and their bow doesn't pitch up and down twenty feet or more. The runway at Long Beach Airport is over ten thousand feet in length, and it doesn't move; the runway on a carrier is probably less than five hundred feet, moves a great deal and is full of steel cables designed to catch jet aircraft that are landing at over one hundred knots. I forgot to mention the weather. These guys fly in all kinds of ugly conditions: low visibility, no visibility until the last few miles, high seas, confused seas (probably worse than high seas), rain, low clouds, and at night.

It takes a big set of balls to do what these guys do day-in and day-out, and I suspect it takes the hand-eye coordination of a brain surgeon and the courage of a blind bull fighter to land a jet on a ship.

One night, while working Southwest patrol, Bill found himself in pursuit of a stolen car. He was very good at identifying stolen vehicles, even recently-stolen vehicles that had not been reported by the owner as stolen. The pursuit was official: red lights, siren and a radio broadcast giving his speed, location and a description of the suspect vehicle, all according to department policy.

The pursuit took him down a narrow alley where he collided with a buried hot-water heater and put a small dent in the car's fender. I don't know exactly why the citizens of South-Central LA buried hot water heaters in the alleys but they did. Bill was doing his job at the time of the incident. He wasn't reckless, he didn't run a stop sign or red light. He was doing what we got paid to do: he was trying to catch a car thief.

The department looked at traffic accidents a little differently. Was it preventable or was it non-preventable? If it was preventable—and the department felt that almost all T/As were—the officer had to relinquish days off.

I believe the going rate for most T/As was four days; so, if the officer was scheduled to have ten days off during a thirty day deployment, he had to give up (relinquish) four of those days, which meant he only had six days off during that deployment. The department got four days of the officer's time off without paying for it.

Several weeks after the incident Bill was called into the Captain's office to be punished for denting a police car while in a pursuit. The captain advised Bill he would, in fact, be given four days off for such an egregious act.

The captain asked Bill if he had anything to say about his punishment. Bill said, "Captain, I have personally destroyed two Marine Corp F-4s trying to do my job. The two planes were probably valued at more than ten million dollars, and the Marines did not have one negative thing to say about the incidents. I put a dent in your precious black-and-white and you want to give me four days off. Do you understand why I'm a little pissed-off about the incident?" I don't know how the captain responded, but I'm sure he had some lame excuse about driving safely on city streets.

A CIGAR—BILL CLINTON WOULD BE ENVIOUS

No, this is not about sex. About once a month a group of local cretins would gather in a large parking lot next to an old, abandoned grocery store. Loud music, dope smoking, drinking and gang rapes were fairly common at these events. In time, if these gatherings continued, I'm certain a homicide would have resulted. It was common for us to receive multiple complaints whenever this group decided to meet. Traffic on the bordering streets was interrupted as drivers were stopped and pulled from the cars, beaten and occasionally robbed.

Whenever we gathered at the location to disperse this mob, we were showered with rocks and bottles. Our gathering of officers usually involved one unit at a time over a period of ten to twenty minutes. The early arriving units took the most heat as they were overwhelmingly outnumbered by an expanding mob.

We finally decided to gather our troops several blocks from the location until we had enough guys to mount a serious presence. Once we had sufficient officers, we'd swoop in at one end of the parking lot and disperse as many people as we could. Most of them would drive away, but a few would run from the lot, on foot, and leave their cars behind. After the dispersal, we'd almost always walk through the lot and check out each abandoned vehicle. It was not uncommon to find weapons, alcohol and drugs.

This went on for several months until it got way out of hand. The group had one thing in common: everyone drove a nice car. They weren't new or expensive, but they were well taken care of. New paint, highly waxed, no dings or dents. It didn't take us too long to figure out how to keep these yahoos out of the parking lot. Somehow a few of these cars got scratched and dented as we walked through the lot, and a few of them picked up nails in their tires.

A divisional copper decided to take up cigar smoking at one of these events; however, it's an ugly habit that he quickly dropped after smoking less than half of the stogie—those nasty things really do smell. Somehow the burning cigar found its way into the back seat of one of the cars. I didn't realize that it took so long for a smoldering cigar to fully engulf a car into flames— I'd say about twenty minutes or longer. As we drove from the location, we were met by several fire trucks, red lights and sirens blaring, that were in far too big a hurry to put out the flames.

Within a short period of time the problem was solved, no more gatherings. I don't think you'll ever see this particular solution on *Adam 12,* but it worked. Having never smoked, I was surprised how bad cigars tasted.

"I SWEAR TO TELL THE TRUTH, THE WHOLE TRUTH AND NOTHING BUT THE TRUTH"

Those are the words you utter each time you testify in court. And most coppers try hard to comply with them; however, sometimes it doesn't work out that way. There was a legendary copper who worked 77th who had a very common first and last name, Don Brown.

Don made an arrest and eventually received a subpoena to testify in court. Seventy-seventh coppers make so many arrests that it's difficult to remember all the details of the arrest based on the name of the defendant on the subpoena. Whenever an officer is subpoenaed, it's his responsibility to pull the arrest report before the appearance date and review it for familiarization; however, officers rarely looked up the report at the station. They usually waited until they appeared in court and then asked the DA for a copy to review.

Don appeared in court at the preliminary hearing on the assigned day. He read and then reread the report but had a difficult time remembering the event. He was sworn in and testified to the facts contained in the arrest report, the actual arrest and the booked evidence. He went through cross examination by the defendant's counsel and was on the stand for over an hour. At the end of the hearing the judge must form an opinion about the strength of the case. Has a crime occurred and does the evidence indicate the defendant was involved. I'm sure the entire process is far more complicated but you get the idea. It's not a rubber stamp hearing but judges usually do a good job of reviewing the case, throwing out the really bad ones and allowing the rest to go forward within the system.

At the end of the prelim, if it's a good case, the judge announces to the court that the defendant is "held to answer" and the case goes forward. Those were the words the judge uttered when Don finished testifying.

He apparently did a good job of explaining the arrest and presenting the evidence. The judge excused Don from court and went on to the next case. Don was subpoenaed, he was sworn in, he testified to the facts and the defendant was held to answer. Good work, but nothing unusual.

When Don returned to the station he still didn't have any independent memories of the arrest. Don usually wasn't bothered too much about details, but this particular case was puzzling. He checked with divisional records and pulled the original arrest report and all the supporting documents. None of those helped, he still had no recollection of the case.

Here's what actually happened: Don received a subpoena to testify and assumed he had made the arrest or was involved in the case. However, unknown to Don, there was another officer with the same first and last name as his working in 77th. The other Don was new to the station and worked a different shift; same name, same division, but different serial numbers. Don was called as a witness, made the brisk walk to the witness stand, was *sworn* in, *testified* to the facts, introduced evidence, and was subject to cross examination by the defense council. After Don's time on the stand, the defendant was held to answer by the court. And Don had absolutely nothing to do with the case!

I heard that the case never went to trial as the defendant copped a guilty plea. I would love to have heard the conversation between the defendant's attorney, a public defender, and the defendant. It probably went something like this: The defendant, *"But it's the wrong cop!"* The public defender, *"I've never heard that excuse before but it doesn't matter and doesn't change the* *facts—*cop *a plea!"* He did; justice in America still exists.

Don was also involved in a famous shooting that took place in 77th Division.

THE SHOOTING

Two suspects wanted to kill an LA copper and attempted to ambush Don Brown and his partner, Mel Bolton, during a traffic stop. They happened to pick the wrong officers. Both men did everything right. The details of the shooting were presented to academy classes as a lesson in tactics and personal safety. Don and Mel were heroes to me, and I rarely use the word hero—it's a word that is clearly overused to describe actions that are *not* at all heroic. Officers like Don and Mel—and so many more—have, in my view, a huge set of "cashews" and all of my respect. As a young policeman, I was nearly speechless the first time I met Don and Mel; I couldn't believe I was actually being introduced to them.

I asked a friend and classmate of mine, Jerry Glade, to fill me in on what actually happened at the intersection of Manchester and Kansas. Jerry worked with Don and knew him much better than I did. What follows is Jerry's recollection of the shooting told to him by Don.

Before I go into details, however, a little background on the suspects might be in order: The two men involved in the shooting were real bad guys. They had killed a New Jersey State Trooper and a New York cop while on the East Coast. Both suspects wore two shoulder holsters. Suspect one carried a .357 revolver and a .45 caliber semi-automatic pistol. Suspect two was armed with another .45 caliber semi and a 9mm handgun. The gunmen used the same or very similar tactics in separate incidents to kill the two officers: In both shootings, the suspects were involved in a traffic stop by patrol officers. After the red lights were activated, the suspects would execute a U-turn—they were now facing the officers—and switch on their high beams blinding the men. Both traffic stops took place at night. As the patrol coppers walked up to the suspects' vehicle, the suspects would open fire on the officers with no warning or reason other than to kill a cop.

After the shootings the suspects drove across the country, committing armed robberies on the way, and continued their crime spree.

I don't have the date of the shooting, but it occurred in the late sixties or early seventies. The incident took place around five in the morning. Don and Mel had been working a "Z-Car", an unmarked vehicle usually driven by detectives and equipped with a red light and siren, both officers, however, were in uniform. My guess is that Don and Mel were working a specialized, crime suppression detail.

Jerry Glade picks up the story from here: Boulton and Brown were traveling eastbound on Manchester Avenue approaching Figueroa Street. They observed a vehicle in the left lane occupied by two male blacks and stopped at a red light. The officers stopped directly behind the suspects' vehicle, and one of the suspects turned around and "made" the unmarked car as a police vehicle. Once the officers were "made", the suspects executed a U-turn at the light and began traveling westbound on Manchester; they turned southbound on Kansas into a parking lot on the southwest corner of Manchester and Kansas. There was a four-foot high block wall surrounding the parking lot. The wall had openings for entrances on both streets. The suspects entered the lot through the Kansas entrance, stopped, and reversed out of the lot and were now facing northbound on Kansas Street. It was clear the suspects were trying to lure the officers into a head-on confrontation, as they had done in the past with the two deceased East Coast officers. Don and Mel, of course, had no idea they were about to stop two suspects who had already killed two officers and who were dead-set on killing two more LA coppers.

During the maneuvering of the suspects' vehicle, Don and Mel had observed the white backup lights illuminate as the car's gear was placed in reverse, and must have suspected something was drastically wrong with this traffic stop. It is unclear if the officers had activated their red lights. Don, who was driving, decided to turn into the parking lot at the Manchester entrance and point the front of his car into the driver's side of the suspects' vehicle, illuminating the left side of the car with his high beams and avoiding the bright headlights of the suspects' vehicle. Don's vehicle was now in the parking lot facing southeast and the suspects' vehicle was stopped on Kansas facing north.

After both cars came to a stop, Don exited his black-and-white and stood behind the open driver's door; Mel left the protection of the passenger's door and took a much safer position behind the block wall fronting Kansas Street. The driver of the suspects' vehicle got out of the car and approached Don. Don ordered him to stop and lie down on the ground. The suspect ignored Don's order and continued to walk toward the police car asking, "What's the problem?" As the suspect neared Don's location, he removed one of his handguns and began firing at Don. Don returned fire and emptied his six-shot revolver into the suspect, killing him in the street.

As Don was firing at the driver, he heard the other suspect firing at Mel and assumed that Mel had been shot or killed. Don's revolver was empty and he had to reload it as quickly as possible. The ammo pouch that is located on an officer's Sam Browne usually holds six rounds; however, by staggering the individual bullets, nine rounds can be crammed into the pouch. Don discovered that staggered rounds are more difficult to reload—especially under fire—than rounds neatly stacked one on top of the other facing the same direction. Don also reported to Jerry that his hands were shaking so badly he dropped three rounds onto the ground during the reloading process.

I suspect that after the shooting, many officers on the department switched to "Speedy Loaders" a magazine-like device that allows the officer to reload a revolver much faster, but takes up a little more space in the ammo pouch. Years later the department transitioned from revolvers to semi-automatics which were much quicker to reload and held far more rounds then the old six-shooters.

After reloading, Don broadcast an *"Officer needs help, shots fired"* radio call and gave the location of the shooting.

Jerry didn't mention this in his recap of the shooting, but I recall that in the middle of the shooting, Don verbally advised Mel that he was out of ammo and was in the process of reloading. I don't believe this was ever taught at the academy, but it showed that Don was thinking clearly while under a great deal of stress.

After Don had reloaded and put out the help call, he crawled around the back of the police car to get a better view of the second suspect. Don reported to Jerry that at this point in the shoot-out he believed Mel had been shot and possibly killed. Mel, believing that Don had been shot and killed, began crawling back to the black-and-white to check on Don. Both men met on the ground crawling toward each other. It's important to know that Don and Mel were veteran, grizzled LA cops. It's a safe bet that neither officer was ever in touch with his "feminine side." These were hard-charging, tough street cops—real men. When they met on the ground, thinking that the other man had been shot and killed, they hugged each other. During this era, LA cops didn't hug one another, especially in uniform, it just didn't happen.

After the reunion, Don and Mel crawled back to the block wall for added protection and to get a better shot at the second suspect. Both officers watched the second suspect walk from his vehicle back toward the black-and-white. It was correctly assumed the second suspect was attempting to "finish off" Don. When the second shooter was between the cars and out in the open, Don and Mel emptied their guns into this asshole. A medical examination revealed the suspect was hit nine times. I don't know how many shots were fired, but it's a safe assumption that a maximum of twelve rounds were discharged at the suspect, possibly less. Nine out of twelve is pretty good shooting, especially under stress.

Both Don and Mel assumed the second suspect was dead. However, after the RA unit arrived, everyone heard the second suspect moaning. The second shooter was transported to California Hospital where he miraculously survived.

LAPD'S AMMUNITION

It was no secret that LAPD used rounds that had very little stopping power. Like a lot of policemen, I know shamefully too little about weapons and bullets, so it's difficult for me to go into detail about the weight, configuration and the load of ammo. But it was no secret that our ammo was not effective. As previously mentioned, the reason we used these subpar bullets was because too many coppers were shot with their own guns, a sad but true fact.

I don't know if it's true, but I've been told that both Don and Mel were using *hot rounds* that had been modified by another officer, a guy who had some expertise in reloading and ballistics. Outwardly the rounds looked like department approved bullets and could easily pass a visual inspection; however, they had been modified to increase their stopping power. The first suspect was killed and the second suspect was clearly stopped. These modified rounds apparently worked, but it would still take several more years before the department changed to a better round. Why the department moved at glacial speeds on so many issues is a mystery to me.

In October of 2013, I observed video footage taken from an Oregon police unit that shows a suspect shooting at an officer making a traffic stop. The officer was hit in the side, but he returned fire and hit the suspect in the chest. After being shot, the suspect ran to his vehicle, jumped in and drove away. He was found thirty minutes later inside his car—dead at the wheel. The officer survived. It seems that Oregon, a liberal state, has not learned the dangers of using ineffective bullets that have little or no stopping power.

THE AFTEREFFECTS

As you might expect, Don, I'm really not sure about Mel, suffered some aftereffects from the shooting. Don told a few of his close friends that shortly after the shooting—whenever he made a traffic stop—he would sweat heavily and shake uncontrollably. Today we refer to it as PTSD, Post Traumatic Stress Disorder, a real medical condition that has destroyed or drastically altered the lives of so many of our military veterans. The psychological damage to these returning men and women has got to be enormous, many of them turned to alcohol or drugs for help, and Don was no different. The shooting had a lasting affect on him and probably destroyed his life.

Several years after the shooting, Don was on medical leave from the department and was not working. During this time I was still working patrol in 77th, and the following broadcast, or one very similar to it, was made over the police radio: *All units, be advised, a retired LAPD officer has indicated that he wants to be shot by an LAPD officer as a way of committing suicide. He has stated that he will be armed and will confront officers in the area of Nickerson Gardens and will not be taken alive.* What a bone-chilling broadcast that was. Obviously, no one wanted to shoot Don. Everyone who knew him loved him and had an enormous amount of respect for him. There was no organized effort to avoid calls in the Nickerson Gardens Housing Project that night, but I suspect very few radio calls to that area were answered. I know my partner and I went directly to the station and started catching up on paperwork. It took us several hours to finish reports that normally only took a few minutes.

Don died several years ago and I'm not certain of the circumstances, but the enormous amount of stress generated by this shooting had to contribute to his death.

THE OPERATION

I had three great kids, but that was enough. It was time to get clipped; yep, I'd be shootin' blanks—a vasectomy. The day of the procedure went well. The doc did his thing and told me to take a few days off or, at the least, go on light duty for a day or two. I foolishly chose light duty. I was still walking on egg shells with a lot of discomfort in my groin, so the idea of working the front desk actually appealed to me.

One could enter the locker room of 77th by walking up a flight of stairs at the back of the station. The upper back door led to a long hallway with offices for Divisional Vice, Narcotics and Community Relations on either side. I carefully and slowly walked up the stairs (I can be a real pussy at times), unlocked the back door and instantly stepped into the scene of a whacked-out, un-handcuffed, combative PCP suspect. His back was to me as he slowly walked backwards down the hallway. A group of about four or five officers was jammed, shoulder to shoulder, into the narrow hallway. They were slowly following him as he walked toward me. The "dusted" suspect, of course, had no idea I was behind him. This guy was clearly out of control and had probably been fighting with the dope cops. But none of them was in a position to stop him. The noise was surprisingly loud. I heard the guys yelling: "Choke him out, cuff him, stop him, don't let him out the back door, kick him in the nuts!" (all these demands were clearly out of the question). The loudest and most frequently heard command was "choke him out!" I was thinking, *you mean you want ME to choke him out?*

I really did not want to get anywhere near this guy. I could barely put one foot ahead of the other. The thought of wrapping my arm around this guy's neck and straining to apply pressure to his throat did not appeal to me. The decision, however, was taken out of my hands as I was the only person between the suspect and the back door. Shit! Fighting with a PCP suspect was never fun, but I was in no condition to deal with this guy. I eventually got my arm around his neck as we backed into the door. The dope coppers piled onto this guy—and me—and eventually cuffed him. I was not a happy camper and immediately returned to my car for a handful of Vicodin.

Most LA coppers would never shy away from choking out a combative suspect. However, under the circumstances, I didn't want anything to do with this guy. Clearly, on this day, I was paying the price in pain for future pleasure.

VIOLENCE, INJURIES AND PSYCHOS

Seventy-Seventh Division was probably the most violent division in the city. In the seventies and eighties, we logged over one hundred homicides each year. They were frequently gang and drug related, but just as often they were as a result of a petty argument that escalated into a homicide.

Serious injuries, of course, are part of a violent community. I've seen a man, who was the victim of a stabbing, walking around in his apartment literally holding his guts in place, looking for cat food for his cat. The paramedics told me that if they forced him to stop, his guts would probably spill out and we'd have another homicide. Somehow we managed to get him into an ambulance and to a hospital.

I've watched paramedics try to remove a large serving fork that had been jammed into the back of a man by his girlfriend. His muscles apparently had tightened around the tines of the fork making it almost impossible to remove it by pulling on the handle. One of the firemen actually placed his knee on the guys back for added leverage and support but the fork wouldn't budge.

I've seen the results of a fight between two gay men, a lovers' quarrel that involved a guitar. One of the men hit the other one with the body of the guitar, the string side not the back. The victim had severe and lengthy lacerations to his face as a result of being cut by the wire strings, plus some additional injuries. I've never seen so much blood from one victim; the pool of blood covered most of the kitchen floor. Chalk-up another murder.

One of the funniest incidents I was directly involved with concerned a psycho, a guy who was completely out of it, and violent. I don't believe he was dusted, he was just plain nuts. With the exception of PCP suspects, he was one of the most difficult guys to control I had encountered. He fought with us, resisted us, kicked at us and was a general pain in the ass.

His family said he was psycho and they didn't want anything to do with him. We eventually got him under control and cuffed; he was so violent that we had to restrain his feet. We took him to an ER where a doctor signed the papers to detain this guy for a seventy-two hour psychiatric evaluation, commonly referred to as a 5150 detention.

Our next stop was the psycho ward that would "evaluate" and house the guy. We brought him into the facility on his own two feet and he appeared to have settled down a bit. However, based on his past behavior, we were still cautious. I presented the patient to the doctor who, without inquiring about why the patient was there, immediately told me to take the cuffs off. I told the doc that it would be a big mistake to remove the cuffs but he insisted. The cuffs came off and the psycho immediately took off running down the hallway yelling and screaming, followed by orderlies in white clothes. The doctor didn't bother to get out of his chair. I told the doc, "Bye, see you later" and started walking out of the facility. The doctor jumped up and said, "Wait a minute, you've got to help us!" We eventually joined in with the orderlies and attempted, once again, to subdue this guy. We had two officers and about six or eight orderlies piled on top of the patient before we could control him. I looked up and saw the doctor walking up to this pile of writhing humanity with a syringe in his hand. I thought: great, maybe now we can control this total psycho.

It was summer and I had on a short sleeved shirt, which, of course, exposed my arms. I was on the guys back trying to choke him out and almost everyone else was on top of me. I felt someone grab my arm and pull it away from the suspect. I also heard an announcement from the doctor that we should try to hold the guy still as he had his arm and was about to inject him with some meds. It finally dawned on me that the doctor had *my* arm and not the suspect's. Now I started to yell, which was difficult to do because of all the noise the suspect was making. We eventually got him under control and knocked out. I generally have a lot of respect for doctors and nurses, but this not so young doctor had a lot to learn.

77th DIVISION

If you really enjoyed cop work, 77th was the place to be. I can only think of one exception, but generally we had very good leaders—Lieutenants Melendres and Woller were two of the best men for whom I had worked—good lieutenants, hardworking detectives and outstanding officers, too many names to list. The officers, however, really made the difference. A few divisions had a fair number of lazy, whiny coppers; 77th was the exception.

Here's a good example of a guy who really loved being a cop: he worked PM watch and was a graduate of an East Coast Ivy League college, Rutgers I think. He was younger than I and had only been on the department for a year or two. He clearly, however, enjoyed the work. He didn't seem to be a typical Ivy Leaguer. There was nothing snobbish about him; he was always eager to put on a uniform and do his job.

We were working together on a busy, hot summer night. End of watch was around midnight and every morning-watch unit that cleared was immediately assigned several radio calls.

The parking lot at 77th was full of black-and-whites. PM watch was returning to the station and going EOW (end of watch). AM watch officers were preparing for the street and a busy night. As we entered the lot at EOW, two hotshot radio calls were broadcast by Communications. Both calls involved a man with a gun. My partner and I looked at each other and without saying a word or notifying Communications, we tore out of the lot and drove to the call. I don't remember the outcome or the nature of the call, but when we were no longer needed, we started to return to the station.

Another hot call was broadcast but there were no morning-watch units available to respond. Again, without discussing it or notifying Communications, we sped to the location and left when we were no longer needed. We responded to hotshot radio calls for the next two hours. We were never officially at any of the calls and avoided all the paperwork. It was great fun and we enjoyed every minute of it.

Things finally settled down around three in the morning and we returned to the station. Neither one of us put in for overtime; it didn't seem right that we should be paid for having so much fun. I don't know what it's like today, but 77th Division in the seventies and eighties was a great place to work and a tremendous learning experience for me. I'd go back in a New York minute.

CHAPTER SIX: METROPOLITAN DIVISION

Metropolitan Division was nearly always described by the LA Times as the Elite Metropolitan Division. The men and women who were selected for Metro were generally hard-working and dedicated. They had good judgment, were outstanding street cops, knew what they were doing and focused on putting bad guys in jail. They were a good group and I was proud to be a part of them. There were a few prima donnas within the ranks, but only a few.

Metro was a mobile crime suppression and special events unit that functioned city-wide. It was composed of four teams: A, B, C and D, as well as a search-dog unit and the mounted unit. Search dogs, used to locate dangerous suspects, not drugs, and the mounted unit were added to the division just as I was leaving the department, so I have very little direct knowledge of their activities.

A-Team was an administrative unit composed of office personnel, B-Team was a crime suppression unit that focused in the Valley, C-Team was also a crime suppression unit but primarily worked the South-end, D-Team was SWAT, special weapons and tactics. Generally when SWAT coppers weren't training or engaged in a SWAT function they too worked as a crime suppression detail.

Crime suppression usually meant a specific crime had gotten out of hand within a busy division: a big increase in gang activity, robberies, stolen vehicles, burglaries and prostitution are a few examples. It's not that patrol officers couldn't handle the upsurge in crime; they were simply too busy answering radio calls to focus on and eliminate the crimes. Metro was called in and we saturated the division with unmarked cars and targeted suspects that might be involved with the specific problem—stated indelicately, that usually meant stopping every swinging-dick in the division who could be involved in the crimes we were trying to suppress. Lots of folks were stopped—usually with probable cause, but not always—and many of them went to jail. Throwing hard-working, dedicated officers at the problem usually worked, and crime was suppressed at least for the short term.

Metro coppers drove unmarked police cars equipped with red lights that could be quickly attached to the dash of the car. A few Metro cars also had removable, magnetized signs that were attached to the outside door. The signs displayed the city seal as well as the motto "To Protect and Serve." These were used when a high-profile police presence was called for. Criminals, of course, knew instantly that these unmarked cars were actually police vehicles. Every black-and-white also had the "To Protect and Serve" proclamation as well as the city seal printed on the side of the car.

An enterprising Metro copper had several magnetized signs made up that contained the city seal as well as the following theme: "To Harass and Kick Ass." Were we harassing criminals, gang bangers and dope dealers? You bet! Were we making life a little safer for the citizens of Los Angeles? Absolutely!

Crime suppression also included targeting a specific suspect who was committing serious crimes. Stakeouts to capture a serial rapist, serial killer or armed robbery suspects are good examples of this type of targeting. It was not uncommon for Metro coppers to spend eight or more hours on the top of a roof or behind a bush waiting and watching for a specific suspect to appear and commit the crime. These types of stakeouts were usually boring until the suspect arrived, which didn't happen that often, but when it did, boring turned into exciting and fun. Capturing a serial rapist or dangerous robbery suspect made the long, uncomfortable hours spent on a stakeout worth the effort.

Metro was also active with motorcade escorts and on-site security whenever a VIP was visiting or traveling through LA. VIPs included the President of the United States and his family members, serious politicians running for President of the United States, heads of state, and anyone considered to be important and whose threat assessment might be quite high.

Being assigned to Metro was a great experience. I had fantastic partners, better than average supervisors and good assignments. I'd like to think that if I hadn't injured my back, I would have stayed in Metro until I retired.

I FAILED THE FIRST ORAL EXAMINATION

The captain of Detective Support Division, Tom Ferry, asked me if I would be interested in working for him as part of his Gang Detail. I really liked Captain Ferry and jumped at the opportunity to work this specialized unit. However, I soon discovered that the officers who worked the unit were disappointing. Many, but not all, were lazy and difficult to work with. And I really wanted to be a Metro copper.

After working the Detective Support Division, Gang Detail, for nine months, I applied for an opening in Metro and was quickly scheduled for an oral examination by a board of Metro supervisors. I fell flat on my face during the first oral. I answered a question honestly, but it was not the answer the oral board was looking for. Here's the question I failed: Would you turn in your partner, a well-respected Metro copper, for damaging a police car after having a few beers at the academy bar? I told the board, no, I'd find another solution to the problem. Wrong answer! I was out the door and extremely disappointed. The department officially expected you to turn in your partner for such minor infractions. Your safety depended on the guy or gal sitting next to you; were you really going to turn them in for denting a police car? Of course not.

I worked for Art Melendres while assigned to 77th Patrol, so he knew me and my work. We had also been on several dive trips together. I have an enormous amount of respect for Art. A month or so after I failed the oral, he contacted me and said that I was scheduled for another one, a second chance. I met with him before the big day and he told me to carefully think about my answers and don't step on my dick during the interview.

I was asked very simple, almost embarrassing questions on the next oral: What's the name of the chief of police? What's the name of the Metro captain? Who's buried in Grant's tomb? (After the Grant's tomb question, I was scared shitless they would ask me if Mickey Mouse was a dog or a cat.) I felt like the village idiot, but I passed the oral.

BAD TIMING

I came to Metropolitan Division in the midst of an investigation that involved many of the C-Team officers and most of the supervisors. The LA Times referred to the incident as a scandal; but the Metro coppers called it the *Eight for Eight* investigation. Whatever you called it, it was not a good time to be in LA's elite Metro Division, especially C-Team, to which I was assigned.

Without going into a lot of detail, the internal investigation focused on a complaint lodged by a Metro officer who apparently was upset with supervision for his own reasons. I don't think this type of complaint would have originated from a 77th Division officer. It turns out that Metro was not quite as elite as I had been led to believe. A few of the officers in C-Team made statements that eventually hurt other officers and supervisors. The supervisors were punished and eventually transferred out of the division. These were great guys and outstanding leaders. It was a huge loss for Metro.

The complaint eventually forced officers to be in direct conflict with one another. The division was divided between officers who supported their supervisors and those who didn't. One group of officers wouldn't talk to the opposing side, and a few refused to work with a specific partner. It was a real nasty situation that could have escalated into fights between old friends and partners. I came into the division after the investigation was initiated, so it had no direct affect on me. However, I found myself on the side of the officers who supported the existing Metro sergeants and lieutenant. I probably should have attempted to stay neutral, but it just didn't work out that way. I had worked for the lieutenant and a few of the sergeants before they went to Metro, while all of us were assigned to 77th, and my loyalty was clearly with them.

First Gun Goes Home referred to an unofficial policy that allowed the first two-man team of officers who recovered a gun—usually from a suspect on the street or in a car—to go home early. About once every two months, during roll call, the watch commander would announce to everyone "First gun goes home" as an incentive to recover an illegally carried weapon. It was a nice reward for doing a good job. After roll call it was a race to see who could find the first gun, usually as a result of a traffic stop.

I've seen a few old-timers who were so good at spotting an armed suspect that they were on their way home after an hour or two at work, which included the time it took to write the arrest report and book the suspect. *First gun goes home* was not unique to Metro;

but it was probably used more often in Metro as we didn't handle called-for services (we weren't assigned radio calls and rarely wrote tickets).

Going home early, of course, was the problem. As far as I know, no one on the department, and that includes the chief, had the power to pay an officer when he was not working, thus the name, *Eight for Eight*. You got paid for eight hours, you had to work eight hours.

The complaint covered a few other violations like driving an unmarked, take-home police vehicle outside the county of Los Angeles. A three-man team of Metro coppers was allowed to drive their police car home as long as the car was properly housed within LA County. Unfortunately, many of the C-Team officers lived in Orange County and it was logistically difficult to leave the Metro car in LA County when they lived in Orange County. Because of the complaint by the disgruntled Metro officer, a lot of C-Team coppers were suspended without pay for out-of-county vehicle violations.

I found myself in an unpleasant working environment, but I wanted to work Metro and eventually SWAT, enduring the turmoil and conflict was a small price I was willing to pay.

MY FIRST PARTNER

My first regular partner in Metro was Bill Dunn. He was a great partner with a mischievous side that was impossible to suppress. He also had a full head of thick, white hair even though he was in his early thirties. The down side to his spectacular hair was that we were always easy to identify: the tall, blond Clydesdale and the young cop with white hair. It was usually hard to deny we were involved in an incident as soon as our description was known.

Senior lead officers and officers who had been in Metro for a long time were usually given the newest and best cars. Metro coppers usually took very good care of their assigned vehicles. They'd wash and wax them at home and even install a nice stereo system in the car at their own expense.

Being fairly new to the division, Bill and I were given an old, green Matador that probably had more than a hundred-thousand miles on the odometer. It was dented, had torn upholstery and was even missing a radio. But we loved it. For some strange reason, however, we kept replacing blown out mufflers. But here's why: Bill would spot two motor cops cruising down one of the streets in LA looking for violators. He would quickly accelerate the Matador past the motor cops and then, just as quickly, back off on the throttle; this caused raw gasoline to be dumped into the engine. At the same time he would shut off the ignition key and then turn it back on. The buildup of excessive gas caused the engine to backfire with a loud explosion—not unlike a 12 gauge shotgun going off. The poor motor cops thought someone was shooting at them. Typically, they would duck, swerve, brake and nearly fall off their "motors." It always pissed them off—I can't understand why.

EVERYBODY LOVES A FIREFIGHTER

Everybody loves firefighters: they don't give you a ticket, they rescue folks in peril, they smile and wave at all the good citizens and they even save your house. Bill Dunn, however, didn't feel quite the same way. He would be driving our dinged up Matador—which actually accelerated and braked very well—and eventually spot a fire engine motoring down the road. Firefighters, in those days, frequently stood on a large shelf located at the back of the truck that was also part of the rear bumper. Bill would get directly behind the fire truck and fall back about one-hundred yards. He would accelerate toward the rear of the truck, and just as he got too close he slammed on the brakes. The Matador would instantly go into a four-wheel locked skid (these were the days before anti-lock brakes) and make all kinds of very unpleasant skidding noises. The firefighters, of course, had no idea there was a police car behind them and thought they were about to be rear-ended and seriously injured.

Their first reaction was to jump-up, as quickly as they could, and land on the stacked hoses that were stored near the back of the truck. Firefighters don't usually move very fast—like cops—so watching them fly up and over the back of the truck was always a treat. To make matters worse, Bill would usually turn the ignition key on and off just about the time we passed the truck. Not only were they going to be squashed by traffic, but someone was shooting at them! As you will see, Bill excelled at pissing off firefighters, motor cops and Metro supervisors.

SCATTERING DOPE DEALERS

Bill had another trick that he used on dope dealers. There were a few locations within the city, sometimes right on a corner, that were known for consistent but small-time drug sales. Bill would surreptitiously check out one of the corner locations to make sure it was active, accelerate to the corner as fast as the Matador would go, slam on the brakes, go into a four-wheel locked skid and stop about even with the corner.

All the dope dealers would drop their stash and takeoff running as fast as they could. They assumed, of course, that we'd be right behind them in a foot pursuit. One of us would step out of the car, collect the dope and casually drive off. We'd usually destroy the drugs rather than book it into evidence. This was fairly effective and efficient: we removed a small amount of drugs from the street in a very short period of time, and we were not tied up writing reports for two hours back at the station. We suppressed crime and saved the city a lot of money.

A KNOWN PCP DEALER

The next incident is a variation on the corner drug dealer, but it requires a little background on search warrants.

Before officers could force entry into a location to serve a search warrant, they had to comply with section 844 of the Penal Code. Section 844 stated before they could force entry into the premises, officers had to knock on the door, identify themselves as the police, demand admittance and explain why they want to enter. In theory this process takes about twenty seconds to complete; plenty of time for the dealer to dispose of evidence, especially liquid PCP. In practice officers serving a warrant for PCP would knock on the door, kick it in and make the verbal announcement—all at the same time. It was a race between the suspect and the coppers as to who would get to the sink first. The coppers frequently lost.

Bill eventually collected enough information to obtain a warrant on a premises where sales of PCP were ongoing. We served the warrant early one morning, but by the time we entered the house the dealer had disposed of the PCP down the drain. We had information that this particular dealer would keep his liquid PCP in an open container placed on the edge of the kitchen sink. If the police came a knockin', the dealer would simply push over the open containers right into the drain. At which point most of the PCP was lost. No evidence, no arrest. All of our hard work went down the drain and no one hit the slammer.

Several weeks later we were receiving reports that the dealer was still in business and was selling PCP as fast as he could make it. Bill had an idea—this usually meant trouble, but I was willing to listen. He wanted to hit the dealer's house early one morning without a search warrant. That was fine with me, but with no warrant it's likely the arrest wouldn't fly. In fact, we probably couldn't get a booking approval. Bill said no problem as we wouldn't be arresting the guy. Bill suggested we park several blocks from the premises, and just before the sun came up—the usual time a drug warrant is served—we'd fire up the red lights and siren and slowly drive right into the suspect's drive way. We'd wait a few minutes and then drive away from the house without getting out of the car.

Feedback from our snitch indicated the dealer poured about a quart of liquid PCP down the drain on the morning of our charade. We employed these tactics several times over the next six months. Never getting out of the car.

About the time the dealer was getting tired of pouring out his PCP, we received enough information from several sources to obtain another warrant. Once again we fired up the red lights and siren and drove right up to the suspect's front door. However, this time we scrambled out of the car, complied with 844 and forced our way into the house. We found the PCP on the kitchen sink, where we expected it, and the suspect was in bed. Evidence secured. Booking approval was granted.

PEPPER SPRAY

The department decided to issue olio capsicum, also known as pepper spray, to everyone in Metro. I was never very enthusiastic about using the chemical. I thought it would cause more problems for an officer than it would solve, and it was just one more item to attach to your Sam Browne. There was so much crap attached to your gun belt that guys were beginning to look like Batman with his carry-everything utility belt. Bill Dunn felt differently, however. He embraced the pepper spray and was eager to find out if it really worked well.

Bill got his chance one night in the middle of winter when the air temperature was in the low forties. We'd stopped two suspects who were not real happy about being stopped. I don't remember why they were so unhappy with us, but they clearly didn't like LA cops. They gave us a bit of a hard time, but nothing too serious. We couldn't find a reason to write them a ticket, and we probably didn't have a ticket book in the car anyway. Writing tickets was not a high priority in Metro. Bill decided to search the vehicle for the usual guns or drugs, but it was clean. However, he seemed to take an unusually long time to complete the search, and he had a big smile on his face when he returned to our car after kicking the suspects loose. I could tell something was up but I didn't know what he had done.

As the suspects drove away, he told me to follow them for a few miles. After only a few blocks, the suspects slammed on the brakes and bailed out of the car. Bill waved to them as we passed their car, which had all four doors open, and he was laughing his ass off.

Bill told me that he had sprayed nearly a full canister of pepper spray into the heating vents of the car. It was a cold night and the heater in the suspects' car had to be on full blast. The fumes from the heated spray must have filled up the interior of the car and made it impossible to remain inside. Bill was, at times, impossible to control, not that I ever tried.

A SEARCH WARRANT FOR A PIRANHA

It was a little odd for LAPD officers to obtain a search warrant for the possession of a piranha, but we did with the help of the California Department of Fish and Game (now known as the Department of Fish and Wildlife).

Bill and I were on loan to one of the divisional dope units, probably Southeast Division. We picked up a hype for being under the influence of heroin. He clearly did not want to go to jail and was ready to make a deal for his freedom. He told us he knew a dealer who lived in Wilmington (Harbor Division) who usually had in his possession a large quantity of drugs and weapons. He told us the dealer was known for being violent and was not afraid to use his guns.

Our hype, based on a buy, provided us with enough information and evidence to obtain a search warrant. He confirmed the existence of a variety of drugs inside the house and several guns. Finally, he reported to us that the dealer told him he would not be taken alive; he would rather die in a hail of gunfire, taking out as many policemen as possible, than go back to prison. We thought this was bullshit, but possible.

We obtained a search warrant for the house and asked SWAT to serve the paper for us because of the guns and the suspect's statement about not being taken alive.

SWAT kicked in the door at first light and made entry into the house. It took about two minutes to secure the suspects and clear the house. No shots were fired and the bad-guy dope dealer turned out to be a real pussy—fairly typical for dope dealers. Bill and I were called into the house to conduct the search and recover the drugs and any guns that might have been inside. We found several weapons, but not an ounce of any illicit drugs. In fact, I don't think we even recovered any aspirin. All that work and we came up with zippo, nada, nothing. We were pissed. All the guns appeared to be legal and we had no reason to arrest the suspects. We kicked them loose and returned to the station; apologizing to SWAT for the inconvenience. SWAT is about the most professional law enforcement organization I'm aware of. The SWAT officers and supervisors assured us that coming up empty on the search was no big deal to them, just another day at the office. We felt a little better about the outcome, but we still knew a dope dealer had gotten away.

We were not sure why the dope was missing. Did the snitch inform the dealer that he was about to be arrested? Did he sell all of his dope the day before? Did he ever have a large quantity of drugs to begin with? We simply didn't know.

Back at the station, Bill asked me if I had seen the aquarium that was inside the house. I told him I did, but so what. Bill said he noticed there was a piranha inside the aquarium. It was a fish and game violation to be in possession of a piranha in California. I said, "Well, so what, we don't enforce fish and game regs." Bill said, "No, but the Department of Fish and Game does." Bill contacted the local F&G office, explained what happened and asked them if they had the time to get a warrant for a piranha violation. Oh, one more thing, could we go along when they served it? Their answer was "absolutely," to both questions.

We accompanied F&G several days later when they served the paper. Not only did they get their fish, we got lots of heroin, speed, cocaine, grass and a little PCP. This very active dealer clearly did not expect us to return, and he didn't know it was against the law to possess a piranha. I'm usually not fond of fish and game wardens, but they came through when we needed them.

TOUGH COPS

I knew a lot of really tough cops, but I think Lenny Munoz was at the top of the list. He was not physically imposing, mean or intimidating; in fact, just the opposite. However, he was physically and mentally as tough as nails. I worked with Lenny at 77th and at Metro. Lenny was well liked by every street cop I knew; however, one or two Metro supervisors, did not seem to like Lenny. I think it was because he was not at all reluctant to go head-to-head with them on any issue. Lenny was also a fighter, literally, and boxed in the Police Olympics.

I know it's obvious, but fighters really are tough guys. When I was younger, I was challenged to box a few rounds with a young, Golden Gloves Hispanic boxer who was much shorter and lighter than I. At first I declined to fight this kid because I didn't want to hurt him. Unfortunately for me, he didn't feel the same way. We eventually put on the gloves and started the match. He knocked me down three times in the first round and I didn't see any of the punches. One moment I was standing up, feet apart, hands ready to throw a punch; the next moment I was looking up at this lightweight from the canvas. That's when I gained a great deal of respect for a trained fighter.

I didn't see any of Lenny's matches but a good friend told me how well he fought. He was tough, quick, never gave up, was not afraid to take a punch and won most of his fights. Lenny could easily have been that smaller Hispanic kid who kicked my ass when I was a teenager.

Lenny was not only physically tough, he was also mentally tough. Nothing seemed to bother him. Clearly, police officers face real physical dangers; however, the psychological dangers can be just as disabling, yet they seemed to have had no effect on Lenny. I knew he was physically tough, I had no idea he was as strong as he was mentally. If Lenny ever felt stress, he hid it well.

Most of the stress to which an officer is exposed comes from the department, not the cop work he or she performs daily. An altercation with a suspect under the influence of PCP will certainly cause the adrenalin to kick in, but it's not especially stressful. What is stressful is an investigation by Internal Affairs about the use of excessive force in controlling that same PCP suspect, or an investigation concerning a damaged black-and-white, or, as in Lenny's case, an investigation regarding the loss of a Department issued handheld radio. I don't remember a lot of the details about the radio Lenny apparently lost, but the Department clearly wanted its "pound of flesh" for the missing equipment. Lenny was extensively interviewed by supervisors; he was threatened with all kinds of punishment and eventually told he had to pay for the missing radio. The Department never missed an opportunity to "pile on" when it came to increasing stress. This is a minor example, but there were many more instances where the "brass" was clearly gunning for Lenny.

THE STRESS OF TESTIFYING

Testifying at court can be fairly stressful, but that too clearly had no effect on Lenny. Lenny and I had arrested a suspect for possession of some type of illicit drug. I wrote the report and booked the evidence. Usually one officer does most of the paper work so that only he is subpoenaed into court. This procedure saves the city a lot of money in overtime and frees-up one officer. The date of the court appearance arrived but I was a no-show. I don't remember why I was absent, but I missed the appearance. Lenny happened to be present in court on another issue and told the prosecutor that he would handle the case. He was clearly covering for me.

Lenny was called as a witness, made his way to the witness stand and testified to the issues. The prosecutor usually has the officer introduce the evidence to the court. Typically, drugs and other forms of evidence are placed into an envelope, sealed with tape and initialed by the officer who booked the evidence; in my case that would have been TEB.

Lenny realized he had a problem with the introduction of evidence as my initials appeared on the envelope, not his. The prosecutor goes through a somewhat dramatic process when he asks the officer—who is testifying under oath—to describe and identify the evidence that *he* booked. In this case, the process went something like this:

Prosecutor: "Officer Munoz, do you recognize the envelope containing the evidence?"

Officer Munoz: "Yes."

Prosecutor: "Would you tell the court how you recognize the envelope?"

Officer Munoz: "It's marked *TEB* (which of course, are my initials) for *Lenny Munoz*."

No one, not even the court reporter, understood the significance of what Lenny had just said, and the prelim continued without a hitch.

Lenny was covering for me while testifying on the stand and under oath. Most guys, and I can't blame them, would have testified that another officer booked the evidence and the case would have been dismissed or held over until the officer who booked the evidence was able to make an appearance. Missing a court appearance without a valid excuse, as I did, was almost always punished by relinquishing days off. Covering for me on the stand didn't bother Lenny one bit; I would have stressed out. Thanks Lenny.

MORE STRESS

Here's another example of the department creating stress: President Reagan was in town for a function. LAPD provided motorcade security as well as on-site security whenever a president was in the city. A motorcade was a wild affair, especially for the officers working one of the scout cars.

The officers in the scout cars—there were usually at least two unmarked Metro cars working as scouts— were responsible for driving ahead of the presidential motorcade and looking for potential suspects that might be a danger to the president. For example, it's likely the scout car would stop an individual standing on the side of a street—on the route of the motorcade—who is wearing a full-length coat on a summer day, or even a guy holding an attaché case or wearing a backpack. These *stops* were different than most pedestrian stops. The scout car would accelerate to the suspect, slam on the brakes, officers would jump out of the car and quickly search him or her for weapons, saying very little in the process, and if nothing unusual was found they would pile back into the car and speed ahead to the next suspect.

Presidential motorcades usually travel fast. They don't stop for red lights and almost always exceed the speed limit. The officers ahead of the motorcade have to work fast and they have to pay attention to the circumstances in front of them. Constant, focused attention to possible suspects lasts as long as it takes the president to travel from point A to point B in a motorcade. Was the assignment stressful, you bet.

The SWAT lieutenant told me I had been assigned to one of the scout cars in a presidential motorcade scheduled for the next day. I should have been flattered; however, I told him I would rather not work the scout car detail. I didn't offer an explanation and he was clearly pissed-off that I had declined the assignment—and it showed. I should have told him the truth: my father had just died and I didn't feel that I was focused enough to work a demanding detail.

The SWAT lieutenant, who I liked and respected, approached a C-Team supervisor, a guy I didn't care for, and told him about my refusal to work the detail. This supervisor called me into his office, closed the door and told me that because of my poor attitude and reluctance to work an important detail, I was ordered to see the department shrink. I'm usually not very demonstrative when it comes to expressing my feelings; however, this incident had clearly gone too far. I explained to the supervisor that my father had recently died, and I hadn't mentioned this to the department or the SWAT lieutenant. I told him I didn't feel I would do a good job in the scout car. The supervisor was very quiet for a moment then essentially told me that I had screwed up and should have informed the department of his death. He went on to say that it wouldn't be necessary for me to see the shrink and then dismissed me. Something was wrong with this scenario. My father had just died, and I was told that I had screwed up. I hadn't heard one word of condolence from this asshole. There were leaders and administrators in the ranks of supervisors on the department; this guy was clearly not a leader. A stressful time in my life just got more stressful, thanks to the department. I was partially responsible, I should have been more forthcoming, but once again the department didn't miss an opportunity to make a stressful job more stressful.

SECRET SERVICE

These guys really earn their pay. We worked with them from time to time, usually whenever the president was staying in LA. They didn't get a lot of sleep, their suits and shirts were usually wrinkled and they could never afford to have a bad day. It's a federal law enforcement agency for which I have a great deal of respect. I can't say the same thing about the FBI, DEA or ATF.

Once in a blue moon we'd have a joint training day with the presidential detail of the Secret Service.

These were all sharp, hardworking agents who were totally dedicated to protecting the president. I have no idea what their formal, academy training was like, but the agency is clearly doing something right when they train their men and women. Each agent appears to be utterly dedicated to giving up his or her life to save the president. Metro coppers were clearly different, not worse or better, but different.

Here's an example: On one of these training days an agent dressed like the president was being escorted on foot from one location to another. There were probably six or eight agents with the president and perhaps an equal number of Metro coppers. My memory is not good enough to recall the exact nature of the event, but I'm guessing the president was supposed to be walking through a large and perhaps not too friendly crowd. At some point during the escort, a "gunman" emerged from the crowd and began firing at the "president" with a handgun. Every one of these agents, without exception, stepped in front of the president and was prepared to take a bullet for the man. A skeptic might say, well it was only a training day; they might react differently in real life. But these guys (I don't believe there were any female agents working presidential details in the early eighties) reacted immediately and without hesitation. This is what they were trained to do and they did it. And that takes some balls.

If you don't think this is true, flashback to the video of President Reagan being shot, each one of the agents in this detail is maneuvering his body to stand between the president and the suspect. Clearly they are trained and prepared to give up their lives to save the president's. In fact, one of the agents nearly did just that; I still have a clear picture of the agent stepping in front of the president and taking a round for his efforts, he wasn't killed but he easily could have been.

Metro coppers reacted a little differently. As the shots from the suspect were ringing out, all of the LA coppers, again without exception, *remained in place* (they didn't step in front of the "president" to take a bullet). Instead, they pulled their guns and made every effort to kill the assassin. The agents were trained and dedicated to protect the president; the Metro coppers were dead-set on taking out the shooter. To me this was an example of two different agencies, two different training regiments and two different philosophies working to protect the president. It's a job probably best left to the Secret Service.

THE SKID ROW SLASHER

As I mentioned earlier, Metro coppers were often used for special assignments and stakeouts. In 1977, Vaughn Greenwood was convicted of slashing the throats of nine victims who lived and hung out in the area commonly known as Skid Row. Fifth Street (the Nickel) was at the heart of Skid Row and probably had the highest concentration of homeless winos and derelicts in the city of Los Angeles.

There was evidence to support an allegation that Greenwood, after slashing the throats of his victims—literally from ear to ear—drank their blood. If evil truly exists, it does so in the form of Vaughn Greenwood.

A massive stakeout, using Metro coppers, was established in the Skid Row district. Coppers were placed on rooftops with a good view of all the alleys and bars frequented by those who lived around the Nickel. As with most stakeouts, the hours of the assignment were in the late-evening to early-morning time frame. Officers assigned to the stakeout were focused on the Slasher and his victims. All other minor crimes had to be ignored.

During one of the stakeouts a team of Metro officers observed two suspects stop and park their vehicle in an alley that was being watched. The driver got out of the vehicle with a baseball bat, approached the other vehicle parked in the alley and smashed out every glass window on the car. He hit both headlights and both taillights and put numerous dents in the hood and fenders of the parked car. There appeared to be no reason for this act of vandalism other than pure meanness. The victim's car was not illegally parked, there was no traffic accident and no confrontation between the drivers. The vandals were just being assholes.

The Metro coppers could do nothing about the incident. They couldn't even report it to patrol officers for fear of scaring off the Slasher. It's quite rare for officers to view an act of vandalism in progress, and it must have been extremely frustrating to watch the windows being smashed out of this car and not being able to stop it. Later in the evening the officers observed the victim as he approached his car and noticed the extensive damage. He was crestfallen and it appeared that he was crying over this senseless act. It was not a new or expensive vehicle, but it was probably the most important asset the man owned. The incident did, however, have a happy ending. When it was time to end the stakeout, the suspects' car was still parked in the alley.

At around four in the morning, when the officers climbed off the roof, they noticed no one was around the car, and the suspects appeared to be down for the evening. Using their heavy aluminum Kel-lite flashlights, every window and light on the suspects' vehicle was smashed and broken. Holier-than-thou administrators like to preach to officers that they shouldn't break the law in order to enforcement it. I suppose I agree with that philosophy, but I'm certain the officers involved in this incident were overjoyed when they were able to inflict a little eye-for-an-eye justice for the victim.

JOHN HOLMES, MEET LAPD

John Holmes was known as the Porno King in Los Angeles. He was an inveterate liar, addicted to cocaine, involved in four homicides and, of course, made porno movies. There was some question about the size of his penis, but it was probably accurate to say that it was close to double the size of a normal one. And he claimed he could keep an erection all day long—don't forget, he rarely told the truth. Okay, I was a little envious. Until I met him. What an asshole!

On July 1, 1981, four people were killed at a residence located on Wonderland Street in Los Angeles. One other person was critically injured and eventually had a portion of her skull removed. The homicides were in retaliation for a robbery that occurred at the residence of a man named Eddie Nash, a big-time cocaine dealer.

Many of the facts are in dispute but the consensus was that Holmes told four or five of his friends that Nash kept a large amount of cash and drugs at his home. The friends armed themselves with a handgun and forced their way into Nash's residence. It was alleged they made off with $185,000 in cash and $800,000 in cocaine. None of these figures, however, can be verified. In addition to taking his money and drugs, they humiliated Nash in front of his bodyguard—who obviously would never make it as an agent for the Secret Service.

Nash apparently forced Holmes to rat-out his friends, who lived on Wonderland Street, and were involved in the robbery. It's likely, but was never proven, that Nash, his bodyguards and maybe even John Holmes went to the location and bludgeoned all five of the residents. Four of them were killed and one was seriously injured. The injured victim, a woman, was treated at Cedars Sinai Hospital and eventually transferred to an LA County rehab hospital. She was protected by officers from Metro while she was at both facilities. As the surviving victim, it was felt Nash would make another attempt on her life. Because of her brain damage, however, she apparently had very little memory of the incident.

At some point in the investigation, the detectives decided that John Holmes' life was also in danger and he would require protection. A room at the Bonaventure Hotel was secured for him; his girlfriend, Dawn Schiller; and his wife, Sharon Holmes. (A room at a Motel 6 would have been more appropriate.) A Metro Sergeant, Jerry Shaw, was placed in charge of the small unit protecting Holmes, his wife and his girlfriend.

We responded to the room and were introduced to Holmes and his "family" by the homicide detectives working the case. After the introductions, the detectives left the hotel and we all settled in for the duration. Holmes made one critical mistake, however. He approached Sergeant Shaw and *told him* how the detail was going to function. He even suggested that Shaw or one of the officers, make a food run for his wife and girlfriend.

Shaw blew up in Holmes' face. He made it clear that he was running the detail, not Holmes, and if he didn't like it, he could always walk out of the hotel. Holmes was clearly afraid for his life and quickly backed down. My admiration for Sergeant Shaw skyrocketed.

The detectives finally focused on Holmes as one of the suspects in the homicides and he eventually went to trial. He was acquitted in the homicides but was forced to spend over one-hundred days in the county jail for refusing to talk to the grand jury about Eddie Nash's involvement in the murders.

Three or four years after the homicides on Wonderland, Holmes died from complications of AIDs. His death may have been a loss to the porno industry, but mankind was clearly much better off.

SERGEANT SHAW vs. THE AYATOLLAH

Metropolitan Division was frequently used to police demonstrations that had the potential to turn violent. In the late seventies and early eighties, Iran was involved in a revolution that pitted the radical Islamists, supported by the Ayatollah Khomeini, against the shah of Iran, supported by the U.S.

There were demonstrations in LA by supporters of the shah and supporters of the Ayatollah. Sometimes the two groups would get together and a miniriot would break out. That's usually when Metro would get involved.

As a general rule, the pro-shah group was well behaved, respectful and did not break the law. The pro-Khomeini group, however, was almost always a problem. They damaged property, and frequently turned to violence to call attention to their cause. I liked the pro-shah group and pretty much despised the radical Muslims.

One interesting observation: the men of the pro-Khomeini group would gather in a circle and surround themselves with their women and children—what a brave group of men. Once carefully protected by their women and children, the men would throw rocks, bottles or anything handy at the anti-Khomeini protestors and the cops.

Led by Sergeant Shaw, Metro coppers would climb over the women and children in order to get at the men. "Stick time"—the use of batons by the police—usually followed the rocks and bottles. Surprisingly, the anti-Khomeini protestors were nearly always law abiding and respectful.

At a different protest I saw Sergeant Shaw approach a group of pro-Khomeini demonstrators, by himself, and make the following announcement: I am

Sergeant Shaw of the Los Angeles Police Department. That's right, Shaw, as in the shah of Iran. I'm here today to make sure you don't break any laws. Please don't forget, my name is pronounced Shaw, just like the *shah.* While making this speech, he would walk up and down the line of protestors and point to his name tag that clearly read Shaw.

He concluded his little speech by stating and *emphasizing* that he was Jewish! And we could tell that this announcement really pissed off the protestors. Once again, I had a tremendous amount of admiration for Sergeant Shaw.

WARRANT SUSPECTS

Metro officers were occasionally criticized by patrol coppers because of a misconception about booking warrant suspects. Metro coppers stopped a lot of suspects while working crime suppression details. Whenever a suspect was stopped, the detaining officers would usually run the suspect for wants and warrants. We were not required to book a suspect if a check revealed that he or she had an outstanding traffic or misdemeanor warrant; felony warrants, however, could not be ignored.

Depending on the attitude of the suspect, most hard-working Metro officers wouldn't bother with a minor warrant suspect and would kick them loose. A few officers felt differently about suspects with warrants.

They would book almost everyone, even those with very minor parking violations. Consequently, a lot of patrol officers felt that Metro, when working crime suppression details, would focus solely on booking warrant suspects. Unfortunately there was some basis for this misconception. Booking suspects with minor warrants, however, was not good cop work and nothing to be proud of.

The following incident, although a bit unusual, is a good example of ignoring arrest warrants.

Bill Anderson and I were working Hollywood Division on a crime suppression detail that involved serious felonies. We stopped a suspect who could have been involved with the crimes we were trying to suppress. A Metro B-Team unit saw us make the stop and decided to standby in case we needed any assistance. We ran the suspect for warrants and discovered that he had over $2,000 in traffic warrants. However, he had no connection to the crimes we were trying to prevent.

After the information on the warrants was transmitted to us—and in the presence of the B-Team officers—I advised Bill that our suspect had over $2,000 of traffic and misdemeanor warrants. I also told Bill I wasn't really interested in booking the guy and knew Bill felt the same way. We kicked him loose. The Metro B-Team officers appeared to be shocked that we weren't going to book this guy.

Our suspect got in his car and left the scene. Bill and I cleared from the stop and continued looking for felony suspects. Moments later we heard the same B-Team unit run the suspect we had just kicked loose. The same warrant information was relayed to the officers and they arrested and booked the suspect for all his outstanding warrants. Was this really good cop work? No, not at all.

Bill and I were doing our job and trying to suppress felonies. The other unit was tied up with this guy, and off the street, for at least two hours. The officers got credit for an arrest, but the arrest had absolutely no effect on the crimes we were trying to stop. Guys like these two B-Teamers gave Metro an undeserved bad name.

A VICIOUS SEARCH DOG

A Metro unit had a dangerous, armed-robbery suspect holed up under a house. Going under the house to capture this guy was really not an option, for several reasons: No one wants to get their uniform dirty crawling around on the ground, and this space is generally full of spiders and other furry critters that are not especially friendly to humans. It's also dangerous and scary as hell to crawl around looking for an armed suspect in a small, dark, confined space.

We tried to talk the guy into giving up but he was not interested. And to make things worse, he said he'd shoot the first officer that tried to arrest him. This guy was turning out to be a real pain in the ass.

We looked at a few options: We could wait the guy out, but that would tie up at least six officers for who knew how many hours; we could call SWAT, but that too would involve even more officers for a long period of time; or we could send for one of the few dog search teams that the department was just putting into service. Unfortunately, the dog and its partner were over two hours away searching another location.

One of the officers at the scene, Steve, had a few hidden talents. He was able to mimic the sound of a barking dog perfectly. He suggested that he be allowed to bark and snarl like some half-crazed dog, while someone else tried to convince the suspect to give up and crawl out from under the house. No one really believed Steve could pull it off, but no one wanted to hang around for half the day waiting for this guy to be arrested. It was decided to give Steve a chance.

Steve and the other officer approached the opening the suspect had used and began to negotiate with him. The negotiator advised the suspect that a K-9 unit had just arrived and gave Steve the signal to begin his routine. Steve growled and barked like a giant, rabid pit bull. I've never seen or heard anything like it. If my eyes had been closed, I would have been convinced this vicious attack dog was real and could have easily ripped out my throat. *The Hound of the Baskervilles* had nothing on Steve's imitation.

Apparently the suspect felt the same way. He immediately told the negotiator that he was giving up and was coming out from under the house. He actually pleaded and begged the officer not to send in the dog.

UNIFORMED OFFICER BUYS MARIJUANA

As I mentioned previously, Steve had a talent for mimicking certain sounds; he seemed to specialize in dogs and dialects, and he was very good. Here's another example of how good he was: There was an old woman who was blatantly selling narcotics, pain killers and marijuana, from her house during daylight hours. Kids in the neighborhood would walk up to a barred gate, which enclosed her front porch, and negotiate a deal for the drugs. The kid would remain outside the house and throw the money through the bars of the gate and into the residence; she would toss the dope out the front door, through the gate, for the kid to pick up. No one ever saw the old woman actually exchange money for drugs, and it's unlikely that she could see the person making the buy.

After getting all this information from a local snitch—probably a competitor who had been losing money to her—Steve, who was also a blond-haired, blue-eyed devil, decided to try his luck at buying dope while in uniform. He approached the gate in the late afternoon and, using his very best black dialect, negotiated a purchase of two-ounces of marijuana. Steve, who was standing behind a pillar next to the gate and somewhat out of sight, threw money into the house, and the old woman tossed out his dope. She clearly thought she was dealing with one of the kids on the block. I was listening to the conversation behind Steve and couldn't believe my ears. He sounded like he had been born and raised in the ghetto. He was perfect and clearly fooled the old woman.

A tow truck was standing by outside the front gate and out of view; as soon as the deal went down, Steve placed a heavy-duty hook and cable on the bars of the gate and told the tow truck operator to wind it up. The winch on the tow truck popped the gate off the wall; we went inside and placed the old crone under arrest for selling dope. She did not believe Steve, a white guy, had actually made a deal with her to buy drugs *while in uniform.* She was certain a black officer or local kid had actually made the deal and wanted to know where and who he was.

THE NEWS MEDIA

Like most officers I was not fond of the news media, which included the print news as well as television and radio. They seemed to lack objectivity and were more interested in selling their product than getting the facts right.

The following incident involved a respected, black TV reporter who could easily have caused a major riot in LA.

A white Metro copper was involved in an altercation with an armed, black suspect in one of LA's housing projects. The suspect blew off one of the copper's hands with a shotgun, and was himself wounded several times in the exchange of gunfire with the police. He was ultimately transported to a local hospital by a city ambulance. The suspect was under arrest and still ambulatory, so a Metro copper rode with him—*in the ambulance*—to the hospital. Two paramedics are assigned to each ambulance; when someone is being transported to the hospital, one paramedic drives and the other one remains in the back with the patient. If an officer rides along with the ambulance, he generally rides in back with the paramedic, not up front with the driver.

The black TV reporter filed his report live from the hospital parking lot on the 11 o'clock news. He stated a reliable, tested source had informed him the suspect had been shot only once by the police before he was transported in the ambulance. This alleged journalist emphasized that the officer got into the back of the ambulance with the patient, as if this were unusual or contrary to policy.

The reporter stated emphatically, however, that while at the hospital the shooting suspect had been treated for three gunshot wounds, not one. The obvious inference was that the copper, riding along in the ambulance, shot the suspect twice more while inside the ambulance. The reporter didn't actually say those exact words, but that wasn't necessary; he had done enough damage with his strong implication.

Fortunately it was the 11:00 p.m. news and not many people in the community had seen the telecast. The department did a good job of gathering the facts and correcting the reporter's blunder before the erroneous news report spread throughout the community.

UNCONSCIOUS CHILD IN A BURNING HOUSE

Bill Dunn, my regular partner, and I were working PM watch somewhere inside Southeast Division. I would guess that about seventy-five percent of our crime suppression details involved South-end divisions: 77th, Southwest, Southeast and Newton Divisions. We were in an area of the division that was not heavily populated. A few open fields, empty lots and very old stately homes. As we passed one of the older, two-story houses, we noticed that the top story was nearly fully engulfed in flames, and not one fire truck was on the scene. The fire had apparently just started and no one reported it to the fire department.

We felt there was a good chance that someone may still be trapped inside the house. We stopped the car, notified communications of the fire and decided to enter the house, if we could.

I know this shouldn't come as a surprise, but a burning structure puts out a great deal of heat, more than you might imagine. We managed to walk to the front door and kick it open. That could have been a mistake, but hey, we're cops not firefighters. Once the door flew open, we could see flames licking from the ceiling and the walls. I didn't smell a lot of smoke, but the flames were impressive; they were rolling down from above like breaking surf, and it was incredibly hot. I really don't know how firefighters can tolerate such heat.

There was a couch in the living room directly under the rolling flames. We could see two, small black legs lying on the floor behind the couch and extending beyond the end. The head, torso and waist, however, were hidden from view by the back of the couch.

The child was not moving and appeared to be unconscious. Shit! Now what do we do? The only thing we could do was enter the house. The heat was too intense to walk into the living room, so we had to crawl on our bellies to reach the little girl, who appeared to be about eight-years old. We didn't think about it at the time, but this incident had Medal of Valor written all over it.

This was a big house and the living room was huge. It seemed like we low-crawled for thirty minutes before we got to the couch. Once there Bill had a good look at the victim: what a doll! Literally, she was a black, plastic doll. Son-of-a bitch. Did I mention it was hot?

We managed to back out of the house and return for some fresh air just as the fire department arrived. The firefighters had quickly figured out what we had done and got a good laugh out of our heroics. We reported the incident to our sergeant and figured we'd at least get an attaboy for our efforts. We found out, however, that the department doesn't hand out accolades for saving a black, plastic doll.

ANOTHER BURNING HOUSE

Sometime later, while working crime suppression at 77th, Bill Dunn and I saw another house that was just beginning to burn. We entered the house and saw a drunk passed out on the couch and food burning on the stove. The fire had spread from the top of the stove to the wall behind it. This time we decided on a plan. We would notify the fire department of the flames and then wait until the fire truck drove up to the house. As soon as the firefighters arrived, we'd drag the drunk out of the house. We were silently sure that our actions would practically guarantee an outstanding rating report on our next yearly review.

There was only one problem: Once the firefighters arrived and we tried to drag the drunk out of the house, he came alive and started to fight with us. This was not part of our plan. The guy really turned out to be a fighter, and I had to choke him out in order to get him out of the house.

This really didn't look good. Two coppers choking out a suspect who nearly burned to death in a house fire. Once again, an attaboy seemed to be out of the question.

A WET STAKEOUT

We worked a lot of stakeouts while assigned to Metro. Stakeouts were usually boring affairs: hours and hours of doing nothing but watching for someone to show up; and then an occasional period of extreme excitement when they finally did.

This particular incident did not happen to me, but a reliable source filled me in on the details.

Two regular partners were assigned to a stakeout involving a suspect wanted for robbery. The guys were watching from a residence that was next door to the suspect's house. A very nice older couple was willing to give up their small but very clean home for them to use as the observation post. The stakeout went a lot longer than most. Day one passed without the suspect making an appearance, and day two was nearly over when one of the guys decided to have some fun and liven up the scene.

One of the officers waited until his partner had to urinate and was inside the spotlessly clean bathroom. At about the right time—when the flow had just begun—the guy outside the bathroom started yelling, "He's here, he's here and he's got a gun!" The suspect, of course, had not made an appearance. After yelling the suspect was here and armed, the prankster jacked a round into the chamber of the shotgun and advised his partner that he was going outside to arrest the bad guy, poor tactics for any officer, so it really got the attention of the guy in the bathroom—I guess you could say it really *pissed* him off.

The guy whizzing couldn't let his partner confront the suspect by himself but he wasn't finished. He only had one option: hang onto his "johnson" with one hand and join in on the arrest. And that's what he did. However, while running through the living room of the house and with all the excitement, the guy holding his wang somehow managed to let go. The very nice living room couch and the new carpet were now sprayed with urine, lots of urine.

I cannot imagine what it would be like to arrest an armed suspect for robbery with your gun in one hand and your dick in the other, but the thought of doing so is good for a laugh. Too bad there wasn't a suspect to arrest.

A LITTLE GIRL WITH A BIG GUN

Jack was a well-liked officer at 77th and Metro. He was also a Vietnam veteran and an outstanding police officer. When you think of Jack you can't help but see images of Clint Eastwood or John Wayne. He was pragmatic, hardworking, tough as leather and occasionally a bit insensitive.

Jack's insensitivity caused him a few days off. I was not present when this incident occurred and it was relayed to me over a beer, so the facts may be a bit off, but not by much. Here's what happened: In the early eighties, female officers were just beginning to show up in the field. At the time, cop work in LAPD was primarily a man's game. And it was probably safe to say that most of the guys working patrol felt that a female partner would be a liability. There were no female officers working Metro, but that would soon change.

C-Team was working a crime suppression detail in the Valley. And Jack was walking down the hallway, minding his own business, when he spotted what he thought was a joke. He saw a very small, very short female officer walking toward him. Jack was about 6'1" and probably hit the scales at over 225 pounds. The two of them, passing in the hall way, made for an unusual sight and quite a contrast.

The brand-new female officer had apparently just cleared roll call and was laden with a brief case, a shotgun, a bag containing a helmet and her Sam Browne crammed with an assortment of accoutrements that Wyatt Earp could only dream of. Her hands and arms were full, her gun belt was full, and to make matters much worse, especially in Jack's eyes, her hat was on crooked and about to fall off. Jack was incredulous; this couldn't be a real live LAPD copper.

Jack was always good for a funny line, so he stopped the young officer and made the following statement, "So, little girl, what do you want to be when you grow up?"

I wasn't there, but apparently the statement caused Jack all kinds of problems. But knowing Jack, I'm sure he didn't back down, in fact, he probably enjoyed all the attention.

WE'RE WAITING FOR SWAT

Once again I was not present at this incident, but my source has proven to be reliable—and maybe prone to a little embellishment. This is another story about Jack and his Clint Eastwood approach to cop work.

Jack was promoted to sergeant and transferred from Metro to one of the patrol divisions. He responded, as a supervisor, to a request by one of his patrol units for a SWAT team. I do not know this for a fact, but I suspect Jack felt SWAT was beginning to be overused by a lot of new officers. When he arrived at the scene, he met the officer making the request and said, "What-da-u got?"

The patrol officer went into a long monologue about how he received a radio call concerning a man with a gun who was apparently holed up inside a residence. The patrol officer stated that no one had actually seen the man with a gun, and no one had reported shots being fired. He went on to report that there had been a long-standing dispute between the man and his girlfriend. The neighbors reported both parties were frequently drunk and the police had been called to the residence many times in the past.

Jack said to the young officer, "What are you waiting for?" The officer stated that he felt the guy inside might have a gun, so this was probably a call for SWAT, and he was standing by until they arrived. Jack was incredulous. This was a slow division and the young officer had probably handled very few man-with-a-gun calls. This type of call was handled almost hourly on a busy night in 77th, and no one, absolutely no one, would think about calling SWAT based on the information received. Jack figuratively kicked him in the ass and told him to handle the damn call. Knowing Jack, he probably said, "And if somebody shoots your ass, I'll call SWAT personally!" Did I mention that Jack could be a little insensitive?

A VERY SPECIAL CAPTAIN

The department had more than a few captains that had a very high opinion of themselves. What follows is a good example:

There were generally three captains assigned to each division, and each one of them had their own take-home car and a reserved parking spot at the station. This sacred parking stall was usually as close to the rear entrance of the station as possible—it apparently was difficult for out-of-shape, overweight captains to walk more than a few feet per day (my apologies to Captain Pat McKinley).

C-Team was assigned to a crime suppression detail at Rampart Division. I was running a little late and took the first parking space I found in the parking lot, very close to the rear entrance, what luck—I should have known better. I pulled into the space, put on my uniform shirt and Sam Browne and made it to roll call just in time.

When it was time to go to work, I noticed that another car, a nice shiny new Plymouth, was parked directly behind my car, perpendicular to the parking space. The parked car blocked me from leaving the space as another car was parked in front of my car in a normal nose-to-nose configuration. Oops, a closer inspection of the parking stall indicated I had inadvertently parked in the captain's reserved space. Even though it was never my intent to park in his space, this had to be an administrative felony. A lowly policeman had the nerve to park in the captain's spot. The fact that he purposely blocked my car showed that he was really pissed and certainly inconvenienced. Now what do I do?

I got the shop number (its identifying number) of the car that was parked in front of me in a regular space and learned that it was assigned to one of the divisional detectives. I located the detective and told him that someone had blocked my car—there was no way I was going to tell him it was the captain's car—and could I borrow his keys so I could move his car to get mine out of the lot. No problem, he gave me his keys, I moved his car and drove my car forward to another parking space. I, of course, promptly returned his keys.

On the way out of the station, I walked past the captain whose car was now blocking an empty parking spot—his own space. The red-faced captain was chewing on the ass of a Metro sergeant because one of our guys, me to be precise, had the personal affront to park in his space. God, I had no idea this captain was so important.

Had I liked the sergeant, who was on the wrong end of a nasty ass-chewing, I would have fessed up and explained what I had done. As it happened, I didn't much care for the guy and rather enjoyed the whole scene.

MY FAVORITE LINE

I'm not going to mention the name, not even the first name, of this officer. He is one of the most highly respected coppers I know. He's a great guy who was not afraid to take on the department when he knew he was right. Unfortunately, I can't go into that story—and it is a good one—as the facts and circumstances could easily reveal his identity. I've probably said too much already.

This Metro cop was an outstanding officer. Later on in his career, after he was promoted, he continued to be admired and well-liked by his troops. More frequently than not, guys would make sergeant, leave the ranks and would do a one-eighty. They would turn into someone you just don't want to be around. They would conveniently forget about their own history and would expect their troops to act like Mr. Clean. It was so hypocritical of them to act appalled whenever an officer stepped over the line, but many of them did.

It was Christmas and time for the Metro Christmas party. It was held in a nice restaurant in Orange County and well attended. Guys, accompanied by their wives or dates, started to arrive around five; dinner was scheduled for seven. Two hours of drinking time was just about right. Drinks were served, stories were told, drinks were served, and more drinks were served. The subject of this story was single at the time but you could tell he really liked his date. She was good-looking, classy and reserved, but not so reserved that she wasn't having a good time. She seemed to enjoy the cop stories and the camaraderie of the men and women who were present. This party, I believe, was their first date.

The officer, who was known to have a drink or two, had a deep, booming voice that was easily heard, even when he whispered. He was never obnoxious, and he projected his deep and distinctive voice without trying.

About a dozen coppers and their wives or dates were sitting on several couches and chairs that were arranged into an informal circle. In front of the entire group, our guy, who was feeling no pain, slowly leaned over to give his new girl a peck on the cheek. She had not had that much to drink and decided that this was not the right time for a kiss. She turned her head away from the man, showed disapproval on her face and fashionably rejected his attempt of affection.

Our guy was undaunted by this rejection and made the following statement in a deep, clear, and loud voice with just the right amount of indignity, "WELL, I GUESS A BLOWJOB IS OUT OF THE QUESTION!"

That comment brought the house down and even she chuckled.

INTERNAL AFFAIRS

Every police department should have an internal affairs unit. It's vitally important that high standards of professional conduct be maintained. I suppose the best way to do that is to have strong supervisors and an aggressive Internal Affairs Division. I have three issues with the department and Internal Affairs investigations: The department is always quick to investigate and discipline officers who have violated department policy. I'm disappointed that the department insists officers cannot have feelings and reactions like any normal human. For example, a male suspect spits in the face of an officer. Does the suspect get away with this behavior? Probably not, it's likely that he will feel some pain for his offensive behavior. Can the officer be disciplined for using excessive or inappropriate force on the suspect? Probably so.

I know it's not a simple issue, but I don't believe officers should be *severely* disciplined for having human reactions. No one should be expected to suppress their emotions to that extent. If politicians were held to the same standards as an LAPD copper, we'd have very few Washington DC scandals. We probably wouldn't have very many politicians either.

The department seems to relish investigating and disciplining street cops for violating department policy, and there's never a delay in going forward with the process. The department, however, is not nearly as eager to investigate high-ranking officers—captains and above. There is something about the concept of "The Goose and the Gander" that eludes LAPD's hierarchy.

The third issue I have concerns the hypocrisy displayed by many of those Internal Affairs investigators. Here's an example: An IAD sergeant was assigned to investigate an allegation of using excessive force on two suspects. The allegation was investigated and the officers were disciplined. In my view, both officers were severely disciplined for doing their job. I wouldn't expect them to get a medal, but the severity of their punishment far outweighed their use of excessive force.

Here's where the hypocrisy exists: One of the investigators involved in this case had a reputation for using excessive force as a police officer. This particular investigator, while he was an officer, was involved in a shooting that was judged to be In Policy and justified. He had fired a shotgun at a suspect who was armed and attempting to shoot an officer. It was reported that after the shooting, the officer, who would later become an Internal Affairs investigator, literally jumped up and down on the suspect's chest yelling, "Die motherfucker, die!" I was not present at this scene, and don't know if it was true, but based on so many other stories about this officer, I believe it to be true.

EIGHT FOR EIGHT AND FIRST GUN GOES HOME

I was not only present at this next case involving IAD investigators; I was a part of it. In the beginning of this section on Metropolitan Division, I mentioned the investigation that centered on the *first gun goes home* allegations. The investigation involved more than going home early. It also involved officers who drove their city police vehicles to their homes located outside Los Angeles County. Many, if not all of these officers were disciplined for this violation of department policy. And it certainly had an affect on their careers.

Metro coppers frequently worked the weekend football games at the LA Coliseum as a regular work assignment. However, the Coliseum would hire off-duty coppers to increase the compliment of men working the game.

While assigned to one of the games—on duty— my partner and I noticed an unmarked police vehicle parked on the street on the Coliseum grounds. We later discovered the car was assigned to two IAD investigators who were working the game while *off-duty.* In other words, the city of LA was paying for transporting two investigators from their private residence to the Coliseum to work an off-duty job. Both of these IAD investigators were involved in the *First Gun Goes Home* Metro investigation. They were violating the very same department policy they had investigated only months before. Did the policy change? No. Did they have a poor memory? No. They were simply taking advantage of the circumstances. Were they disciplined? Not that I am aware of. Last I heard, they had been temporarily reassigned to a desk position in IAD.

The IAD investigators weren't kicked out of the division. The Metro supervisors, however, were sent packing. Again, senior management seems to have forgotten about the "Goose and the Gander."

I actually learned a very good lesson from this incident. When my partner and I discovered the identity of the two IAD investigators, I phoned the watch commander of Southwest Division, the division in which the Coliseum was located, and reported the incident. I did it anonymously, which I now know was a mistake. I should have come forward and reported the incident to my supervisor. However, I was afraid that the complaint would be ignored or swept under the rug by management. And I think it essentially was.

I was verbally admonished by a Metro sergeant for not reporting the incident to a Metro supervisor. There wasn't much they could do to me, however, as I observed a violation and reported it to the watch commander, who had jurisdiction over the area. As far as I know, however, there was no requirement to report the incident to *my* supervisor.

I phoned the watch commander anonymously, but I did not keep it a secret from the coppers working that day. In fact, I was a bit joyous about catching two IAD investigators—especially the two who conducted the Metro allegations—violating department policy. Practically the same policy violations they had investigated only months before.

I eventually discovered one of the Metro officers, let's call him Snitch, who knew I had phoned the watch commander with the allegation, went directly to a Metro supervisor and reported that I was the one who made the anonymous complaint. Once again, I was disappointed with a Metro copper. Snitch was supposed to be one of the good guys, he wasn't. He was just trying to curry favor with the boss. He was just another Metro copper who proved to be untrustworthy. Fortunately, there were very few officers like Snitch.

MR. PRESIDENT

The nineteen-eighty presidential election was about to come to an end, and the first Tuesday in November was only days away. Governor Reagan was in town to do some last-minute campaigning and Metro was providing on-site security as well as motorcade security. Secret Service, of course, was primarily responsible for his protection.

The governor was scheduled to give a speech at the Bonaventure Hotel and Metro coppers had been assigned to several locations within the hotel that Secret

Service was unable to watch. I was assigned to a large hallway somewhere in the back of the facility. We were not aware of the route the governor would be taking through the hotel, but I was alone and no one, absolutely no one, was near my location. Most of these assignments were boring and usually uneventful. Typically an officer would spend several hours inside a stairwell making sure no unauthorized personnel entered the area, pretty ho-hum stuff. I was sure this detail would turn out the same way.

Just a few minutes into the assignment, I looked up and saw a group of about eight men walking toward me. The one in the lead set a quick pace, walked with swinging arms, exuded confidence and stood about a head taller than anyone else in the group. The big guy was Governor Reagan. I had always admired the man and it was exciting to see him in person.

As he passed my location I said something really stupid. I uttered a firm, "Hi Mr. President." I don't believe he said anything back to me, but I do remember seeing a huge smile on his face. The big smile and rosy cheeks were certainly iconic and unforgettable. I sincerely hope I wasn't being rude by addressing the future president of the United States with a "hi."

I know it's highly unlikely, but I would like to think I was the first person to call Ronald Reagan, Mr. President.

LAPD BRASS

I've been pretty hard on several captains in these stories about LAPD, but the department had some fine leaders within the ranks: Captain Pat McKinley, Captain Smitson, Captain Tom Ferry, Captain Brennan, Deputy Chief Jesse Brewer, Chief Ed Davis and Chief Daryl Gates. All these fine men were examples of outstanding leaders. I've undoubtedly left some men (and now women) off the list, but only because I didn't know them or know of them.

Metro had its own future captain, Ron Sanchez, working in the ranks of C-Team officers. He too was an outstanding copper. He was smart, quiet, unassuming and a martial-arts expert.

Metro had just been issued a new baton called a monadnock. It was supposed to be superior to the old, wooden night sticks made of hickory. And like anything new, a lot of guys had their doubts about this improved baton. The monadnock was made of fiberglass, was shorter in length than the wooden batons and had a short handle, about six-inches long that stuck out perpendicular to the main "stick." They looked like an elongated "L" with a short tag at the bottom of the L, which was the handle of the baton.

C-Team had been assigned to beef-up security at the annual Puerto Rican Independence Day held in San Pedro (it seems to me that Puerto Rico was not fully independent, so I don't exactly know what they were celebrating).

As usual there was too much sun, too much beer and too many people in attendance. A fairly small brawl broke out under a tree near the entrance to Cabrillo Beach. I'm guessing there were about twenty people involved in the melee. C-Team gathered its troops and were prepared to move in and stop the fighting.

Ron, who was very familiar with the monadnock, told our sergeant that this would be a good time to demonstrate to all the doubters just how effective the new baton was. He asked permission to enter the fight—by himself—with his new plastic stick. One against twenty seemed to be stretching the odds a bit, but we had at least ten or so troops standing by in case Ron needed some help. Turns out we weren't needed. We watched, fascinated, as Ron made his way through this hostile crowd swinging his baton just below shoulder level and single-handedly breaking up the miniriot. A few arms and knees got dented and bruised, but no one was seriously injured. The new stick worked.

RITALIN

There is nothing funny about this next incident, but it does show what a person will do for drugs. I was surprised to learn that Ritalin, a stimulant given to hyperactive kids, was sought after by a few drug abusers.

Bill Dunn and I were on a side street very close to Wilshire Boulevard. Bill observed a small, black woman walking down the street with her arms extended out from her body as if she were a walking-T. This obviously was not an everyday sight, so we followed her for a few minutes. We were behind her and she didn't know we were present. She walked up the stairs to an apartment building, her arms still extended, and into an open apartment. We stopped the car and followed her into the apartment. We discovered her sitting on the toilet in the bathroom. She was heating a substance that had been dissolved in water, just like a heroin addict would prepare heroin. This however, was not an opiate; it was Ritalin.

Neither Bill nor I had ever heard of anyone injecting Ritalin, and there are some very good reasons for not doing so. It was unknown to us at the time, but Ritalin injected into the skin causes an enormous abscess at the injection site. Her open sores were over two inches in diameter and at least one-quarter of an inch deep. Both of her tiny arms were covered in wet, runny abscesses. She was walking down the street with her arms extended to dry them.

This woman was covered in deep, painful sores on each arm and probably other parts of her body unseen to us. In spite of this painful condition, when we saw her sitting on the toilet she was in the process of injecting the same drug that had caused her so much pain and discomfort.

Over the years, because of various injuries, I've taken enough opiate-based pain killers (Vicodin, Oxycodone, and codeine) to understand just how appealing and alluring this type of drug can be, but I was surprised to learn that injected Ritalin apparently had a similar effect.

We learned the woman had a hyperactive son who was prescribed the drug. She was, however, injecting his Ritalin in order to satisfy her needs. This is pure speculation on my part, but I believe this woman was addicted to practically anything she could lay her hands on. Heroin was somewhat difficult to obtain and expensive; Ritalin was readily available and probably free to her. I doubt that the "high" was the same, but it must have had some mood-altering effect on her that made it appealing.

We weren't sure what to do with this woman. She wasn't under the influence of an opiate and the crime she was committing, if she was committing a crime, would have been difficult to identify. I think Bill and I both felt sorry for her and we kicked her loose.

HYPES, BODY LICE AND FLEAS

If we were not involved in a serious crime suppression detail, Bill Dunn and I would frequently look for a hype to book. The feeling on the street was that if you booked a hype you probably prevented a burglary. True or not, booking hypes was not a waste of time. It frequently led to the arrest of drug dealers and was often a valuable source of information.

Newton Division was having a serious burglary problem so Metro was invited in to help suppress the crime. Once we hit the street, we immediately began looking for hypes. Bill observed a guy walking down the street with a gait that had hype written all over it. We looked at each other as if to say, "this is just too easy."

We stopped our car a short distance behind the suspect and shouted at him to stop walking. He turned around to face us as we approached on foot. Before we had a chance to say a word, the guy made the following admission, "Hello officers, I gotta tell you I'm under the influence, I just got *down*, and I'm infested with body lice." Everything was perfect until he mentioned body lice.

Again, Bill and I looked at one another and Bill said, "Thank you very much for letting us know, and we hope you have a nice *high.*" We immediately turned around and got back into our car. We rarely let hypes go, but we recently had a confrontation with fleas, and we figured body lice would be much worse and a hell of a lot more difficult to explain. Was he *bullshitting* us? We'll never know and we weren't about to find out.

The flea incident occurred in Harbor Division. We were backing up a unit that was serving a search warrant on a drug pad. We were asked to go to the rear of the house as the serving officers made entry through the front door. As the primary unit quickly made their way up the steps leading to the second story apartment, we rushed to the back yard, our assigned area, and discovered it really wasn't a back yard. No swing set, no manicured lawn, no barbeque. In fact, the area resembled a small jungle in Panama: tall grass, muddy dirt, weeds and dead leaves covering every inch of the ground.

We didn't know it at the time but it was a perfect breeding ground for fleas. We positioned ourselves below the upper story windows—a perfect location from which the suspect could dispose of drugs—and waited for the officers in front to make entry. And we waited and waited. For some reason they were delayed. All of a sudden our ankles started itching, then our arms began to itch and finally our necks and heads were on fire. Son of a bitch, we were being eaten alive by thousands of fleas. We knew the entry team was about to go in, so we couldn't leave our little jungle in case the suspects attempted to escape or dropped his dope. We were stuck.

We finally got a code-4 from the entry team and couldn't get out of the back yard fast enough. Once on the street, we started slapping at fleas. It didn't seem to do much good, so we removed our uniform shirts and that made things worse. Picture this: two guys in blue pants and white T-shirts wearing Sam Brownes and guns, slapping at invisible bugs. It didn't do any good, we were covered in fleas. I told Bill I knew there was a drug store not far from us where we could get some bug spray. We jumped in the car, turned on the red lights and siren, and beat feet—code-3—to the store. We stopped in front, probably in a red zone, ran inside and got a spray can of Black Flag Ant and Roach Killer. We sprayed our entire bodies, our clothes and the inside of the car. That seemed to kill the little bastards, but both of us had hundreds of flea bites.

Body lice and flea bites. It was not what I signed up for, and I don't recall any classes at the academy on the subjects, but it was good for a laugh.

SPIT AND POLISH

Metro's grooming and uniform standards were higher than most patrol divisions. Because we were frequently assigned to VIP details, our uniforms were generally in good shape, no patches, no frayed collars or cuffs, highly shined badges, and spit-shined shoes. Haircuts and mustaches were nearly always perfect.

Sergeant Woller, who would later make lieutenant and transfer to 77th Division, was assigned as the watch commander when an officer new to Metro happened to walk by his desk. As previously mentioned, Woller had been a Marine Corps gunnery sergeant and was no stranger to spit and polish. As the officer passed Woller, the sergeant yelled out, "Hey Elvis, if you want to be a hippy, get a dog and a van; if you want to work Metro, get a haircut!" I didn't hear the incident (it was told to me by Dave Reynolds) but I think I knew the sergeant well enough to know that it is exactly what he would have said.

CHAPTER SEVEN: THE UNDERWATER DIVE UNIT

There were two Underwater Dive Units that existed at different times within LAPD. The first group of divers was in place sometime during the mid-sixties; the second unit was formed in the mid-seventies. The first unit probably ceased to exist due to a lack of work. However, prior to the formal establishment of the second unit, a bomb had gone off on a ferry that was moored in LA Harbor. LAPD had no way to conduct a formal, underwater investigation into the explosion of the sunken ferry. By coincidence, one of the investigators assigned to Criminal Conspiracy, the unit responsible for investigating bomb blasts, was a certified diver. The name of the diver was Sergeant Arleigh McCree. Arleigh volunteered to dive on the ferry and conduct a preliminary investigation into the blast before the vessel was raised.

Diving inside a wreck is almost always dangerous, but diving on a recently blown-up vessel is far more hazardous. Visibility is reduced because of the sediment (although the water in LA Harbor is rarely clear), broken pipes, severed hoses, and loose wires are nearly everywhere, and navigating deep within an unfamiliar wreck is so disorienting that a diver can easily get lost. The only good news about the dive was that it was in relatively shallow water; I'm guessing thirty feet would probably have been Arleigh's maximum depth.

Somehow he completed the dive—by himself, I believe—and determined the ferry had in fact been sunk by a bomb. Arleigh eventually left Criminal Conspiracy and transferred to the Bomb Squad. In 1986, Arleigh and Ron Ball were killed while trying to disarm a booby-trapped pipe bomb. It was a personal loss for me as he was a friend, and a huge loss for the department.

Because of the sunken crime scene and a clear need for divers who were skilled at locating and identifying evidence, the department decided it was time to resurrect the Underwater Dive Unit.

Captain Tom Ferry, the head of Detective Support Division, was selected to develop the new unit. I submitted my application for the Dive Team as soon as

I learned of its formation. I had been scuba diving since I was eighteen and had been certified as an instructor at the age of twenty-eight. After going through some testing that was not especially demanding, I was selected to be a member of the team.

This was not a full-time assignment, however. The men who were selected continued to work their normal jobs; I was still working patrol, but was given time off for training and call-ups. I really enjoyed sport diving, but I soon learned that diving in LA Harbor had almost nothing in common with diving for lobster, abalone and fish. But it was still fun.

What follows are a few sea stories that I hope are interesting and maybe even a little funny.

CAPTAIN TOM FERRY

Tom Ferry was a terrific leader. He was not a huge physical specimen, in fact, he was of medium height and fairly slender. Years later I learned he was an outstanding high school athlete. For some unknown reason, he took a liking to me. Policemen generally didn't have a lot of friends who were captains, but Tom was a friend—and I almost never use the word *friend* casually, it has a special meaning to me.

Under Captain Ferry's leadership, the dive team was formed and we became a functioning unit—a little rag-tag perhaps—but we got the job done. I mention rag-tag because even though we were an official team, we received very little money from the department for equipment and dive gear. We didn't have a boat, we used our own gear and we had to "borrow" large plastic barrels that were used as floats. Several years ago I attended a reunion of the old dive team and was introduced to the new unit. What a difference. As a result of 9-11, the new team had several dive boats, department furnished dive gear, underwater communications equipment and a trailer to haul around gear—there was even a microwave oven inside the trailer. These new, young studs are trained well, have good equipment and I'm sure they do an outstanding job.

Captain Ferry did manage to obtain a van from the department that we used to transport gear and other equipment. We kept a supply of oxygen inside the van as a safety measure. We did, however, have a problem with our oxygen bottle. It seemed the tank and regulator were constantly leaking. There was no real evidence of a leak, but the pressure gauge, over a period of several weeks, would go from full to about half-full. It would never go completely empty, which seemed a little odd. We had to refill the tank, which had never been used, about once a month. We even exchanged our tank and regulator with another unit and had the same problem.

We eventually found out why the tank was "leaking." Early one morning, before it was time to go to work, someone caught Captain Ferry taking hits off our "leaking" oxygen bottle. Bill Anderson had told Tom that it was not uncommon for a Marine fighter pilot to sit in the cockpit of his F-4 and suck-up as much pure oxygen as possible just before takeoff. The oxygen would help clear the pilot's head after a hard night of drinking. If it was good enough for the Marines, it was good enough for Captain Ferry, who was known to have a drink or two after work.

Years later, I was fortunate enough to visit Tom in the hospital just before he died. He was very sick, but the huge smile on his face suggested that he recognized me. He was unable to speak, but I'd like to think that a visit from an old *friend* gave Tom a little pleasure for the remainder of the day.

THE DRAIN PIPE

We had a training day set-up for the canals that are found in Venice Division, now known as Pacific Division. The canals are man-made and were created by a developer to increase sales. There were a series of connected ponds and canals, controlled by sluice gates that formed the entire system of canals. The sluice gates were used to control the flow of water and the water level of the ponds.

This particular training day found Arleigh McCree diving by himself in one of the ponds. He had only been in the water for a short time when we heard him yelling and screaming. We couldn't see him, but we recognized his voice and knew it was Arleigh. We eventually discovered his voice was coming from a grate that covered a vent leading into a large drain pipe. That large diameter pipe was part of the drainage system of the canals and ponds. He was caught in a wire mesh that prevented large objects from traveling from one canal to another, and there just happened to be a vent—and air pocket—directly over the wire mesh. Arleigh kept yelling for us to cut off the flow of water. We didn't know it at the time, but a city maintenance worker had opened the sluice gate that allowed water to flow from one canal to another. The slow but steady flow of water forced Arleigh into the pipe and pinned him against the wire mesh. We finally got the worker to close the gate and he swam out of the pipe on his own, none the worse for wear. Nothing seemed to bother him, but it didn't take a genius to figure out that if the vent had not been in that location, or had been smaller, Arleigh would have drowned.

A RECOVERED VOLKSWAGEN

We knew we were going to have a Dive Team call-up that was actually a training day. We didn't, however, know when we were going to be called up. At around midnight my phone rang and I was advised to report to a certain pier in the harbor and bring all my dive gear. It was raining heavily, dark as the inside of a cave and the wind was probably blowing over twenty knots. I'm sure the boss thought these were perfect conditions.

When we were all assembled, we were briefed on the reason for the call-up. We were supposed to locate a stolen Volkswagen that was used in a homicide and probably contained a weapon. In addition to locating and searching the car, we had to secure cables to the vehicle so that it could be returned to dry land.

When I looked over the side of the pier, I noticed that there was a fifteen foot drop from the top of the pier to the water, so the entry would be a little difficult. I was actually more concerned about getting out of the water than jumping into it.

Two of us managed to get into the water and began the search. While at the surface, I noticed all kinds of debris that had been washed into the harbor. A tampon, floating in the current, actually got hung up on my wetsuit glove, and that's when I realized this was not going to be a fun dive.

We had underwater lights, but they really are not that effective in murky water. They'll light up an object, if it's within a foot or so of the light, but they have very little penetrating power. Diving in the harbor in these conditions was like diving in a huge mug of hot chocolate. You could feel an object but you couldn't see it until you were right on top of it.

We killed about half a tank of air and finally located the VW. It was on its side in about forty feet of water. The harbor waters are deeper than you might expect, and that's because some large ships draw close to forty feet; super tankers draw even more. After locating the car, I tried to communicate to my partner to hold open the door while I went into the passenger compartment. I was a little afraid the door would shut and I wouldn't be able to get out.

I left my dive buddy with the open door in his hands and made my way into the cramped VW. Fortunately, Captain Ferry had the good sense to have the interior seats removed before he pushed the car off the pier. As soon as I was inside, the door closed. Shit! My stomach was tied in knots and I was on the verge of a full-blown panic. I checked the door and it opened easily from the inside. I eventually found the gun and made my way out of the now open VW.

After marking the location of the car with a buoyed line, we swam to the surface, removed our dive gear and climbed the ladder to the top of the pier. When we were on the pier, I asked my partner why he let go of the door; he told me that he had lost his grip and the current had pushed it closed. I was not a happy camper but we had found the gun and another team had recovered the car.

We almost always critiqued our dives once we were on dry land. This particular critique included

Captain Ferry, a lieutenant, a psychiatrist that was affiliated with the department (and was actually on the team), and the divers who were at the scene. I explained how we located the car, and told everyone how the door closed after I had entered the vehicle. The doctor asked us if we were scared. I believe I said something like, "You bet your ass I was scared, scared shitless!" My partner said he wasn't frightened at all. That really pissed me off, but I didn't say anything.

I was not afraid to admit that I was more than a little scared while inside the VW, and I think that's when Captain Ferry and I became friends. I was honest with him when I could have easily said, "No, I wasn't afraid."

HEY, YOU IN THE SKIFF, DID YOU CALL FOR A TOW?

The next incident, though not falling-down hilarious, made us all laugh. I'm afraid I'm not talented enough to make this sound as funny as it was, but I'll do my best.

We were gathering our gear in preparation for a training dive in the harbor. We were adjacent to the main channel that was almost always full of ships entering and leaving the port. Small boats had very little business inside the channel among the big ships, but a few dimwits always managed to find a way to interfere with the movement of these enormous vessels. They quickly found out a huge tanker, full of oil, could change course about as fast and effectively as a glacier.

Just as we were about to enter the water, we saw a guy in a rowing skiff that was about eight-feet long, and way too small to be in that area of the harbor. He was attempting to row *across* a fairly narrow channel that was full of underway ships. This guy had to be nuts, drunk or suicidal.

From among these huge ships, we saw an ocean-going tug that had to be close to one hundred and fifty feet in length—with an engine big enough to pull a train—slide-up to the skiff and make the following announcement over his PA system, "Hey, you in the skiff, did you call for a tow?" The incongruity of the entire event was almost impossible to believe or understand. And to top it off, the guy in the skiff shook his head back and forth, as if to say no, not me. How people like this managed to stay alive will always be a mystery to me.

BUMPY BILL

The guys on the team started calling Bill Anderson Bumpy Bill. The bumps were actually muscles that had been worked hard at the gym. He lifted weights to get stronger and did not appear to be interested in looking like the freaks that appear on the front page of muscle magazines. Bill had no interest in becoming a pretty boy;

he wanted to get strong and stay strong. And even though he's now approaching seventy, he's still as strong as a bull and spends hours in the gym.

As I mentioned previously, Bill was shot down during the Vietnam War. He was flying at a very high speed when he had to eject from his F-4. During the ejection, he sustained a minor shoulder injury, but for the most part was unhurt. He attributes his lack of significant injuries to weightlifting; he feels his strength enabled him to minimize the flailing of his arms and legs as he rocketed, literally, from the cockpit of his jet.

Bill frequently dived with twin scuba tanks that had a built-in harness and buoyancy compensating device. This set-up, though not unique, also had a compartment designed into the backpack that contained close to twenty-five pounds of lead; it was called an Attpack. In total the twin steel tanks, backpack assembly and lead probably exceeded one hundred and twenty-five pounds. I've watched Bill grab both tanks and the heavy assembly in his hands and lift the entire unit over his head and drop it onto his back—while *out* of the water. I could barely do the same thing with a single tank that contained no attached lead while I was *in* the water.

I've seen Bill effortlessly walking around with these same tanks on his back on a boat that was pitching and rolling in heavy seas. Of course, I remember watching Mike Nelson on the TV series *Sea Hunt* doing the very same thing. There was, however, one difference,

Mike Nelson's tanks were a product of Hollywood. They were made of balsa wood and were used for shooting above water scenes; I doubt they weighed more than fifteen pounds.

I met Bill while we were going through the selection process for the Dive Team. We became good friends and remain so today. Men like Bill Anderson, Bill Dunn, and Danny Rockwell—like so many LA coppers—were not afraid to risk their own skin while trying to save yours. I would consider myself a good cop if all the men I've worked with felt the same way about me.

ALASKAN STATE TROOPERS

Two Alaskan State Troopers joined us for a training day. The idea of joint training days, of course, is to share information and perhaps learn something new. I definitely learned something new: new respect for the men (and now women) who worked up north. I cannot imagine jumping into saltwater that has a temperature below freezing. I can see them now inventorying their dive gear: dry suit, fins, mask, tanks, regulator, BCD (buoyancy compensating devise), *ice ax*! I've taken a lot of equipment into the water, but never an ice ax. No thanks. These guys had some cashews, no doubt about it.

It apparently was not uncommon for them to dive on the hulls of oil tankers in the frigid northern waters.

Oil leaks, freezing water, poor visibility, strong currents, hurricane-like winds and no sunlight for weeks were normal conditions for these police divers.

They dived in extremely hostile conditions, and their above water environment wasn't much different. LAPD coppers could almost always count on help that was only seconds away. An Alaskan trooper could easily find himself or herself alone and hundreds of miles from assistance. A response for help could be measured in days not seconds.

We enjoyed spending time with these very unassuming and humble troopers. I especially enjoyed hearing about an officer-involved shooting that one of them had experienced. The incident doesn't have anything to do with the Dive Team, but it's an interesting story.

The trooper involved in the shooting was responsible for an area that covered thousands of square miles. He was advised that two poachers had been working an area within his jurisdiction that was several hundred miles from his normal patrol area. The remote site could only be reached by airplane as there were no roads leading to the poachers. The trooper, who was also a pilot, climbed into his state-owned airplane—by himself—and flew to the last know location of the suspects. He circled the area in the plane and noticed a rough camp had been setup and was apparently still occupied. He landed the plane and approached the campsite on foot. As he neared the camp, multiple high-powered shots rang out; these hardened, backwoods poachers had ambushed him and were intent on killing him. Poachers normally knew how to handle a rifle, but, fortunately for the trooper, alcohol may have influenced their ability to shoot accurately.

City coppers would have put out a help call and waited about 30 seconds for scores of officers to arrive. That wasn't going to happen in this remote area of Alaska. The trooper advanced on the shooters and eventually killed both of them with his own big-bore rifle.

I was absolutely fascinated with the story. As mentioned before, whenever an LAPD officer is involved in a shooting, a specialized team of detectives descends on the scene and conducts an extensive investigation into every detail of the incident. One of the responsibilities of this team of investigators is to determine if the shooting was in-policy or out-of-policy. They also look into the tactics used by the officer to determine if his actions contributed to the use of deadly force. In a nut shell, was it a good shooting or a bad one?

There was little doubt in my mind that the team investigating the trooper's incident would come back with an in-policy shooting. However, curiosity got the better of me and I asked him if it was a good shooting. He said, "Yes, definitely." I also asked him, because of the great distances involved, who completed the officer-involved shooting investigation? His short response, "Well, I did." He wrote the report and it was approved by his supervisor, who was probably hundreds of miles away. Alaska was not only a spectacular state, it was also the home of some amazing troopers; like Secret Service agents, they have my respect and admiration.

EPILOGUE

South-Central Los Angeles is one of the most violent areas within the city. Blacks and Hispanics still account for a majority of the homicides in LA, and over half of those are gang related. Grim numbers, but Los Angeles still has one of the lowest crime rates for any major city in the country.

Here are the significant stats: In 2000, there were 550 homicides in the city, by 2012 the number had dropped to 299. Robberies during that same time went from 15,527 to 8,983. The same held true for rapes, they went from 14,590 to 8,983.

Traditionally LA has accomplished this with fewer coppers per capita than any major city in the U.S. The Los Angeles Police Department has 10,000 police officers and a population of 3.9 million. New York City has 35,000 officers with a population of 8.4 million.

The crime stats from Chicago tell a different story and I suspect the numbers in New York will begin to increase as there is political pressure for the police department to become less aggressive when stopping and searching obvious gang members or suspects who appear to be involved in criminal activity.

Who will pay the price for this "soft" approach to cop work? Law-abiding citizens.

Why is Los Angeles more efficient? I believe the answer is simple: The men and women who make up LAPD are some of the finest big-city coppers in the country. Other big cities have fine police departments, but I don't believe they compare to Los Angeles.

GLOSSARY OF TERMS

ADW	Assault with a Deadly or Dangerous Weapon
Air Unit	Police Helicopter
BCD	Buoyancy Compensating Device, keeps a diver afloat and maintains neutral buoyancy
Called For Services	Request by a citizen for a police response
Code-3	Police unit traveling with activated red lights and siren
Code-4	No further assistance is needed
Code-6	Off the air and investigating an incident or location
Code-30	A burglary alarm has been activated
CVC	California Vehicle Code
Deuce	Driving under the influence
DSD	Detective Support Division
EOW	End of Watch
F I Card	Field Interview Card, also known as a shake
IAD	Internal Affairs Division
IOD	Injured On Duty
MLK	Martin Luther King Hospital
Nichel, The	Fifth Street
P-2	A policeman who is no longer on probation
P-3	A training officer
PCP	Phencyclidine also known as Angel Dust or "dusted"

PIC	Parking and Intersection Control
PR	The person who called the police
RA	Rescue Ambulance with paramedics
RD	Reporting District
RTO	Radio Telephone Operator, dispatcher
Sam Browne	A belt that contains the officer's gun, handcuffs and extra bullets
Sap	A lead-weighted miniature baton, sometimes spring loaded
SWAT	Special Weapons and Tactics
T/A	Traffic Accident
Tac-2	Radio frequency used to communicate between two or more police units
UDU	Underwater Dive Unit
15-7	A report that explains an incident but is not part of a crime report
181	A report that initiates a personnel complaint against an officer
187	The Penal Code section for homicide
211	The Penal Code section for robbery
415	The Penal Code section for disturbing the peace and a general catch-all section
459	The Penal Code section for burglary
502	The old Vehicle Code section for driving under the influence, a deuce
647F	The Penal Code section for being drunk in public

ABOUT THE AUTHOR

Thomas Blandford (Tom) was a member of the Los Angeles Police Department from 1972 until he was medically retired in 1983. After leaving the department, he was employed as an investigator for Boeing Aircraft in Long Beach, California.

He retired from Boeing in 1996, and spent four years aboard his trawler, with his wife Judy, cruising from Los Angeles to Panama. He has contributed magazine articles on boating to several national boating publications. He and his wife have a home in Arizona but spend time in Colorado, California, and aboard their boat in San Carlos, Mexico

AUTHOR'S NOTE

If you are a police officer, deputy sheriff or an investigator in any jurisdiction—active or retired, local or federal—and you have a story that belongs in volume II, please contact me by email at mvgracias45@gmail.com.

If you live in California, Colorado or Arizona, we might be able to get together over a beer. Cop stories are always better with a cold beer or a shot of tequila.